W9-BIY-224

FLORIDA STATE
UNIVERSITY LIBRARIES

JAN 31 1995

TALLAHASSEE, FLORIDA

TRANSFORMING HUMANITY

Kumarian Press Library of Management for Development

Selected Titles

Breaking the Cycle of Poverty:
The BRAC Strategy
Catherine Lovell

The Challenge of Famine: Recent
Experience, Lessons Learned
John Osgood Field, editor

In Defense of Livelihood: Comparative
Studies in Environmental Action
John Friedmann and
Haripriya Rangan, editors

Democratizing Development: The Role of
Voluntary Organizations
John Clark

Getting to the 21st Century: Voluntary
Action and the Global Agenda
David C. Korten

Growing Our Future: Food Security and
the Environment
Katie Smith and Tetsunao Yamamori,
editors

Intermediary NGOs: The Supporting Link
in Grassroots Development
Thomas F. Carroll

Keepers of the Forest: Land Management
Alternatives in Southeast Asia
Mark Poffenberger, editor

Managing Organizations in Developing
Countries: A Strategic and Operational
Perspective, Moses N. Kiggundu

Management Dimensions of Development:
Perspectives and Strategies
Milton J. Esman

Opening the Marketplace to Small Enter-
prise: Where Magic Ends and Development
Begins
Ton de Wilde and Stijntje Schreurs,
with Arleen Richman

Primary Health Care: Medicine in its Place
John J. Macdonald

Promises Not Kept: The Betrayal of Social
Change in the Third World, 2d edition
John Isbister

Voices from the Amazon
Binka Le Breton

Women at the Center: Development Issues
and Practices for the 1990s
Gay Young, Vidyamali Samarasinghe,
and Ken Kusterer, editors

Working Together: Gender Analysis in
Agriculture, Vols. 1 and 2
Hilary Sims Feldstein and
Susan V. Poats, editors

TRANSFORMING HUMANITY

The Visionary Writings of
SOEDJATMOKO

editors
Kathleen Newland
Kamala Chandrakirana Soedjatmoko

Foreword by Clifford Geertz

Kumarian Press

HD
75
S645
1994

To Danya,
Soedjatmoko's granddaughter,
and her generation

Transforming Humanity: The Visionary Writings of Soedjatmoko.

Published 1994 in the United States of America by Kumarian Press, Inc.,
630 Oakwood Avenue, Suite 119, West Hartford, Connecticut 06110 USA.

Copyright © 1994 Kumarian Press, Inc. All rights reserved. No part of this book
may be reproduced or transmitted in any form or by any means, electronic or
mechanical, including photocopy, recording, or information storage and
retrieval system, without prior written permission of the publisher.

Cover design by Mary Crombie. Cover photo by Martha Stewart.

Production supervised by Jenna Dixon

Text design by Jenna Dixon
Copyedited by Linda Lotz
Typeset by Pro Production
Proofread by Jolene Robinson
Index prepared by Alan M. Greenberg
Printed in the United States of America on recycled acid-free paper by
Thomson Shore, Inc. Text printed with soy-based ink.

Library of Congress Cataloging-in-Publication Data

Soedjatmoko, 1922–
      Transforming humanity : the visionary writings of Soedjatmoko / editors,
Kathleen Newland, Kamala Chandrakirana Soedjatmoko.
          p.   cm. — (Kumarian Press library of management for
development)
      Includes bibliographical references and index.
      ISBN 1-56549-025-8 (alk. paper). — ISBN 1-56549-026-6 (pbk. : alk.
paper)
      1. Economic development—Social aspects. 2. Economic development—
Religious aspects. 3. Developing countries. 4. Education, Higher.
5. International organization. 6. Humanitarianism. I. Newland, Kathleen.
II. Soedjatmoko, Kamala Chandrakirana, 1960–   . III. Title. IV. Series.
HD75.S645   1993
338.9—dc20   93-5181

98   97   96   95   94   5   4   3   2   1
First printing, 1994

Contents

Foreword

There is, in the modern world, a dilemma that faces people who, as Soedjatmoko did, wish to serve their country not by flattering it or dominating it or extending its power but by recalling it to its proper self—to what in a less embarrassed age one would unashamedly call its soul. One needs to remain connected to this inner life with an intensity that gives one's words and actions the weight and resonance that come with commitment to something more than mere ideas—to a place, a time, a history, and a form of life. And one needs, at the same time, to transcend those things, to develop a richness of experience and a range of concern that allows one to maintain a distance from them and avoid the parochialism, the self-righteousness, the romanticism, and the distrust of change that is the the downside of patriotism everywhere. There is no one in our time—not Adam Michnik, Desmond Tutu, Abba Eban, or Octavio Paz, in whose diverse and particular company he clearly belongs—who managed this dilemma more effectively than Soedjatmoko. Rooted to the end, he was cosmopolitan to the end, and it is that which gives his writings their enormous force.

The rootedness came not merely from his childhood in the court city of Surakarta, the heart and center of Javanese high culture, but from his deep involvement, once he left it as a young man, in every phase of his country's evolution as an independent state. He conspired in the student movement during the Japanese occupation. He fought in the revolution that freed his people from the Dutch. He participated in the negotiations at the United Nations that established the international reality of the new Republic. He picked his way through the rising delirium of the Sukarno period—when Muslims, Communists, and the military clashed, plotted, and killed until, stirring popular hatred, they produced popular disaster. He served the quieter, more deliberate, and—at least in the beginning—less personalistic Suharto regime (which emerged after the massacres) as its first ambassador to the United States and then had a falling out with it over its hardening autocracy. And he ended his career in Yogyakarta trying to reawaken in a new generation the hopes and ideals that had inspired his own. For nearly half a century, his life and that of his country seemed internally fused. It is hardly possible, at least for those of us who found ourselves caught up with them both, to think of them apart.

The cosmopolitanism came from Soedjatmoko's conception of himself—which was there from the beginning but grew stronger with time—as a world citizen: a Third World intellectual with something to say both to other Third World intellectuals who were trying to be heard in the global centers of power and to those who were harder to reach but more closely connected, at least culturally, to such centers from the First and Second Worlds. That extraordinary early embassy to the United Nations in the late 1940s, when he was only twenty-five and had not been outside the country since early childhood, launched a career not merely of representing Indonesia's interests abroad (which, after all, a lot of people have done) but of exemplifying its ideals— what it wanted to stand for, and what it wanted to stand against, in the postwar, postcolonial, post-laissez-faire world. (There is, to this day, a group of now aging American and European friends of Indonesia who still proudly boast that they met "Koko"—as everyone who ever encountered him, however briefly, always called him—in those electric early days in New York.)

Later, of course, his stature on the world stage grew a great deal larger and the audience of his admirers a great deal wider— as ambassador, as rector of the United Nations University in Tokyo, as a member of the Board of Trustees of the Ford Foundation, and most of all as a tireless traveler to and speaker at international public events, scholarly conferences, program planning sessions, and the like. (One of the last times I saw him was at a meeting in Princeton, set up by the Rockefeller Foundation, to stimulate interaction among Third World scholars working on development who were otherwise isolated from one another. The program turned out to have an important effect in connecting African, Middle Eastern, and Asian scholars directly, without the paternal intermediation of Americans and Europeans.)

Some of the results of all this activity are presented in the following pages from which the tone, the range, and the force of his mind can be grasped. But there was much more—his work on Southeast Asian historiography, on the comparative study of culture, on the role of the mass media in shaping political life. I never knew him when he wasn't up to some project, plunging into some subject, organizing some discussion. As inward and reflective a person as he was, he gave his life to the public world. Just a couple of years before he died I had some discussions with him in connection with his coming to that ivory tower of ivory towers, the Institute for Advanced Study at Princeton. The plan was that he would spend two or three years there to recollect in tranquillity and write up at a distance what he had learned from his political and scholarly career, what conclusions he had come to about himself, his country, this century, and the world. He was passionately, almost desperately, eager to do this (though he worried about how so much quiet would affect him after a lifetime spent in the middle of things). He began to project chapters, propose subjects, outline issues that he wanted to discuss with me and other scholars, particularly young ones. He kept saying, yes, I really *must* have time to bring my experiences together, to express my views in a sustained way. But right now there is so much that I need to do in Jakarta. Things are really beginning to move. Everything is changing or about to change. Maybe next year . . .

I am not, alas, one of those who knew Soedjatmoko during the New York days. I first met him in Jakarta in October 1951 when I arrived, together with some colleagues from Harvard, as a young, largely ignorant, and wildly overconfident graduate student about to embark on a two-year study of religion in central Java. It was the day after the first attempted coup—or half-attempted coup—in the new state's history, the now largely forgotten October 17th affair. The city was tense, with various military personnel in the streets and various rumors in the newspapers. But Soedjatmoko, who as a stalwart of Sjahrir's socialists was disappointed in the turn of events, sought us out not for political reasons but for intellectual and personal ones. We spent, as I remember, the entire night talking with him and some other younger Socialist Party of Indonesia figures about Indonesia's history and culture and about the value our work might have for its future. What I remember most besides the warmth and, at a difficult time, the optimism is the total candor of Soedjatmoko and the other Indonesians. He, and they, simply assumed that we were as we represented ourselves to be, that we wanted the country to prosper, and that we could be trusted and talked to as friends, not merely "dealt with" as possibly useful, possibly troublesome, foreigners. It was an extraordinary introduction to a man and a country. And after all that has happened, much of it not pretty, this is how I still think of him, and of it.

For me, that long and miraculous night was the beginning of what has been more than forty years of work on and in Indonesia with Indonesians. During those years I had many other intense and mind-shaking encounters with Koko—in Manila, in Tokyo, in Princeton, and again in Jakarta. In the pages that follow, the reader can catch something of the man I knew as well as at least the outlines of the summing-up book that he was too dedicated to all of us to take the time from us to write.

Clifford Geertz
Institute for Advanced Study
Princeton, New Jersey

Acknowledgments

The editors would like to express their thanks to Ivan Kats of the Obor Foundation, a long-time friend and colleague of Soedjatmoko's, who urged—indeed insisted—that we assemble this collection. He offered helpful advice and encouragement at every stage of our effort.

We are also grateful to the Soedjatmoko Foundation for its support of this project as part of its effort to preserve and develop Soedjatmoko's intellectual legacy. The foundation was established in 1990 to serve public welfare and promote social learning in the spirit of Soedjatmoko's commitment to humanity.

Our thanks go to Prof. Miriam Budiardjo, Soedjatmoko's sister, for reading the introduction to check biographical details.

Krishna Sondhi of Kumarian Press made publication of this collection possible. We are grateful for her interest and her patience.

Our thanks also go to the original copyright holders of those sections of the book that have been published previously. Chapter 1 is reprinted with permission from the Asia Society; "The Role of the Intellectual in a Developing Nation" was given as a lecture in 1970 under the auspices of the Indonesia Council of the Asia Society. The first part of Chapter 2 originally appeared as Parts I and II of an article entitled "Religion in the Politics of Economic Development" published in *The Stanford Journal of International Studies* 6 (Spring 1971); it is reprinted with the permission of that journal. The second part of Chapter 2 is the Hans

J. Morgenthau Memorial Lecture on Morality and Foreign Policy, originally published by the Carnegie Council on Ethics and International Affairs (New York 1981), and is reproduced with the council's permission.

The first part of Chapter 5 is included with the permission of Universitetsforlaget AS. It appeared in *Studies in War and Peace,* Oyvind Osterud, ed. (Oslo: Norwegian University Press, 1986). Chapter 6 includes a piece originally published as an Occasional Paper of the Institute for the Study of Diplomacy, Edmund A. Walsh School of Foreign Service, Georgetown University, under the title "Policymaking for Long-Term Global Issues: The Oscar Iden Lecture," and is reprinted with the institute's permission. The second part of Chapter 6 is reprinted with the permission of MIT Press; it was originally published as "Values in Transition," *The Washington Quarterly* 9(4): 67–72 (1986). Chapter 7 includes Parts III–V of "Religion in the Politics of Economic Development," *The Stanford Journal of International Studies* 6 (Spring 1971).

ABOUT THE EDITORS

KATHLEEN NEWLAND is a Washington, D.C.-based consultant on refugee and migration issues. Her experience includes serving on the international relations faculty of the London School of Economics and as special assistant to Rector Soedjatmoko at the United Nations University in Tokyo. She has a number of publications to her credit, most recently *Gender and International Relations* (Indiana University, 1991, with Rebecca Grant).

KAMALA CHANDRAKIRANA SOEDJATMOKO, the eldest daughter of Soedjatmoko, holds an M.A. in development sociology from Cornell University and a B.A. from Sophia University in Tokyo. She has been involved in research on the urban informal sector in Jakarta.

Introduction

Soedjatmoko was an Indonesian thinker who believed that, as a Third World intellectual, he had the responsibility and the right to contribute to the debate on the future of the global community. He saw his role in life as that of a free intellectual whose disinterest in attaining personal political power allowed him to focus on the interests of the weak and the marginalized as well as those of humankind as a whole. He aspired to a role akin to that of the traditional Javanese sage, the carrier of basic values of society and humanity. He believed that his inherited cultural values and his experience with nation building and development in a Third World country gave him insights that could be useful to a world undergoing rapid transformation. He was also convinced that he was participating in a process by which non-Western cultures would take their rightful places alongside Western civilization to enrich and strengthen an interdependent, crowded, and fragile world.

The product of a particular time and place with which he identified closely, Soedjatmoko was condemned to being slightly ahead of his time and apart from his own society. He was a man of many apparent paradoxes: profoundly Javanese but a committed internationalist, an intellectual mystic, a gregarious loner. Although he spent long periods of his life in self-imposed or externally enforced isolation, he insisted that, for him, thinking was a social process.

Soedjatmoko was troubled by the state of the world as he saw it. Reflecting on the performance of the post–World War II development effort, he could not help but express his disappointment. The world, he declared, remained conspicuously beset with unacceptable suffering, want, and strife as the gap between the rich and the poor continued to widen. Structural inequality was to him a tragic legacy of our time. He saw political conflict, economic recession, and environmental pollution spilling across borders and throughout the international system. These were the facts of interdependence. But he was alarmed that no society seemed to have mastered the dislocations of the twentieth century with its dizzying growth of populations and massive movements of people, its instant communications, alienating technologies, shrunken spaces, and horrifying destructive power. He saw that despite its great diversity, all humankind was united in a common vulnerability to violence and the destruction of the earth's life-support systems.

Despite his dark view of the present state of the world, Soedjatmoko refused to indulge in apathy. He was confident that once societies recognized their common vulnerability and the inseparability of their futures, the first step toward humankind's survival would already have been taken. He had no panacea to solve the world's problems; he did not believe in panaceas. Rather, he thought that we should consider ourselves as undergoing a process of mutual learning in which everyone is both teacher and student. It is the capacity to learn, more than any other single factor, he believed, that would determine the viability and integrity of our societies.

Soedjatmoko focused much of his work on issues of development, though not to the exclusion of other issues of global transformation. His work on development departed from much of the conventional thinking—or perhaps carried it forward. Although never underestimating the seriousness (and destructive potential) of material deprivation, he was equally concerned with intellectual, cultural, and spiritual impoverishment. His work turns our attention to dimensions of development that are too often neglected: Freedom, democracy, human rights, and tolerance were as crucial in his view as capital-output ratios and export targets. He was quite certain that the industrialized countries still had developmental tasks ahead of them and that they had things to learn from the Third World.

He arrived at an extraordinary synthesis of ideas through a lifetime of intellectual effort. That effort was to fit together the shifting, kaleidoscopic patterns of simultaneous social, economic, and political change at levels ranging from the minutely particular to the cosmic. No field of inquiry failed to interest him, from chaos theory in physics to psychiatric interpretations of culture, from economic development modeling to Islamic architecture. He was often described as equally at home in Western and Eastern culture and discourse. It is probably more accurate to say that he was fully at home in neither, for he could always see the missing piece in any self-contained explanation derived from a single worldview.

From the tensions within him he derived enormous creativity and provided enormous stimulation to others. His ability to see a number of sides of a problem simultaneously made him a valuable and valued interlocutor to Indonesians coming to grips with the challenges of nationhood, to others from Third World countries grappling with the issues of development, and to those from North or South engaged in the serious business of trying to comprehend—and perhaps even manage—the often convulsive transformations of the age.

When Soedjatmoko died in 1989, he left more than a hundred pieces of writing—the legacy of a lifetime of rigorous thinking about the future of Indonesia, the developing world, and humankind as a whole. This volume presents a selection of his work produced between 1970 and 1987. Bringing these pieces together in a single volume permits an integrated reading of his work and shows the breadth and complexity of his thinking.

Soedjatmoko's writings cannot be characterized in terms of conventional disciplinary categories or approaches. This is partly because his education was eclectic. He learned to distrust the fragmentation inherent in "scientific" method and was wary of what he perceived as overspecialization in the academic disciplines. He was uninspired by absolutes and would not offer simple answers to the complex problems with which he was concerned.

Soedjatmoko's writings, instead, are characterized by a syncretic use of major works of scholarship. He gave equal consideration (though not necessarily equal weight) to the works of Nietzsche and Ibn Khaldoun, to Metternich and Gandhi, to Vivekananda and Thomas Merton. The synthesis at which he arrived was unique. Often described as an interpreter between East and West or North and South, he was much more than that, for he brought to the issues of the day a distinctive analysis born of his personal search for understanding.

Skeptical of "solutions," Soedjatmoko valued the process of searching for solutions as much as or perhaps even more than the outcome of the search. His was the approach of someone who had no desire to impose ready-made answers or to foreclose undiscovered options. And while he labored to establish a viable sense of direction, he knew how difficult it is to predict the consequences of our actions. Too often he had seen unanticipated outcomes overwhelm intended results; hence his emphasis on qualities of responsiveness, resilience, restraint, and open-mindedness. At the same time, he was keenly aware of the fallibility of human beings. It was only natural for him to voice a reminder that there would always be room for failure, and even tragedy.

Soedjatmoko's writings reflect his own perception of the role of the intellectual. In a paper he wrote on Third World intellectuals (Chapter 1 in this volume), he expressed his view that the role of the intellectual is:

> to define the problems of their societies . . . to sharpen the vision of the kind of society they want theirs to transform into, to relate emerging value patterns to changing social realities, to illuminate the road ahead, to identify pitfalls and constantly to search out alternative roads, to find the significance of each new development in relation to the common goals.

The intellectual, he believed, had the responsibility to defend the common goals of freedom and justice—a task that required

> a strong moral commitment . . . [and] a clear vision that is armed with a firm grasp of the economic, political, social and cultural contexts within which the struggle [for freedom and justice] is to be waged.

In light of these views, the value of scholarship is not to be judged simply by precision and elegant presentation but by its relevance to the common good. To a fellow Indonesian intellectual, he once said, "we think not for ourselves . . . [but] for the people . . . [so] they will be ready to have their rendezvous with history."[1]

Soedjatmoko lived his life in pursuit of the challenges he himself set for intellectuals. Perhaps because he never earned the degree that would have stamped his education "complete," his thirst for knowledge was unquenchable. All his life, he seized upon new (to him) authors and arguments with relish. He loved the give-and-take of vigorous debate. Sometimes he would pause and grin in the midst of it, as if carried away by the sheer fun of it—or, sometimes, by his own eloquence. The exchange of ideas was as vital to him as breathing—a fact that made the narrowing of political debate in Indonesia particularly painful. He especially loved the fierce and passionate commitment of the young. In maturity, he urged his contemporaries in positions of authority not to fear it or seek to suppress it. Since his death, his stature as a "sage" has continued to grow. He is seen as a model of the free intellectual by many of those to whom he dedicated his thinking: the younger generation.

At various stages of his life Soedjatmoko worked as a journalist, a diplomat, and an international civil servant, but he was first and foremost a humanist. Human growth and well-being were at the core of his concern; they were, in his view, the ultimate purposes of any endeavor and the standards by which human achievements were to be judged.

Soedjatmoko was brought up with the idea that one must strive for freedom. This was at the core of the education Soedjatmoko received from his father, one of the most influential people in his life. Soedjatmoko's father, Saleh Mangundiningrat, was a medical doctor—one of the first generation of Indonesians trained in Western medicine and one of the few with a doctorate from Holland. He was also a well-read intellectual and a Javanese mystic. Political freedom ranked high in his scale of values, but not higher than inner freedom of the mind and spirit. His life was filled with the pursuits of his intellectual curiosity and spiritual longings.

Dr. Saleh, as he was commonly known, was an avid reader. His library contained books on world history, philosophy, the development of science, and literary classics.[2] His collection included writings by Western thinkers such as Hegel, Marx, and Nietzsche and by Indian intellectuals such as Krishnamurti, Gandhi, Vivekananda, and Ramakrishna.[3] Dr. Saleh encouraged in his son the habit of reading and supplied him with a wide range of books. His father's library became an increasingly important source of learning for Soedjatmoko as he grew older. By the time Soedjatmoko entered school, his father had already taught him the value of self-motivated learning and open-mindedness.

Dr. Saleh was also deeply spiritual. He meditated regularly and journeyed into the world of mysticism. Although he believed in the centrality of religion, he would not treat one religion as truer than another. A Muslim himself, he did not hesitate to put his children into nondenominational schools, for he believed that all religions had valuable messages to impart. It was Dr. Saleh who first planted the seeds of Soedjatmoko's spirituality, humanism, and hunger for knowledge.

Soedjatmoko's further intellectual development was closely entwined with Indonesia's history. He came of age in the final years of Dutch colonial rule in Indonesia. In 1940, at the age of 18, he moved from Surabaya, in eastern Java, to Jakarta to attend medical school. Through student activists in medical school, Soedjatmoko was introduced to leaders of the nationalist movement such as Sukarno, Hatta, Sjahrir, and Amir Sjarifuddin. He was immediately recruited to the top circles of the movement.

It was also during this time that Soedjatmoko first saw the face of extreme poverty in the slums of Jakarta, taken there at the initiative of one of his student-activist friends. Night after night he saw men, women, and children sleeping on the streets and in railroad cars. It was a terrible shock to him. "Then, only then," Soedjatmoko later recalled, "I realized that there was that kind of poverty. . . . The discrimination of the Dutch [colonial system] became very clear."[4] From that time, he became deeply committed to the struggle against poverty and structural inequality. For these goals, national independence was, he believed, a prerequisite.

During World War II, the Japanese defeated the Dutch in Indonesia and took over control of the colony. They arrived with promises of independence for Indonesia. Soedjatmoko was among the small number of people in the nationalist movement who were suspicious of the intentions of the Japanese forces. His proficiency in German allowed him to read European fascist literature. He saw the commonality with Japanese ideology of the period and was determined to resist Japanese domination of Indonesia. During this period, Soedjatmoko saw many of his more radical nationalist friends embrace the Japanese, motivated by a blinding hatred for the Dutch. This reinforced Soedjatmoko's skeptical attitude toward radicalism.

After two years of medical school, Soedjatmoko was arrested for organizing a student strike against the Japanese authorities. He was put in prison, where he experienced brutality first-hand—an experience that stayed with him throughout his life, reinforcing his sense of the tremendous vulnerability of the human person. Upon release from prison, he was expelled from medical school and barred from enrolling elsewhere. This marked the end of Soedjatmoko's formal education. (A brief stint at Harvard in the 1950s was cut short by the call to take up responsibilities in the newly recognized, independent Indonesian government.)

After his release from prison, Soedjatmoko returned to his parents' home in Solo, central Java, where he stayed for two years, until Indonesia's proclamation of independence in 1945. Throughout that time, Soedjatmoko was kept under surveillance by the Japanese military police. These two years in Solo were spent in virtual exile. It became a formative period of contemplation and intellectual journeying for the twenty-one-year-old Soedjatmoko.

He read voraciously during this time, benefiting particularly from the Japanese campaign to raid the homes of Dutch missionaries. These raids were responsible for the availability of books on Western philosophy and theology in the local flea market that Soedjatmoko frequented. His reading list included Jaspers, Bergson, Scheler, Heidegger, and Kierkegaard. He also explored Eastern philosophies, developing a particular interest in mysticism in Hinduism, Islam, and Catholicism, and especially in his own Javanese tradition.

After months of total absorption in reading the writings of the world's great thinkers, Soedjatmoko found himself losing his sense of self-confidence and indeed his sense of self. He questioned his passive reception of the great ideas he had read. This frustration culminated in Soedjatmoko's decision to abandon what had been his most valued source of learning: He refused to read another book until he could regain his sense of self. After six months of painful and at times agonizing reflection, Soedjatmoko finally reached a new understanding of the meaning of knowledge. Reflecting on that time, he said, it was only then that I understood the value of knowledge as a manifestation of one's inner force. Before, I simply absorbed [and] gathered knowledge; [after that], I had begun to view knowledge as an extension of one's inner self, an extension of one's mind and soul.[5]

He came to view knowledge as "a tool of understanding that would not have meaning without sincerity and a desire to know, to understand, and ultimately, to [express] love to humankind."[6]

It was after this painful soul-searching process that Soedjatmoko began to feel "liberated from the grip and domination of knowledge" and was able "to face the world's greatest thinkers . . . as fellow seekers of truth."[7] This was a turning point in Soedjatmoko's development as an independent thinker. From this moment on, he saw himself as "a person of Indonesian culture who is also a world citizen."[8]

In 1945, the Japanese surrendered, and the nationalist leaders of Indonesia issued a unilateral declaration of independence. Direct confrontation with the Dutch entered a new phase. Soedjatmoko, then twenty-three years old, was summoned to Jakarta to work for the revolutionary government. He first worked under Amir Sjaruffudin, who was then Minister of Information, as Deputy Head of the Foreign Press Department. The following year, Prime Minister Sjahrir appointed Soedjatmoko as chief editor of a Dutch-language weekly, *Het Inzicht,* which was published to maintain a channel of communication between the revolutionary government and the Dutch. In these early experiences, Soedjatmoko became aware of the need to balance the power of government. He later cofounded a weekly magazine, *Siasat,* which was intended to be an independent and critical journal of opinion for intellectuals committed to the revolution.[9]

Through his work with the revolutionary government, Soedjatmoko realized the centrality of international forces in the fulfillment of Indonesia's nationalist aspirations. In his first assignment he was asked to take charge of foreign journalists who came to Indonesia to cover the revolution. Their depiction of the struggle and its protagonists would help determine the degree of support or opposition the nationalists would gain from the outside world. In 1947, Prime Minister Sjahrir assigned Soedjatmoko to his first diplomatic mission. Anticipating an attack by the Dutch military, Sjahrir asked Soedjatmoko and two other young men to find their way to the United States in order to present Indonesia's case at the United Nations. In 1949, the new independent nation of Indonesia gained international recognition. Soedjatmoko then helped to establish the first Indonesian diplomatic missions to the United Nations, the United States, and Great Britain.

The success of Indonesia's struggle continued to be linked to international political realities. Soedjatmoko saw, for example, how the U.S. position toward Indonesia, and Asian nationalism in general, changed only after the so-called fall of China in 1949. This was the beginning of his complex appreciation of the interconnectedness of international, national, and local realities and his preoccupation with the dynamics of international governance in general.

Soedjatmoko made two intellectual journeys before he returned to Indonesia in 1952. The first was to the American South. Finding much to admire in the United States, he also felt strongly that he could not leave that country without witnessing for himself the realities of racism there and its impact on the living conditions of black Americans. His second journey, which lasted almost a year, took him to Western and Eastern Europe. Seeing the postwar world divided into two ideological camps, Soedjatmoko wanted to find out for himself what the societies and leaders of these two camps had to offer for newly emerging nations such as his. Eastern Europe was of particular interest to him, because ideologies of the left were prevalent among Indonesian nationalists with whom he was closely associated. Indeed, Soedjatmoko considered himself a socialist, although by this time he was no longer certain what it meant to be a socialist. He felt the need to determine his political position before returning to Indonesia.[10]

After eleven months of traveling and meeting with European politicians and thinkers, Soedjatmoko was unimpressed. A Europe exhausted by war and rent by competing "isms" seemed to be out of ideas for the future. In all his meetings he had found neither vision nor any alternatives that seemed relevant for Indonesia. In a last attempt, Soedjatmoko decided to visit Yugoslavia, a country that had just broken away from the Soviet orbit. Here, he met the one person who made a strong impression on him: Milovan Djilas. Soedjatmoko was inspired by Djilas's conviction that the monopoly of the world by the two superpowers would not last, and that the other nations of the world would gradually learn from both camps and proceed with their own paths. After his conversation with Djilas, which lasted three hours, Soedjatmoko felt that he had found some of the answers he had been seeking. He finally felt ready to return home.

It was in the period after his European journey that Soedjatmoko began to take a more active intellectual role in Indonesia. He became editor of the daily newspaper *Pedoman* and then of the weekly political magazine *Siasat*. Through these and other outlets, he shared the lesson he had recently learned: that answers to Indonesia's problems were not limited to a choice between capitalism and communism. He stressed, instead, the need to throw off the bonds of ideological dogmatism and search for uniquely Indonesian answers rooted in indigenous creative capacities. He maintained that the essence of Indonesia's independence and freedom lay in both the possibility and the imperative of constantly penetrating, understanding, and recreating from its own past and its own traditional cultures.[11] It was in the same spirit that Soedjatmoko later spoke to wider audiences about the importance of cultural rootedness and the inevitability of diverse and culturally specific solutions to global problems.

Soedjatmoko came back to a highly politicized Indonesia where almost everyone was immersed in interparty and ideological battles. In this climate, Soedjatmoko insisted on the importance of giving priority to economic development. Ultimately, he believed, success in overcoming structural poverty would be the measure of the viability of any political system. He cautioned that without economic development, the gap that divided the newly independent nations and the industrialized countries would continue to widen,[12] ultimately robbing the former's political independence of real meaning.

In the same breath, however, Soedjatmoko stressed that it would be misleading to think of development as simply an issue of economic growth. It is also, he insisted, "a process of social change, a process of transformation of the soul, the creative adaptation of [a] culture."[13] It is a difficult and painful process, generating widespread anxiety as old values are challenged before new ones have crystallized.

Despite his mistrust of ideology, Soedjatmoko joined the Socialist Party of Indonesia (PSI) in 1955 and was elected a member of the Constituent Assembly a year later. Yet even as he took his place in the Assembly, he witnessed the deterioration of

Indonesia's political system. The creation of a democratic society—which to him was the ultimate purpose of the nationalist movement—was being abandoned for authoritarianism. Political conflict among segments of society continued to escalate without signs of resolution. Poverty, supposedly to be overcome with the end of the colonial system, was still widespread.

Soedjatmoko was forced to rethink: What role could he and fellow intellectuals play in the midst of their society's disintegration? He refused to take part in an underground movement because he believed in an open political process. But he was unsuccessful in an attempt to create changes through a democratic league. Nevertheless, he maintained his stance against radicalism, which he believed could mislead people, and remained loyal to his principle of restraint and "intelligent flexibility." He believed that intellectuals should play an active role in facilitating dialogue between and within social and political groups in conflict rather than participating in partisan politics. He also saw the need for intellectuals to help direct the concerns of these groups away from traditional preoccupations and relate them to the more urgent problems of society as a whole. For this purpose, disinterest in political power—a quality that demonstrated independent thinking—came to be seen by Soedjatmoko as crucial for intellectuals.

Soedjatmoko also recognized the vulnerability of the intellectual, who "easily falls into the role of the articulator of dissent."[14] Nevertheless, he continued to stress the need for intellectuals to persevere "as watchdogs of democracy," to "push back the limits to freedom and nurture the will and the capacity to defend each hard-won expansion of it."[15]

A political turning point came for Soedjatmoko in 1957. President Sukarno,·by then well advanced along the road of "guided democracy," asked Soedjatmoko to join his cabinet. Soedjatmoko refused. Sukarno was furious. Soedjatmoko was blacklisted in official circles. During the same period, the Socialist Party was banned. A short time later, *Pedoman* and *Siasat* were closed down. Soedjatmoko remained effectively unemployed for almost four years.

The polarization of the Indonesian society reached its peak in 1965 in one of the bloodiest incidents in recent history. In the wake of an abortive coup, as many as half a million people were killed in an orgy of intercommunal bloodletting. To

Soedjatmoko, the massacre imposed painful lessons about the fragility of social structures, particularly in heterogeneous societies. He saw the ease with which disintegration and violence can overwhelm orderly processes of change. Along with this awareness of unintended consequences came a reinforced conviction about the need for effective mechanisms of conflict resolution and strengthened social resilience.

A new regime took control of Indonesia in 1966, and Soedjatmoko was appointed ambassador to the United States in 1968, signing beforehand an agreement that he would not remain a civil servant after his appointment ended. He proved to be an effective and highly respected diplomat in his three years in the United States, gaining the attention of both President Richard Nixon and Secretary of State Henry Kissinger for his insightful views on international politics. He also earned the attention of many members of Congress by traveling widely throughout the country, including the small towns, speaking with their constituents.[16]

Soedjatmoko also used the time in the United States for intellectual pursuits. The best part of being an ambassador, he later said, was that he could invite practically anyone to lunch. He was able to engage in discussions with many of the thinkers and policymakers he most admired. Edward Shils, Robert McNamara, Zbignew Brezinski, and Thomas Merton were among those with whom he developed relationships. Senior journalists, international development practitioners and decisionmakers, and university scholars also became his colleagues in dialogue. Eager to understand the military dimension of the world political order, Soedjatmoko initiated discussions with people in the Pentagon and think tanks such as the Rand Corporation.

Few people who had the opportunity to listen to him came away unimpressed. His great personal charm attracted an audience; his intellectual power and breadth kept it. It is probably fair to say that no Indonesian thinker has had such an impact internationally. From the 1970s onward, he was in tremendous demand as a speaker at an array of conferences, meetings, and public events. He was even more in demand as a member of deliberative bodies; the scope of those in which he participated reveals the range of his contribution. Among many others, they included Olof Palme's Independent Commission on Disarmament and Security Issues, the Independent Commission on International Humanitarian Issues convened by Prince Saddrudin

Aga Khan and Crown Prince Hassan bin Talal, David Rockefeller's Williamsburg Group, and the jury of the Aga Khan Award
for Islamic Architecture. He was the first person from the Third
World (and only the second foreigner) to sit on the board of the
Ford Foundation. In 1978, he was awarded the Magsaysay Award
for International Understanding—the so-called Asian Nobel
Prize. His reputation grew largely by word of mouth, for he never
published an overview of his thinking in a unified book that
might have gained him a large audience.[17] His public had to seek
him out, and did.

The flood of honors, awards, and invitations continued
throughout his life. He took each one seriously, aware of the risk
of spreading himself too thinly and of the dangers of tokenism.
He refused to be a figurehead. In each forum in which he
agreed to participate he was fully engaged. And he derived enormous stimulation from the range of contacts to which his travels
exposed him. Nevertheless, he was not unconscious of the irony
that as his international reputation grew, the scope for direct
involvement in Indonesia narrowed.

When Soedjatmoko returned to Indonesia from Washington
D.C., he found the country single-mindedly led toward economic
growth and political stability. It disturbed him to see how, for the
sake of growth, order was given priority over justice, freedom sacrificed to control, and popular participation abandoned for efficiency. Structural inequality, still at the center of his concern, was
dealt with only halfheartedly. He questioned the economic models that dominated policymaking, believing that they were unable
to take account of the complex dynamism of social change. His
critical stance once again marginalized him from the chambers
of government decisionmaking and gave further impetus to his
international career. Given his long-established concern with
development and humanitarian issues, this was a natural shift for
Soedjatmoko.

In his travels throughout Asia, Soedjatmoko shared with his
fellow intellectuals the lessons learned from Indonesia's recent
attempt at nation building. He reminded them that economic
development meant not only greater efficiency and growth but
also social and political dislocation. Although nation building
generated hope and visions of a better future, the rapid social
change that went with it could also cause disorientation, frustration, and despair. Having witnessed for himself the fragility of

social structures, particularly in conflict-ridden pluralistic societies, he stressed the imperative of maintaining a dynamic balance among growth, security, and social justice.[18] He reaffirmed that the purpose of attaining political independence and implementing the development effort was, above all, to create "the material conditions in which human freedom could become meaningful."[19]

Soedjatmoko also shared his conviction that Asian civilizations could offer alternative models of development that were distinct from those offered by the dominant Western ideologies. He wrote:

> This may imply a concept of modernization that does not emphasize competition, but cooperation; a concept of development that does not aim at affluence, but at sufficiency; and a concept of individual rights and ownership that is limited by the public good.[20]

To his Western colleagues, Soedjatmoko underlined the persistence of the structural disparity between the nations of the North and those of the South. He suggested the need for a redefinition of North-South relations by creating

> an international order that is not simply a global projection of particular ideologies . . . [but one that is] capable of facilitating the major structural changes that will be necessary to ensure the survival of freedom, justice and civility in a world of scarcity, without doing violence to the pluralism that is an essential precondition for the viability of any international system.[21]

In Indonesia, Soedjatmoko's audience was largely drawn from outside the state structure, from among intellectuals, students, and people in the arts, most of whom were of the younger generation. The country was then dominated by planning based on Western economic models and by pressures to conform to a single way of thinking. Once again, Soedjatmoko found himself defending independent thinking and called for vigorous and critical examination of Indonesia's own cultural values and historical past.

As Soedjatmoko gained popularity among students and disenchanted intellectuals, he was increasingly perceived as a threat to those who saw open debate as a challenge to power. In 1974, he was falsely accused of masterminding a student-led riot against the visiting Japanese Prime Minister Kakuei Tanaka. After a few weeks of intensive interrogation, Soedjatmoko was exempted from imprisonment but banned from leaving the country for two and a half years. During these years he continued to write about education, religion, and culture as well as about structural poverty and the development of a centralized and authoritarian bureaucratic state.

In 1980, Soedjatmoko was offered the position of rector of the United Nations University (UNU). He accepted it with a heavy heart, for in doing so he acknowledged that there was little space for him to contribute effectively as an intellectual in Indonesia. This position at the UNU, an institute for global learning, allowed Soedjatmoko to fulfill a need he had perceived in 1969:

> Because of the interdependence for survival, there . . . [is] an urgent need for an intensified international cooperation between . . . intellectual institutions the world over. Without cross-fertilization and cross-cultural illumination it will become impossible to develop those concepts and that vision which will be acceptable to the world at large. . . . If such a close cooperation could be developed, this international network of universities and research institutes could yet become the intellectual infrastructure of a new world and a new world order.[22]

The eighteen papers presented in this volume, all originally written in English, have been consolidated into eight chapters. The papers were chosen for their relevance to an international audience and because they show the evolution of a cluster of overarching concepts that Soedjatmoko developed over the course of his career. They show the importance that he attached to qualities such as resilience, restraint, tolerance, the ability to live with complexity, and a sense of solidarity among diverse peoples.

In Chapter 1, Soedjatmoko writes about the intellectual in a developing nation "as he is defined by his dilemmas." He explores the thinker's uneasy relationship with power and tradition, looking for ways to protect integrity and creativity while making the compromises necessary to translate ideas into reality. It also reflects Soedjatmoko's personal views of his own role as a Third World intellectual.

Chapter 2 presents two pieces that explore the broader dimensions of the development process. Written a decade apart, they demonstrate Soedjatmoko's effort to connect the economic, social, cultural, and spiritual dimensions of change and to place them in a moral framework.

In Chapter 3, Soedjatmoko characterizes development as, above all, a learning process. The failures of the development experience show that material approaches to progress do not automatically bring justice or dignity in their wake; explicit strategies for democratic structural change to enable people to liberate themselves from dependency and powerlessness must be learned. Beyond this, communities must learn to prepare themselves to live in the future and cope with new technologies, new political forms, and new demographic patterns.

In Chapter 4, Soedjatmoko insists upon the importance of the humanities in development. A thorough grounding in the humanities has the capacity to endow people with the self-confidence that comes from understanding their own cultures. It also encourages tolerance and empathy by acquainting people with other civilizations and the commonality of human experience and aspirations. Social science has two functions, which may sometimes appear to conflict: to provide tools for social management and to provide keys to self-understanding. Soedjatmoko also considers how higher education can remain rooted in specific cultures while addressing global problems and preparing people to live with change. For the universities, this implies a change of objective, emphasizing the habit of continual learning rather than the transmission of received knowledge.

The destructiveness and easy availability of modern weaponry have given the problem of violence a new urgency in our times. Chapter 5 looks at the patterns of armed conflict in the Third World in the international context and demonstrates how a policy of restraint—in both seeking and providing external intervention in localized conflicts—can limit the duration and the destructiveness of wars. He then goes on to argue the case of nonviolence not simply as a moral imperative but as a practical and effective means of struggle and a building block of the essential quality of social resilience.

The issues of governance discussed in Chapter 6 encompass the aggregate of forces, systems, institutions, disputes, and arrangements by which human beings cooperate and compete. The crucial question is how to reduce the human cost of the necessary and, in many cases, desirable convulsions associated with social change. How can the need for change be reconciled with the need for order and for justice? And what scope for freedom is defined by the dynamic equilibrium among these three?

Soedjatmoko insists in Chapter 7 that there is no necessary contradiction between science and spiritual values; both assign the highest value to the search for truth. One problem remains, however: How, in a period of growing religious intensity, can religions heal the breach between ethics and policy without opening the door to dogmatism and intolerance? He also argues that religion can play an integrative role in the often disorienting process of rapid social transformation. The forward movement of a whole social system depends on a broad consensus on goals and means based on a shared vision of the future that is capable of arousing new hope.

The final chapter proposes an expansion of the international consensus upon which a common ethical framework for action could be built. A broader consensus requires a search for the highest common values that are widely shared among cultures, drawing on non-Western as well as Western legal, moral, and philosophical traditions. The idea of human solidarity implies an almost Copernican change of perspective, from a view centered around the nation-state to one in which the state system revolves around the commonality of human interests, with human well-being as its primary goal. This chapter represents in many ways the culmination of Soedjatmoko's thinking.

It would be possible to trace Soedjatmoko's preoccupations in a number of different ways through his writings and in relation to the major influences on his thinking. One of the major themes that emerges from his work is freedom. In his reflections on freedom, one can see the blended influences of Eastern and Western intellectual traditions, lived and observed realities, abstract and concrete concerns.

Soedjatmoko's readings in Western liberal philosophy highlighted freedom for the individual as the goal of political organization; the study and practice of Eastern philosophies and religion revealed inner freedom as the highest aspiration of the one who seeks truth. But he saw the social dimension of freedom too, and recognized that it went beyond individualism. In his view, to free people from powerlessness and dependence was the ultimate purpose of the independence movement, of nation building, and of the search for a more equitable international order.

Looking back over his work, one finds a remarkable consistency in tone and in the themes that concerned him from his earliest writing to his last. The sophistication that characterizes the later works is built up of layers of observation, experience, contemplation, comparison, and relentless pursuit of understanding. Although he saw the human race participating actively in its own destruction, he retained a lurking optimism about the possibility of eliminating the causes of destructive behavior: poverty, ignorance, insecurity, fear of the unknown. He did not believe in the perfectibility of human society or human beings, but he did believe in the cultivation of civic virtues such as restraint, civility, tolerance, self-respect, and respect for others.

To those trained in the detached, rationalist, Cartesian thought patterns of the European Enlightenment, he insisted on the dynamic uncertainties of engagement; to passionate radicals committed to action, he urged the value of analytical approaches. His rejection of simplistic responses did not make for an easy life. He was accused both of encouraging the kind of ill-considered actions of which he disapproved and of being too slow to act. But for Soedjatmoko, the highest duty was to comprehend and explain. His last official position, as rector of the United Nations University, was one that allowed professional scope for this sense of vocation. His farewell address to the University Council expressed his hopes for the UNU in terms that showed how closely his personal aspirations were invested in his work there:

> Ultimately, we may hope that the United Nations University will make a contribution toward the emergence of a universalism beyond pluralism, based not on the lowest common denominator but on the highest common values that we share as human beings. Our mutual dependence and mutual vulnerability demand this, and both are daily growing. I have always felt that the United Nations University is ahead of the times. But now, I feel, the times are catching up. We must be ready for them.[23]

This sense of urgency never left him. He always felt that humankind was in a race between its intelligence and its destructive impulses. He was enormously encouraged by the end of the Cold War but anticipated the explosion of suppressed nationalism and ethnic conflict that would follow. Today, his pleas for restraint, tolerance, and resilience have greater resonance than ever.

1

....

The Role of the Intellectual in a Developing Nation

Soedjatmoko maintained a lifelong preoccupation with the relationship between thought and action, political power and personal integrity. They were not abstractions to him. At a number of points in his life he had to make a choice between a form of political engagement that would have compromised his principles and withdrawal—or ejection—from political influence. He refused a position in Sukarno's cabinet, as "guided democracy" became increasingly authoritarian, and was blacklisted as a result. But he also refused to join the underground resistance, maintaining that open debate was essential to political development. The change of government in 1966 brought him back into an official position. In 1970, as ambassador to the United States, Soedjatmoko gave this lecture at Asia House in New York to members of the Indonesian Council of The Asia Society. It is both a philosophical exploration of the role of the intellectual and a very personal credo.

The Intellectual in a Developing Nation[1]

The sociologist Edward Shils gave what is possibly the earliest in-depth picture of the intellectual in a developing nation.[2] Since

This chapter is reprinted with permission from the Asia Society.

then, a number of other studies have appeared, some dealing with the impact of foreign education on such an intellectual. After the collapse of parliamentary government in a number of developing countries and the emergence of regimes dominated by the military, a spate of studies was published dealing with the intellectual in uniform.

In most of these studies, the intellectual is portrayed as the modernizer, the formulator of new goals and purposes, as well as the articulator of dissent. Intellectuals often emerge as people tormented by their own sense of alienation, stemming from the clash between the two cultures to which they feel they belong; the classic statements on this subject were made by Nehru and Sjahrir. Part of this picture of intellectuals is also the manner in which they see themselves performing the function of relating universally held human values to the concrete situation in which they find themselves and to the methods by which they seek to pursue their goals. In this respect they are continually and crucially concerned with the cultural and moral or normative problems of identity and expression, purpose and direction, structure and meaning, perception and motivation.

A great deal of time has passed and a great many events have taken place since Shils started to draw attention to this general topic. This passage of time has been characterized by the collapse of many of the illusions that Shils's intellectuals held when they entered into the era of independence. Simultaneously, there have been considerable changes in the general intellectual climate of the world, from which the Third World intellectual in part draws sustenance. Third, many of these men and women have had the previously unfamiliar experience of entering into positions of responsibility. And fourth, a new postindependence generation of intellectuals has emerged, bringing with them a different sense of life, a different *lebensgefühland*, and, often, a more nativistic orientation. Another look at the beast, therefore, seems justified.

Rather than utilize the sociological perspective as Shils did, I will try to describe Third World intellectuals as they are defined by their dilemmas, by looking at them from the inside rather than from the outside, by examining their internal conflicts rather than the external pressures to which they are subject. Although this is not meant to be an occasion for self-revelatory posturing in the manner of Rousseau, there is, inevitably, an Indonesian and a personal cast to the following description.

Despite all the political changes in many of the new nations, the basic role of the intellectual has not changed, mainly because the process of social transformation in which the nation is involved is still going on. Thus the intellectual is still faced with essentially the same dilemmas analyzed by Shils. But there have been some important shifts in perspective and, consequently, some changes in the intellectual's sense of self-awareness and in the resulting responses.

The first and foremost dilemma remains that of the relationship of intellectuals to power. Insofar as they have clear ideas about the future of their countries, the goals that have to be pursued, and the manner in which those goals should be pursued, they are inevitably fascinated by power as the unavoidable means to translate their ideas into reality. At the same time, the ambivalence of their own attitudes toward power has remained the same. They must come to terms with the slow pace of change, the inevitable compromises that go with administrative responsibility, and the need—in order to buttress their power bases in any political structure—to cater to popular prejudices and preoccupations that they are unable to share. These adjustments do violence to the clarity of their vision of the future and to the directness and vigor that they see as an essential condition for successful implementation. These conditions all seem to threaten both their integrity and their continued creativity as intellectuals.

Moreover, political and administrative responsibility is concerned with order and, insofar as change is concerned, with orderly change. New ideas always constitute a threat to the established order. Although administrators or political leaders may be well aware of the contribution that intellectuals could make to the success of their regimes, they are also suspicious of the potential danger that intellectuals and intellectual freedom pose to the need for order.

For many intellectuals, this dilemma was at its sharpest immediately after the attainment of independence. Then there was an urgent and legitimate need to man the government services, help lead the political parties, staff the newspapers, and so forth. Over the years, the pattern of such adjustments has remained much the same; still, it would be interesting to study possible shifts in the relative percentages of those intellectuals who became mandarins in the highest sense of disinterested service, those who became sparkless bureaucrats, those who descended to the level of cynical apparatchiks serving self-perpetuating power, and those who preferred unstructured influence to power. Different categories of political style have also remained: the populist, the elitist, and that dynamic combination of the two, the Jacobin.

What changed in the light of postindependence experience was the intellectual's awareness of power, its function, its limits, and its character. Among intellectuals there is now a greater awareness of the need for a strong central government capable of pursuing the goals of nation building and economic development in the face of intractable obstacles posed by tradition, ignorance, and backwardness. There is also a greater awareness of the need to establish and develop countervailing forces within the society that can limit abuses of power and ensure voluntary popular participation, initiative, and organization. The intellectuals of developing nations have aligned themselves on both sides of this dividing line, their places determined mainly by temperament and incidental factors. But whatever their place, it is clear to all of them that a sufficiently large number of intellectuals should stay outside of the government, outside of direct political involvement, to strengthen and nurture the intellectual institutions and voluntary associations needed to secure a balance between state power and the power of society. This is a precondition for freedom and civility in the political system.

One of the sobering lessons many intellectuals have learned since independence concerns their personal interest in gaining power: that the reach of their persuasiveness in their own country often has little to do with the validity of their arguments or the correctness of the positions they take. They find it very difficult, if not impossible, to break through the reserve with which their ideas are greeted beyond the boundaries of their own solidarity group or community of origin. During the struggle for independence, the risks involved in defying colonial rule made the power role of the activist-intellectual more broadly accepted. Many have now made the ironic discovery that in new nations, where deep communal cleavages and suspicions exist, the more convincing the intellectual's disinterest in political power, the more his or her political ideas are taken seriously beyond the boundaries of a narrow communal group of origin. This certainly is no balm to the intellectual's ego, but it does strengthen the belief that ideas have legs. It is conceivable, at least in some cultural traditions in Asia, that there is an inverse relationship between influence and involvement of the intellectual in the power game. It springs from the recognition on the part of the general public that the intellectual's role harks back to older, more easily recognizable roles in the traditional system: the role of the prophet, the seer, the sage, the carriers of the basic values of a society, in all cases characterized by a disinterest in power.

The difficulties of setting economic development in motion, especially in some of the larger developing nations, have made many intellectuals realize that power is not an indifferent commodity that can be applied to all problems and all tasks. It has become quite obvious that not all forms of power lend themselves to the solution of development problems. The manner in which power is built and its constituency welded together, the nature of the appeals used, the rhetoric and later the doctrine articulating that power all determine which tasks can be undertaken by the application of that power and which tasks are almost a priori precluded. For example, in Indonesia, Sukarno's appeal to certain emotions precluded the possibility of success in solving the basic structural problems of Indonesia. Similarly, the Indonesian Communist party in its quest for mass support paid a high price for soliciting millenarian impulses among the Javanese masses, thereby infusing an alien and uncontrollable element into the internal dynamics of that party. Therefore, intellectuals may find themselves in the paradoxical situation that if they want to seek power themselves, they can do so only by sacrificing in the quest for mass support the very motivations that they need to mobilize more widely in order to achieve their goals of modernization, which were the reasons for seeking power in the first place. Under circumstances in which tradition has remained rigid, the intellectual as modernizer is often precluded from seeking power for himself or herself. If, through historical accident, power is thrust upon intellectuals, they can only make do with what is available as best they can and, in the meantime, try to stimulate the modernizing impulses within society. It is only after they have helped the modernization process further along that they can hope to build up the kind of power with which they can fully identify.

The continued inability of many nations to overcome economic stagnation, despite all the national efforts for development, has pointed up another important role for the intellectual: to link up more closely, broadly, and deeply the primordial solidarity groups of family, village, clan, or ethnic group to the life and purposes, goals and problems of the new nation-state. Failure to overcome stagnation in some countries has made many people fall back on the traditional structures of social organization—on the security of their community or their tribe—thus trading the insecurity of a new orientation and the pursuit of new goals for the safety and emotional comfort of tradition. This regression reinforces other obstacles to social progress, and the country is locked permanently in the vicious circle of underdevelopment. It is only through their intellectuals that communal groups can increase their capacity to come to grips with the new problems of modern existence and with the life of the nation. It has become very clear that the role of intellectuals is crucial in helping their communal groups develop a national vision—and the new overarching loyalties that go with it. A national vision must encompass the modern goals of development and redefine traditional values broadly enough to accord a place and role for all communal groups on terms that are meaningful to them.

No less crucial is the role of intellectuals in establishing and nurturing continuous dialogue with their peers from other solidarity groups. In the absence of these cross-communal dialogues, there is very little chance of achieving the kind of cooperation at all levels of national life that is required to mobilize the forces necessary to get development going. This requirement suggests how important it is for the intellectuals of developing nations to develop a strong and separate identity as intellectuals, which can cut across the traditional divisions in the society without cutting their roots to their own traditional groups. It also shows the need to develop strong national, transcommunal, intellectual institutions.

If the cross-communal dialogue in a new nation is reduced to polemics in newspaper editorials, without personal communication among the intellectuals of the communal groups involved, then a serious danger point in the life of the nation has been reached. Without deliberate efforts by the intellectuals of all communal groups to maintain a continuing dialogue, it will become impossible to secure any degree of civility in the resolution of serious political conflict. The fragility of the social preconditions on which the political consensus of the new nation-state rests also becomes more obvious. It has certainly forced many intellectuals to take another look at the question of dissent in a developing nation.

Because they are always concerned with diverse possible courses of action and the formulation of alternative choices, intellectuals easily fall into the role of articulators of dissent in a society. This is an essential and creative function in a new nation-state. But how can dissent be brought into the political system to play a constructive role if the political culture is traditionally unfamiliar with the notion of a "loyal opposition" or if, conversely, dissent is too particularistic to grow easily into that role? What space can be found for dissent in countries where independence was attained only after a long and violent struggle that put a premium on loyalty, solidarity, and disciplined conformity? The fragility of national unity in cases of economic stagnation or political rebellion or threats of secession with or without foreign support has made the intellectuals in many of these countries deeply aware of both the need for self-restraint in intellectual pursuits and the obligation to take into account the social and political consequences of their actions.

Intellectuals' experiences of civil war, or the bloodletting resulting from the total collapse of traditional social mechanisms for conflict resolution, have added to their sense of social responsibility. They have become aware that for a long time to come it is unlikely that they will find themselves in a situation sufficiently in accord with their basic values and intellectual sensibilities for them to feel comfortable, without problems of conscience or intellectual integrity. Of course, it is always possible to avoid involvement and responsibility and in that way keep one's hands clean while wallowing in a sense of self-righteousness and waiting for things to run their course. Disengagement can be accomplished either by a retreat into silence or through the kind of defiance that leads to imprisonment, exile, or martyrdom.

However, given the instability and heterogeneity of the power structure in most developing nations, as well as the fluidity of the constellation of forces underlying it and the inefficiency of its bureaucracy, the intellectual's options are not necessarily limited to the two extremes: to join the dictator's stable of intellectuals or to go to jail. Even when freedom is officially disenfranchised, the intellectual can in some cases and up to a point still work with a certain degree of effectiveness, although perhaps less openly, by trading the broadside delivery of new ideas for their pinpointed injection into the interstices of the power structure and of society in general. This requires, apart from a cool head, an understanding of a country's situation and the general direction of developments as well as a sensitivity to the politics of instability. Even with a highly developed understanding and tactical skill, the intellectual may misjudge the level of tolerance or may have to draw the line at some point beyond which he or she is not prepared to withdraw. But of course this is not the only example of an occasion in life when rational calculation ceases to be decisive.

In any case, whatever role intellectuals choose, they are bound to pay a price for it. What is more important is that those who stay outside—as well as the insiders—work to establish meaningful alternatives out of existing potentials. To do so they may have to dirty their hands, to involve themselves in situations that are bound to expose them to criticism and ridicule. In pursuing this course, they may lose their souls as well. But I think it is a measure of the vitality of a nation that enough intellectuals can find it in themselves to take such risks—or at times to give in to certain pressures so as to avoid more serious compromises—in order to maintain the continuity of the struggle.

The problem of whether to meet a threat to the basic freedoms of a society frontally or indirectly, of whether to bring about changes by working outside the system or within it, is a continuing dilemma that is not limited to developing societies, although the risks in developing countries may be a little greater. The brittleness of civility in many new nation-states has brought home to the intellectuals the depth, power, and potential violence of the emotions; the passionate hopes and fears; the fervor and the desperation that go into the building of a nation and that lurk below the level of day-to-day normalcy. It has made intellectuals realize more deeply the force of irrationality in the life of a nation; it has made them realize the extent to which their rational manipulations of situations touch only the tip of the iceberg—or the volcano. It has also made them realize that many notions of modernization are doomed to remain lifeless constructs unless they can be connected to the deep-seated sources of feeling, drive, and purpose that lie embedded in the subconscious of a nation. This has led intellectuals to look at tradition with new eyes and with a new respect.

Among the many illusions that modernizing intellectuals have had to shed since the attainment of national independence is the notion that tradition as a barrier to modernization can be overcome by frontal attack, or can at least be neutralized and circumvented. The strength and pervasiveness of tradition have taught many of these modernizers that unless they are willing to develop some kind of relationship with tradition they will find themselves isolated or at best relegated to the sidelines. If one was willing to use totalitarian methods it might be otherwise, but even then one would most likely find that a power apparatus built up for that purpose would in some unexpected way be imbued by the very elements of tradition that one wanted to fight. How can one develop a modus vivendi with tradition without becoming a captive of it? Experience in inducing change has undermined the notion that tradition is a monolithic entity and has opened the way to speed up the modernization process through the deliberate stimulation and mobilization of specific elements of tradition.

It gradually became clear that modern ideas and institutions fail to come to life unless they can fit into new structures of meaning that link developmental goals to prevailing perceptions. The next step was the realization on the part of many intellectuals that any development plan, any movement toward modernization, would have to make use of existing impulses, skills, values, and symbols. Providing this linkage, helping to reinterpret traditional values or rearrange them in new patterns of meaning, is therefore a crucial intellectual task. And although a close relationship to tradition has its risks, it has led to greater effectiveness for those who were able to maintain their modernizing impulse simultaneously.

It should be realized, however, that the modernizing intellectual's better understanding of the dynamics of tradition does not obviate the need for structural changes in society. Without these, modernization as a self-sustaining process cannot be achieved. Greater respect for tradition has coincided with the emergence of more sophisticated notions about the modernization process itself. The inapplicability of the communist model, the irrelevance of various scholarly development models, and the growing awareness that the Western history of modernization is just one of several possible courses have led many older intellectuals to be less self-conscious about their own experimentation and tentative notions. In this respect, the relationship of many Third World intellectuals to the West has undergone significant change.

It is now being realized how culture-bound is the notion that modernization automatically implies the Western model. The Soviet and Japanese models had a liberating effect on the narrow concepts previously held by many Third World intellectuals. Equally important in their emancipation was the general collapse of faith in the great ideologies of communism or capitalism throughout the world, especially faith in their applicability to modernization efforts in the Third World. The emergence of new problems, unforeseen by the doctrines of either East or West, and the complexity of international problems made Third World intellectuals realize that the major ideologies has lost their "magic"; in the search for answers to the problems of their nations, they would have to stand on their own feet. Gone now is the inclination to look over one's shoulder for the benign nod of approval from one's mentors—at the London School of Economics, Leiden University, or the Sorbonne, or on the editorial board of the *New Statesman* or *Nation*. The younger generation of postindependence intellectuals was never bothered much by this type of relationship with the outside world. Less erudite, less cosmopolitan, but—most important—imbued with a greater self-confidence, they are not concerned with the psychological need to find outside approval for their intellectual activities. Nor are they bothered by the same torment of alienation—the sense of belonging to two opposing cultures—that tore at the souls of older intellectuals. They seem to be more firmly and less self-consciously rooted in their own societies. The accusation of being an "uprooted Western intellectual" is seldom leveled anymore.

This shift in attitude may also be a function of the much larger number of intellectuals who have been exposed to the same influence and a much larger domestic audience for these intellectuals. Thus it might reflect the rapidity with which the modernization process has advanced. Although, on the whole, the younger postindependence generation has shown a lack of interest in the ideologies of the 1920s and 1930s, they are showing a considerable interest and faith in the social sciences, especially in what social science might do for the modernization of their countries. This is the natural result of more of them being trained in the social sciences. The contribution that science could make to speeding up modernization is, of course, beyond dispute. Modernization implies the application of science and the use of rationality in employing the resources of the country to solve its problems. However, many intellectuals—those who are concerned with basic cultural and moral evaluations and with problems concerning the public good—find themselves unable to develop a blind faith in the social sciences or in the superficial pragmatism that can stem from it. To those intellectuals it is only too obvious how many of the fundamental problems of nation building, modernization, and development have not been adequately dealt with by the social sciences.[3]

There are a number of flaws in existing development theories and strategies that impede their coming to grips with the basic problems of stagnant societies. One is that they avoid dealing with basic normative issues, with cognitive questions of an essentially ideological nature. Second, they ignore the central questions of power and the relationship of social change to the power structure. Third, they are not linked to political dynamics and thus fail to recognize the political preconditions for development. Equally serious is the historical one-dimensionality of these models. After all, we are not concerned here with stable situations and linear growth but with processes of fundamental historical change that frequently involve the violent collapse of political and social systems. We are concerned with what one might call the politics of instability, which has its own particular dynamic. There could be no greater danger for young social scientists in the Third World than to lose themselves in the kind of social research that is a mere extension of the traditional academic concerns in the stable, developed countries of the West while remaining blind to the more basic issues that will have to be identified and defined by the intellectuals of the Third World themselves.

To define the problems of their societies in terms of their new sense of national purpose, to sharpen the vision of the kind of society they want theirs to transform into, to relate emerging value patterns to changing social realities, to illuminate the road ahead, to identify the pitfalls and constantly search out alternative roads, to find the significance of each new development in relation to the common goals: These are some of the intellectual challenges that have to be faced. And it is in this framework that social scientists will have to reorient their research in their own countries.

These are some of the dilemmas that intellectuals in many parts of the Third World face in performing their functions. This essay has brought out the complexities of their relationship to power, to reason, to tradition, to nation and community of origin, as well as to dissent. The self-restraint that grows from a deeper awareness of these dilemmas does not necessarily diminish the strength or the depth of the intellectuals' commitment or reduce their willingness to struggle.

Increasing rationality, widening the area of freedom and emancipation, nurturing civility in politics, building respect for basic civil and human rights, maintaining the pressure for modernization: These are the continuing commitments of intellectuals. The impossibility of finding clear and unambiguous answers to the dilemmas that they face has led to greater sobriety and greater realism. To win the fight against stagnation requires not only courage and tenacity but intelligent flexibility and a deep and sympathetic understanding of one's own society. Intellectuals cannot fail to be aware of the wholly political nature of their commitment and of the need for political engagement. The nature of their political roles remains a matter of personal and subjective choice for each. Whether this role should be an evolutionary or a revolutionary one depends on the particular situation each one faces.

Still, intellectuals have come to realize, despite their continued fascination with power, that as intellectuals they should not lose themselves entirely in waging the political battles of the day. It is clear that their most important, most enduring contributions lie in changing the nation's perception of the problems it faces, in changing the capacity of the nation to respond to new problems, in changing the terms on which the political struggle will be waged. These functions, in turn, will help define the issues around which political forces will range themselves and change the criteria for selecting and evaluating leadership.

In the end, this role in changing perceptions may be more decisive in putting a country on the road to development than the question of who or what combination of forces wins office. The basic concern and responsibility of intellectuals is the modernization of politics as a prelude to the depoliticization of modernization. In performing this function, they will have to operate on a national level, in the communal framework, as well as in the area of transcommunal relationships.

Intellectuals have one other crucial function to perform, one other linkage to make. This is the linkage with the rapidly changing outside world, a world that is itself in crisis and that is bound to affect the fate of their countries, for better or for worse. It is no longer enough to think that as soon as modernization and development have taken place, the countries of the Third World will automatically be able to take their rightful place in the world. The world will have moved on, and the requirements for survival, security, and equality will have changed as well. While intellectuals remain firmly convinced of the need for more rationality in the lives of their nations, they cannot but be deeply affected by the strength of the backlash they observe in developed societies against too much uncompensated rationality and against the resulting existential emptiness of much of modern life. Like it or not, they are forced to think through once again the assumptions on which their ideas of modernization are based.

The collective capacity of the nation to understand the nature of the changes in the world, to evaluate properly the direction of its movement insofar as that is possible, and to plot a course that is in line with the interest of its people is a capacity that is dependent on the quality of its intellectuals and the breadth of their interest.

The future of new nations also depends on the kind of world that humankind can construct. The reduction of international tension, an international peace that will allow a fundamental reallocation of world resources away from armaments, and progress in combatting domestic and international poverty are among the ingredients necessary to lay the foundation of a new international order that will not only free us from the scourge of war but also reflect a new sense of international social justice. These are the direct concerns of the new nations in the Third World as well. Very few of the problems that will determine whether the world of the late twentieth century will be a livable place can be solved unless they are addressed collectively by all the nations of the world, rich as well as poor, and on a global scale.

In developing the conceptual tools of comprehension and language that will enable humankind to come to grips with these problems, the intellectuals of the Third World will have some significant contributions to make. The fact that they, like their colleagues of the developed world, will have no ready answers only emphasizes the extent to which all of us are in the same boat, dependent on one another when it comes to facing up to the great and urgent problems of the near future. The different perspectives emerging from different cultures and experiences of life may help us sensitize one another to different modes of living, other forms of social and political organization. They may enrich the common fund of human experiences from which the elements will be drawn to shape a new and, one hopes, more tolerable life in the decades to come.

Does this account exaggerate the importance of intellectuals in a developing nation? It may, to the extent that it describes not the roles that they are playing but the ones that they should play. Such a description defines the challenge more than it describes the actuality. Certainly the life of an intellectual in the Third World is not without its risks. The dangers and penalties are not just jail, unemployment, or loss of integrity but also irrelevance. The last of these could be the most humiliating experience.

The challenge to intellectuals is clear. The freedom that they crave and need in order to function properly as intellectuals will have to be fought for. The strength of intellectual institutions, the standards and criteria of performance by which intellectuals should operate, will have to be created by the examples of their own performance.

Hubris is commonly perceived to be an affliction of intellectuals the world over. But intellectuals in developing societies have come to realize too vividly the strength of the irrational forces involved in the process of nation building for them to be able to afford the luxury of arrogance. Moreover, the big issues of politics and the human condition are in truth intractable. The answers we seek to give to these problems will not prevent them from arising again in different forms. Still we keep throwing stones into the stream. Big or small, these stones will disappear with scarcely a ripple, without influence on the course of rushing water. Still, we are bound to keep on tossing our pebbles or our boulders, for it is not success or failure that is the measure of the meaning of a person's life. And if this statement summons up echoes of the *Bhagavad-Gita*, it is not entirely inappropriate for a modernizing intellectual of a developing nation to be deeply aware that it is within the stream of historical continuity that he fulfills his destiny.

2

....

Development and Transformation

Throughout the 1970s, Soedjatmoko engaged in a struggle to grasp and explain the complexities of the development process. The limitations of purely economic approaches had become clear in the previous decade. In particular, the convulsions that Indonesia experienced demonstrated that a neglect of the social strains induced by change could derail progress comprehensively. Soedjatmoko began to see economic development as one element of a larger process of social transformation. To comprehend the interwoven spiritual, cultural, philosophical, social, and moral dimensions of change required strenuous effort, which is revealed in the two pieces reproduced below. The first is taken from a paper presented to the Asian Ecumenical Council for Development at a meeting in Tokyo in 1970. Ten years later, Soedjatmoko was asked by the Council on Religion and International Affairs to give the first memorial lecture in honor of American political scientist Hans Morgenthau. In it, he returned to a discussion of the moral dilemmas presented by fundamental social change.

The first part of this chapter originally appeared as "Religion in the Politics of Economic Development, Parts I and II," *The Stanford Journal of International Studies* 6 (Spring 1971). The second part was the Hans J. Morgenthau Memorial Lecture on Morality and Foreign Policy, Carnegie Council on Ethics and International Affairs (New York, 1981). Reprinted with permission.

Beyond Economics:
Social and Cultural Dimensions of Development[1]

Our concern with the development process bears a resemblance to the search for the "elixir of life," which is part of traditional folklore in most cultures. The search concerns the revitalization and rejuvenation of nations and societies. The social sciences have helped us identify many of the factors and some of the basic relationships that are involved in development. However, the secret of what breathes life into it, what sparks the revitalization, is still to be unlocked.

Most of us are familiar with the various theories of economic development. They start by identifying factors that have a bearing on the growth rate of the net domestic product and on savings and investment rates and capital output ratios. However, many of the theoretical models that have been designed with the use of these indices, although useful in increasing our understanding of economic development, say nothing about how to get development started. Also, they tend to read into the development process a simple rationality that increasingly proves to be far removed from real life. Essentially, they deal with the externals of the development process and its measurable symptoms. The compulsion toward increasing refinement of measurements and the craving for theoretical elegance add to the irrelevance of these models. One gets the impression that the various development strategies that have been suggested were designed from hypotheses that, consciously or unconsciously, only try to explain the failures of less developed societies to launch self-sustaining growth or to conform in their process of change to the benchmarks of the historical Western model. The strategies of balanced growth on the one hand and of the "big push" and unbalanced growth on the other tend to fall within this category, as do strategies concentrating on so-called leading sectors to the exclusion of others. Theories of political development have also been elaborated as we have come to realize that development is not only an economic process. Crucial cultural, social, and political elements must also be considered. But most of these models seem to be based on a very limited number of variables. Their unilinear explanations operate within a single system. The impact of such variables on a system in the process of transformation will undoubtedly be different from their impact within a static system. For instance, factors whose impact on the growth rate can be measured under fixed assumptions may turn out to have only limited relevance in a rapidly changing society. It is significant that there are few theories that try to relate economic development to the process of political change.

We still do not know how the development process can be set in motion, much less at what point growth can become a self-sustaining process. There is no doubt that our understanding of the development process has greatly increased as a result of the empirical and theoretical work that has been done. Nonetheless, people who have a stake in the development of their nations are acutely aware of the lack of operational guidelines that might help them in their efforts to overcome the sluggishness or stagnation of their societies and the frustration and despair that go with it. However intellectually stimulating, there is a lifeless quality about the models and the theories on which they are based.

In wondering why these products of the social sciences show this sterile quality, four points suggest themselves in answer. First, they remove the problems of development from the reality of power and politics. In this way, they seem to reduce the decisions that have to be made to simple technocratic and bureaucratic ones. But each of us knows how intensely political the choice of the site for a dam or a factory in our own community can be, or the choice between a weapons system and a road and harbor system. Also, social change and development are bound to have political implications which will have a bearing on the distribution of power. Likewise, the degree of power a government is able to exert significantly influences the range of economic policy options open to it. Therefore, until the economics of development is more directly related to the political process, much of the operational irrelevance will remain.

Second, most models overlook the importance of the cognitive factors in development and growth. Humans are future-oriented animals. Their visions of the future and their hopes, fears, and expectations determine their actions in the present, though awareness of the past influences them as well. It is impossible to understand the dynamics of a social system responding to new problems and challenges (and this is what development is all about) without some understanding of the aspirations and sense of identity of the people within that system. Until we take into account how people in a given society perceive their own problems, interests, and goals, we really have no clue as to how and why they will react in one way and not another. In our search for understanding of the dynamics of development and for operational relevance, we should therefore concern ourselves with the perception of values, goals, and purposes underlying the organization of a society; with motivations to social action; and with the dynamic implications of national and group identity.

Third, economic development cannot be understood in isolation. It is part of a more general process of social transformation. At no point is that process simply concerned with the attainment of economic goals or the creation of a new economic system. We are dealing with major changes in a society, with the building of a new nation, with painful processes of disintegration and reintegration at various levels of society. Nation building has its own requirements, its own priorities, as well as its own dynamics flowing out of the history, the cultures, and the geopolitical situation of a nation. Decolonization has left a number of Asian nations with a heritage of unresolved conflicts resulting from or aggravated by the arbitrariness with which colonial boundaries had been drawn, the preferential treatment accorded certain ethnic or communal groups, and the existence of unintegrated minorities. National independence now requires as a condition of national survival the welding of these often quite disparate elements into a single polity capable of coping with the requirements of the twentieth century. Inevitably, the goals and priorities, the phasing of economic development, and the feasibility of specific economic policies are deeply affected by these requirements of nation building.

The transformation of old societies into new nations inevitably leads to some of the ultimate questions that a nation and a culture must face: questions about the meaning of life on this earth, the legitimacy of the pursuit of material improvement, the relationship of the individual to other people, and the human relationship to the divine. This is especially true in Asia where, generally, religion has determined the inner shape of traditional society and structured the social system. Most particularly, the traditional purposes of the state have had little to do with the pursuit of material goals but rather with a transcendental order. Nation building and development raise some basic questions of a moral and normative character whose answers are far beyond the capacity of available social science models.

Fourth, the models that we have are one-dimensional in character. This is a weakness that afflicts much of the social science research relating to less developed countries. It is important to realize that in nation building and development we are not dealing with unilinear processes of gradual and rational adjustment and redirection, but rather with discontinuities, strains and stresses, conflict and disorder that put to the test the viability of whole social and political systems. We have to take into account the possibility of the collapse or the deliberate destruction of such systems and the chaos and almost inconceivable violence attendant to such historical convulsions. It is important, too, to be sensitive to the possibility of failure, for there are risks and dangers involved in any process of social transformation. We should also be aware of the depth of the human emotions involved, whether hope and fervor or fear and despair. History is replete with examples of the terrible violence and cruelty of which humans are capable in extreme historical situations. Only intellectual arrogance could blind us to the role irrational forces play in such processes of transformation and in the life of nations.

Our discussion about the development process cannot and should not be removed from the magnitude and urgency of the problems that threaten to overwhelm most Asian developing societies and that may destroy their social and political fabric: the pressure of population growth on resources, the massive and rapidly growing unemployment problem, the pressures resulting from urbanization and from inadequate educational systems that are incapable of coping with changing needs and are unsuited to serve developmental purposes. All these problems make rapid development an essential precondition for the viability of many new Asian states—irrespective of their politicoeconomic systems.

From this background some general observations on development as a problem of social dynamics follow. These reflections are necessarily shaped by the Indonesian experience but perhaps have some broader relevance as well.

Development obviously does not occur in a political vacuum. Unless there is a strong commitment from government, no sustained development is possible. Such a commitment implies the willingness to avoid war, external or internal, and to avoid expenditures that only satisfy the craving for grandeur that is so often rooted in a deep national inferiority complex. It also requires the political courage to bring about administrative reform and the forging of national discipline. Both are necessary for the effectiveness of any set of development policies. That courage—as well as a sufficient power base—will also be necessary to implement the unpopular measures that may be crucial to the success of the development process.

Above all, a commitment to development requires the will, the courage, and the ability to organize the whole nation for development, not only economically but also politically. In many cases this involves structural changes in the economic, social, and political fields. Tax reform, for example, may increase the government's capacity to mobilize domestic resources; land reform may increase productivity and lead to higher levels of production. Both are means of releasing new developmental impulses in the society at large, but they are also profoundly disturbing and politically hazardous. Economic growth can take place, up to a point, without radically disruptive changes in the social system. However, it would be an illusion to think that the point of self-sustaining development could be achieved without any change in economic and political structures. Structural change is not only a condition for development but also a product of it. Developmental change inevitably brings in its wake shifts in the distribution of power. The "green revolution," for example, affects the composition of the labor force in agricultural villages. The establishment of farmers' cooperatives leads to changes in the local balance of power and is likely to have repercussions on regional and national balances of forces. The emergence of more goal-oriented organizations on the various levels of transitional societies is bound to lead not only to growing political awareness but, more importantly, to the formation of new centers of power. Rapid change significantly aggravates intergenerational conflict. The emergence of a new generation in such a situation becomes a dramatic episode, a quantum jump. It constitutes both a serious challenge and a new opportunity to the prevailing political and social system.

The ability of a government committed to economic development to stay the course and maintain the momentum it has developed also depends on whether it has the courage and wisdom to absorb the political consequences of development. These may well include some degree of damage to its own power base. Unless a government shows the skill to appeal to and recruit the new elements of power that emerge in successive phases of development, frustration and disaffection are bound to occur. In the extreme this may lead to the collapse of the development effort and the government that had initiated it. Development continually creates new constituencies that must be integrated into a continuously expanding or shifting power base. The political risks to a government are obvious. The political system that made development possible may itself change. Furthermore, economic growth often leads to new or increased inequalities. Unless adequate political compensation is made for these inequalities and the sense of injustice that they evoke—in terms of a more equitable distribution of both burden and benefit, or of a different sense of legitimacy—the momentum of development will be threatened, and serious challenges to the government will be inevitable. In sum, development does not immediately lead to political stability. It is inevitably accompanied by some measure of instability, which the political system must develop the capacity to absorb.

Although we have spoken of the need for political strength and support as a launching pad for development, the history of most developing nations has shown the very obvious limits of governmental power. Irrespective of whether such power is structured at the center as a democracy or an autocracy, the low level of managerial effectiveness and the general inefficiency of bureaucracy put distinct limits on the implementation of developmental policies by governmental fiat. It is therefore obvious that self-sustaining economic development cannot rest on the government bureaucracy alone. Only to a limited extent can these bureaucratic limitations be circumvented by entrusting specific developmental policies to special autonomous agencies outside the traditional governmental bureaucracy, unencumbered by rules and regulations. There is very little hope that developmental plans can take on life and reality unless governmental leadership succeeds in setting in motion widening areas of self-generated activity geared to the development of the social system as a whole. Change from above is insufficient, unless change from below helps to sustain the development process. The importance of ever-broadening popular participation and the organizational revolution that is required to achieve this end is an essential element in the developmental process that is too often overlooked.

In the final analysis, self-sustained development and modernization involve the capacity of the entire social system to deal rationally with new problems and challenges. The establishment and development of voluntary associations for specific new purposes—such as small business groupings, trade unions, cooperatives, credit unions, school associations, and community service organizations—are just as important as the strengthening of governmental capacities. Such networks of voluntary associations constitute the new emancipating forces, the new instrumentalities capable of harnessing the spontaneous impulses for change and progress in the society at large. Finally, it is these networks that will lay the foundation for the redistribution of power that will make possible the growth of an increasingly open society.

A government's capacity to initiate and sustain the development process depends on more than the amount of power and popular support available to it, or even the strength of its commitment and its political courage. Success equally depends on the quality of its political leadership; its ability not merely to suppress the conflicts and tensions that are bound to develop in the course of the development process, but to use them creatively for further action. Such dynamic leadership cannot be guided solely by a shallow pragmatism, even when mobilized around an overall growth target or by calculations aimed at the perpetuation of power. Development is a matter of social dynamics, to be nurtured through the manipulation of shifting combinations of economic, political, and social factors. The willingness of a leadership to take the necessary risks implicit in continuous adjustments of its power base is a function of the clarity and persuasiveness of the social vision that motivates it.

Power and Morality in Global Transformation[2]

One of the most important things humankind must learn if we are to survive and progress in this increasingly insecure, perilous, and fragile world is the art of existing in a state of rapid social change, accompanied by a great common vulnerability and a new sense of limits. Hopes of entering the next century as a viable, just, and equitable world community hang on our ability to manage our lives at such a rate of change.

The sweeping global process of transformation brings to the fore a number of ethical dilemmas with which we must wrestle in seeking to determine how to use power wisely. Change is inevitable. This fact raises the profound moral question of how to allow inevitable change to occur without drifting into chaos and violence. What actions to keep a measure of order and stability could be considered morally acceptable, while permitting the march toward a new and more just international order to continue?

A particular imperative is the need to make this swift process of global transformation less frightening. It has been observed by my good friend Kenneth Thompson that when historians try to sort out afterwards why a war started, most often they find that fear was a major factor. After the next conflict we may not have the hindsight of historians, since the stockpiling of nuclear weapons poses the ultimate threat of extinction of all life on this planet. We therefore dare not become prisoners of fear, striking out at shadows. We simply must find ways to live with and manage our fears in such a way that all countries, strong or weak, will have to accept a high level of vulnerability as an inevitable feature of global interdependence.

The urgency of this need is further underscored by the world's growing capacity to inflict violence and destruction—in sheer number of arms as well as in their increasingly deadly sophistication. With the means to maim and kill our fellow men and women becoming more numerous and more easily acquired, violence—by individuals, groups, or, indeed, by society at large—has become a common feature of our daily lives.

The spread of nuclear weapons is increasingly likely, and their possible proliferation has now led to the use of violent force against that perceived threat. Everywhere we look around the globe we see appalling evidence that violence begets further violence.

The reality—or should we say pathology—of the world as an armed camp confronts us with some of our most wrenching ethical dilemmas. The issue is one of unilateral nuclear disarmament versus the development and emplacement of tactical nuclear weapons: Basically it asks the question whether or not, under certain conditions of perceived vulnerability and threat, certain nuclear weapons are morally justifiable. To what level of deadliness and destruction would we accept such justification? No matter how ugly they seem, these are certainly questions that any student of Morgenthau's analyses of power and morality is compelled to ask.

The developing countries face particular moral dilemmas born out of the same sense of vulnerability and the quest for security. Should they, for example, pursue development with all economic resources at their command, even at the sacrifice of freedom, or must they devote scarce foreign exchange to the purchase of arms and the buildup of their military? If arm they must, how far up the ladder of destruction should their arms reach to ensure a sense of self-protection?

In a world that tends to answer such disquieting questions with increasing militarism, surely the time has come to think about more relevant concepts of security—ones that offer the hope of domestic freedom and international peace at lower levels of armaments. We need, for example, to evolve more effective methods of conflict resolution that are not based on the implied threat of the use of violence. Ways should be devised to make more transparent the actions considered by nations against real or perceived threats—which is to say that nations must develop a greater ability and willingness to communicate with one another. We ought to encourage more deliberate efforts to correlate the national interests of countries at the international and regional levels and to cooperate in works for peace—such as the development of international or regional hydropower for the generation of electricity and irrigation. Above all, we need to reduce the great structural disparities, at both the national and international levels, that are such relentless breeders of violence.

All these would be important steps in enhancing our capacity to use power more wisely and more humanely than we have in the past and would be grounded in the perception that there must be voluntary limits in the application of power. This is a vital need at a time when conflicts can be waged with such terrifying and deadly weaponry and can engage the emotions of whole populations. But I fear that we will not develop this capacity for wiser use of power unless and until we also come to recognize and adopt a set of shared human values—values that honor both the rich diversity and the overarching universality of our global society—unless, in short, we learn to undergird our use of power with morality, a central thrust of Hans Morgenthau's philosophy.

I have been rereading some of Morgenthau's works in recent weeks and have been struck anew with the continuing importance he assigns to morality as power's ethical guidepost—that which gives power legitimacy and acceptable meaning and purpose. What Morgenthau demanded of morality, however, was that it be grounded in the day-to-day operations of the real world: "The choice [he stressed in *In Defense of the National Interest*] is not between moral principles and the national interest, devoid of moral dignity, but between one set of moral principles divorced from political reality, and another set of principles *derived from* political reality."

Note that Morgenthau did not say "depending upon" but "derived from" political reality. Thus his is no endorsement of situational morality but, rather, a call for a set of workable ethical standards to help guide humanity's efforts to regulate its affairs.

But what are we to consider "workable" in today's world of fragmentation, drift, and danger? The old world system—where the individual interests of nations worked to determine a more or less stable set of regulations, based on a given order and accepted legal rules of the game—is simply no longer viable or, in the view of a large part of humankind, morally acceptable. That system may have served the interests of certain powerful states and provided a workable, if often uneasy, balance of power, but it is in no way reconciled to the emerging hopes and aspirations of the hundreds of millions of marginalized and voiceless people around the globe, some of whom are on the move and are beginning to assert themselves. It is not a workable model for a world caught in the turmoil of inexorable, fundamental change, groping for a more just, humane, and equitable order.

In attempting to come to terms with the conflicting demands and goals that this search for a new order will inevitably encounter, we will again be confronted with a number of ethical problems. They have to do with the actions and the roles of the various actors on the international scene and the trade-offs they will have to make. When, for example, is a nation morally justified in taking certain actions in its self-interest that jeopardize international peace? Is it morally acceptable in today's world for any country to act unilaterally in response to unilaterally perceived threats to its own security? As the growth rate of the world economy slows down, which nations or which segments of society should bear the heavier burden of adjustment—the rich or the poor, the strong or the weak?

Of course, none of these situations is new to history. What is new, however, is their urgency, the breadth of their implications, and the frequency with which we are likely to encounter them as our populations grow, our resources are depleted, and the expectations of more and more people continue to mount. Unless we are able to find the means to answer these sorts of deep moral dilemmas in a just and equitable fashion, the present crisis in the world system will certainly become all the more acute.

Implicit in our capacity to find these answers, I believe, is the notion that we can no longer afford the luxury of separate moral standards and values tailored to the perceptions and ideologies of separate societies or cultures. Interdependence and technology have opened virtually all national boundaries to the flow of information and ideas, increasing the impact of decisions made outside one's national borders. Standards will have to be fashioned and adopted that are acceptable across a wide spectrum of cultures and ideologies. Embodied in these standards will be the notion of the human species as a single and indivisible but pluralistic unit constituting the global society in all its cultural, social, racial, and religious diversity.

The urgency of our need to develop such standards becomes particularly apparent when one considers the other side of the coin of power in today's world—not its frightening ability to unleash unlimited destruction and violence, but its increasingly apparent inability to resolve a growing number of problems of our age. All societies, the strong and the weak, are now exposed to many forces and processes beyond their control. Power and military might, it is increasingly evident, are unable to command authority, impose any particular ideology, or provide any lasting solutions to problems. Power has shown itself incapable of coping with the many inexorable forces of social change and profound shifts in values that are upsetting the political equilibrium both nationally and internationally. And power, it seems, has little or nothing to do with our ability to stabilize the international economic scene.

There are also problems of massive population movements within and across national boundaries of developing as well as industrialized countries—by migrant workers, illegal immigrants, refugees, and others. These problems cannot be solved by power alone. All signs point to one inescapable fact: No one is in control, and no longer can one nation or group of nations chart the course of the world.

The industrialized countries are experiencing great political and economic difficulties in adjusting to the growing industrialization of the South and the shifting configuration of economic power. Their political and social institutions—political party machines, trade unions, and government bureaucracies—were created largely as responses to other, older problems than those we face today. Aggravating these difficulties are profound cultural and value changes that affect basic attitudes toward nuclear arms, nuclear energy, and environmental degradation or are manifested in such things as the search for new life-styles, the rise of a new religiosity, and altered concepts of work.

The Third World countries evince equal fragmentation, disarray, and swirling force for change. They are caught up in sharp conflict—socially, politically, economically, and culturally—both at home and abroad.

Just where all this fragmentation and change are taking us may at times be extremely difficult to discern, for it often appears to be pulling in opposite directions. For instance, consider the rise of interest in religion. In some of its manifestations, this can be read as a healthy searching for the transcendent in human life, as a reassertion of the human person as a moral being, and perhaps as recognition of the need for human values that can encompass humankind's wide diversity. In other forms, however, the new religiosity seems bent on imposing the views and beliefs of a particular group on the larger society, on turning away from true morality and espousing its mirror opposites— moral self-righteousness and intolerance. We need to search for ways to match this greater religiosity with a greater capacity for tolerance.

Whatever the current forces for change now at play, a great many of them seem rooted in the vast global disparities that abandon hundreds of millions around the globe to lives of squalor, injustice, and despair. The need to balance the requirements for effective development strategies with respect for justice and liberty; to balance the right of participation of the hitherto marginalized millions with the urgencies of efficiency; to balance the use of resources for development with the general need to protect the earth's life-support systems; and to keep conflicts over access, rate of use, and control of natural resources from developing into a new "geopolitics of resources," in which once again the weak will be manipulated and exploited—these are some of the moral dilemmas we have to face in a more crowded, competitive, and limited world.

Whatever solutions we turn to—whether in attempting to cope with hunger, energy demand, environmental degradation, or rapid population growth—the ultimate answers are not going to come from only the experts and the technocrats. They will arise from our ability to relate their recommendations to the hopes, interests, and aspirations of those who, until now, have been marginalized and powerless. New patterns of food distribution and consumption, new allocations of energy and other resources, new configurations of power, new concepts of work and leisure time—all, in the long run, will be fashioned out of countless millions of decisions by individuals around the globe, decisions made within the perspectives of their own cultural values, societal customs, and moral guidelines.

Neat and tidy packages prepared by experts to describe the appropriate future energy "mix" will avail us little unless they are socially and culturally acceptable to the people being asked to use them and make them part of their daily lives. We have already seen how attempts to include a nuclear component in a country's energy scenario threatened or actually brought about the fall of government. Energy options must be treated as essentially political and cultural choices, not merely technological ones.

So too with management of the environment, the small day-to-day decisions by individuals will count the most. The decision, for example, by millions of individual farmers and villagers that they must cut down another tree to cook their food or heat their homes is the kind of choice that will ultimately determine the ecological well-being of this planet. We must find ways to incorporate the reality of such decisions—ones that intimately touch on daily human existence—in our scientific and technological planning.

Clearly, then, science and technology alone are not going to provide the answers to the new kinds of problems we are facing. They will have to be firmly rooted in the customs and mores of local cultures and societies. They will have to take account of new perceptions of the problems by new generations rising to take their place in society. Out of all this, new solutions, speaking to real needs, will have to be fashioned.

Science and technology alone cannot help us reshape the social structures in which hunger, poverty, and injustice are embedded unless we strive to make science and technology serve social and ethical purposes. Those of us who are concerned about a more humane, just, and secure world would do well to remember Morgenthau's counsel in *Science: Servant or Master?* that "the ultimate decisions that confront the scientific mind are . . . not intellectual but moral in nature."

To make such decisions, however, we will need to know a great deal more than we do now about the myriad social and cultural elements of the problems we face. We need, for example, to know about the dynamics of community participation, village self-management, and farmers' associations. We must pay fuller attention to many hitherto unheard voices—the marginal farmer, the landless laborer, women, and other disadvantaged groups in the countryside. These are voices that governments and bureaucracies have thus far generally ignored.

These voices are now clamoring for our attention on a worldwide scale, and they are becoming a major force for transformation and value change. The roots of these yearnings can be traced in part to the liberation movements during and after World War II, and they have since been manifested in a number of ways: the civil rights movement here in the United States, the environmental and peace movements, the women's movement, and the evolving workers' and peasants' associations in many parts of the world. In seeking to position the power-morality equation within the framework of global transformation, we must not only ponder how morality should be a checkrein on power but also recognize the ethical necessity of granting power and legitimacy to these movements from below.

These expressions of desire for change, for having a vote in one's own future, are at the same time eroding the capacities of existing institutions and governments, for they are sharply questioning the existing order on which many of those governments are based. They pose a severe moral test to bureaucrats, planners, and others who are wedded to the idea that efficiency and order—not noisy, unruly mass participation—should rule the day.

This is, of course, much the same dilemma that the founders of the American Republic wrestled with two centuries ago, and the Alien and Sedition Acts of 1798 might be taken as an indication of how severe a problem this was judged to be in the early years of the Republic. But Third World countries today do not have the luxury of time and space that the United States had as it set out on its journey to nationhood. Those who were discontent with the prevailing order in eighteenth- and nineteenth-century America could pick up their axes and their new ideas and head farther into the virgin frontier to carve out a new life. There are no longer such frontiers for the poor, hungry, and despairing masses in the Third World.

It is thus all the more important that we listen to their voices and recognize that they may have something profoundly significant to say. They represent, after all, the hopes of vast numbers of humankind for a more decent life and control of their own destinies. And we may find much that is fresh and original in their challenges to old assumptions about development and economic growth. We may, in fact, find today's new frontiers.

Here let me express my personal belief that, while we assuredly face a troublesome, turbulent, and disquieting march into the twenty-first century, the ultimate consequences of this journey are by no means totally bleak and despairing. Indeed, I believe that we may now be beginning to recognize that out of all the confusion, fragmentation, and disarray may come development strategies and trajectories of industrialization that are basically different from those we have followed to date and more consonant with the essential values inherent in our culture. We may be witnessing the unfolding of a historical process that could lead to the emergence of alternative, non-Western, modern civilizations in various parts of the world—possibly the Sinitic, Hindu, and Islamic, as well as others. They are bound to take their rightful place side by side with Western civilization and could enrich and strengthen an interdependent, crowded, and fragile world.

This brings me once again to the underlying and compelling need I expressed at the outset: the moral imperative of somehow arriving at an overarching set of shared human values beyond our particular parochialism to guide us during this perilous but also hopeful period of global transformation—when the strong, however grudgingly, see power slip from their grasp and the weak reach out for the promise of new power.

In the past, we were able to turn to religion and a sense of divine wisdom to help us set rules for living with our fellow human beings. As society diversified and expanded, religious influence waned, societies and systems grew more secular in character, and the rule of law came to be accepted as a way to regulate and order our lives. But now we have to develop an international legal infrastructure that will enable us to manage our globe peacefully, equitably, and effectively at a time when many countries are experiencing internal contradictions that are eroding the moral consensus on which respect for law is based. The difficulties encountered in gaining acceptance and securing implementation of the UN covenants on human rights and the plans of action adopted at the various UN global conferences, and now the difficulties with regard to the negotiations on the law of the sea, demonstrate the wide differences that have to be bridged and the patience and persistence required.

In the end it is not only governments or experts that will shape these decisions. A great deal will depend on the capacity of common people everywhere to practice moral reasoning, which comes from the enlargement of our capacity to communicate with one another, to empathize with our fellow human beings, and to recognize ourselves in others. The achievement of this capacity will undoubtedly come hardest to those who are still strong. American theologian Reinhold Niebuhr warned us that "love for equals is difficult. We love what is weak and suffers. It appeals to our strength without challenging it." There are those who would challenge his view, contending that too often we despise the weak or turn our heads and pretend we don't see them. But the point I want to make is this, and I am now paraphrasing economist Barbara Ward: Unless we learn to love our fellow human being—whatever his or her culture, color, ideology, relative strength, or social status—we may all very well perish.

We could perish because there is so little space available for expansion in our lives, for maneuvering our hopes and aspirations without their clashing. Growing population densities, improved communication technology, and above all the means of violence now at our disposal have combined to make the only frontiers available those of communication and communion with our fellow human beings.

What it comes down to essentially is accepting the fact that the whole globe has become a very small island. This will mean learning what people living on small islands—or in conditions of extreme population density—learned long ago: that under such circumstances it is foolish to seek complete control over one's neighbor or total victory over one's adversary. In small, crowded places, people's lives collide and rub and jostle too much for a continuing state of conflict and tension to be bearable. Living on our small island Earth, with its growing billions, we will have to learn a great deal more about the art of tension management and the management of social harmony.

Our capacity for moral reasoning, however, is still badly eroded by the fragmentation of our perception of ourselves and our ultimate value. To rediscover this moral and ethical capacity and to reassert it in ways that will speak to the real needs of a pluralistic world remain a daunting challenge. It is not that knowledge is lacking. Indeed, it is perhaps rather that too much of it presses in upon us and overwhelms us. Nor is intellectual ability in question. Instead, and again I turn to the wisdom of Hans Morgenthau, "the refusal to make morally relevant use of that intellectual ability is the real deficiency of scientific man."

Because of this refusal, the explosion of knowledge that has taken place has not necessarily added to our capacity to solve some of the pressing problems of our age.

3

....

Development as Learning

Development has often been characterized as an almost mechanical process, to be accomplished by following certain steps and achieving certain targets. Soedjatmoko argued forcefully against this conception. In 1985, he was invited to give the Vikram Sarabhai Memorial Lectures, which commemorate the Indian industrialist who was one of Mahatma Gandhi's earliest and most important supporters. The lectures took place in Ahmedabad, cradle of the nonviolent Indian independence movement. Soedjatmoko, who identified strongly with Gandhian methods, chose the occasion to elaborate his view of development as a process of empowerment. Development, he insisted, is not something that we *do*, but something that we learn. The two lectures develop the concept of social learning, which was central to Soedjatmoko's thought.

Lessons from the Development Experience[1]

No reasonable observer of development is content with what has been achieved to date. Today, more than three decades after the post–World War II development effort was launched, the world remains conspicuously and tragically beset with unacceptable suffering, want, and strife as the gap between rich and poor continues to widen. The reasons advanced as to why development has not worked as it should are many—economic, social, ideological, and historical. But perhaps the most important of all the lessons to be drawn is recognition of the failure to deal effectively with the problem of poverty. If anything, the scale of poverty worldwide is even larger today than it was in the past, despite the relatively higher growth rates some developing countries have achieved.

According to the World Bank, average per capita income in the poorer countries of Africa fell throughout the 1980s. As many as 100 million Africans are affected by hunger and malnutrition, and one out of every 200 Africans is a refugee. These facts are symptomatic of a process of economic and environmental decay that, compounded by political instability, has turned drought into famine. Average per capita income has also been falling in much of Latin America. It has now dropped to the 1976 level in Brazil and below the 1970 level in Argentina. Here, the proximate cause is debt, not drought, but long-term processes are also at the root of the problem.

These failures have led to the search for alternative development theories, including the bottom-up approach, the participatory approach, and the basic needs approach. None of these constitutes a full-fledged development strategy; all require enabling national policy frameworks for them to be effective.

What is at stake essentially is the social, economic, and political capacity for growth at all levels and in all component parts of a society. Only this will enable the nation to reduce poverty, unemployment, and inequality and to survive and evolve in an unstable, complex, and increasingly competitive world. In short, we need to think of development not as something that we *do*—through actions or acquired skills—but as something we *learn*.

Learning, in this sense, is the individual and collective enhancement of a society's ability not only to adjust to change but also to direct change toward its own purposes. It involves learning to break out of the frame of mind that accepts passivity as the only relevant response to centuries of oppression and powerlessness; learning that the individual has rights and learning what they are; learning that people have the right and the potential to use new opportunities; learning, as a community, to organize for the attainment of goals that may not have been part of traditional life; learning, as a society, to make timely course corrections.

It will not suffice to cast new learning strategies within the framework of traditional development models and approaches.

Our world today would be virtually unrecognizable to the early practitioner of development from the 1950s. The degree of change associated with development is far more fundamental than was originally assumed. The development effort of these past three decades has been trying to hit a moving target.

The current of change itself can be divided into two broad streams. The first encompasses those flowing from the development process itself—that is, from the impact of science and technology, from uneven patterns of growth, and from the intrusion of alien cultures and values into traditional societies. In the second stream are changes in the national and international context within which development takes place—including increased population density, heightened political awareness, the growth of international communications systems, large-scale migrations of peoples, and sharply altered life-styles and life situations. Although these are in some measure also induced by development, they are for all practical purposes autonomous and cannot be willfully altered or reversed.

Both sets of changes pose their own learning needs. Those that result from the development effort itself call for mastery of skills that permit modern science and technology to be handled constructively and adapted appropriately to social needs. Other skills are needed to keep the inevitable disparities in rates of development manageable and within morally acceptable bounds. This is particularly important within the pluralistic societies characteristic of many developing countries—especially when, as is so often the case, political organization follows communal divisions.

The secular changes in the context of development provide rigorous tests of, for example, the ability of people to live together in much greater population densities; the willingness of the established to bring hitherto marginalized groups into the national mainstream without raising levels of social tension unacceptably; and the understanding of how to benefit from the information revolution without further fragmenting cultures or fanning new instabilities. If not used wisely, the new information technologies can accelerate social change to such an extent that the integrative abilities of cultures are pushed beyond their limits.

The interactions between these two sets of changes in the specific setting of each country make any generalization about their dynamics extremely difficult. The positive or negative responses of a given culture to either internally fueled or externally induced changes are prefigured by the deep structure of each culture and shaped by the worldview underlying it as much as they are affected by the economic and social conditions prevailing in that particular country.

Development is not a linear process, but a complex of closely interlinked changes. The top-down approach to development has been thoroughly discredited by hard experience. In reaction to it, the bottom-up, or grassroots, approach has gained passionate advocates, and their insistence on the importance of participation is an insight of lasting importance. Yet even here, enough bitter experience has accumulated to suggest that participation by itself is no panacea. Participation without learning can be a fruitless exercise, leaving the parties involved disillusioned and frustrated over their lack of success.

It is possible to distinguish two broad sets of learning needs—one that looks back, the other ahead. The failures of the past and the daunting challenges of the future hold the present in a viselike grip. These two kinds of learning may, if mastered, allow us to escape that immobilizing grip. One kind consists of the lessons from the successes and failures of postwar development. The second is anticipatory learning, responding to the transformation of the human condition now under way.

The two sorts of learning needs—those that derive from past experience and those that anticipate the future—are not set in rigid channels. They mingle and overlap, jostling for attention and priority. Similarly, the changes that arise from development and those that act on development are not neatly distinguished.

For purposes of analysis, however, the remainder of this section considers the lessons of the past three decades of development. In the following section, "New Learning Pathways to Development," the focus shifts from learning from the past to learning for the future; that is, to the new learning needs and opportunities that are emerging from the information revolution.

These needs are not abstract, offering idealized prescriptions of what might be desirable or pleasant in some future utopia. The need for new forms of learning springs from a very real and tragic urgency. We are now seeing, in many parts of the Third World, whole communities on the verge of breakdown. Societies are beginning to come apart at the seams. The despair, frustrations, and rage of the have-nots meet the fear, reluctance, or intransigence of the haves to erupt into religious, ethnic, tribal, racial, and class violence. The rapid increase in urban criminality in many of the world's impossibly overcrowded cities is an additional manifestation of the urgent need to come to grips with the problem of domestic and international poverty. This urgency is underscored by the fact that the prevalence of poverty seriously reduces the margin of adjustment that is open to a society. Particularly in pluralistic societies, the rapid economic growth of some sectors while others lag behind may strain the resilience of the political system beyond its limits—leading to polarization, the collapse of the moderate center, and, eventually, to a mutual escalation of violence. This is especially true now that arms and explosives are easily available to any group that dreams of imposing its will on other groups.

To consider the development experience to date does not mean to overlook or belittle the considerable accomplishments of the past three decades. There have been great successes in the developing countries. India offers a number of examples of those successes. Indian science today has world rank, and various elements of Indian society enjoy a much-improved lot over that of three decades ago. A number of Third World countries have been able to move from dire poverty into the range of the comfortably middle class.

The record of the development effort is mixed. There have been successes and failures. Yet one fact dominates any general assessment: The problem of poverty still stalks this earth on a vast and unacceptable scale. Hundreds of millions remain in an intolerable state of degradation and despair—ill-housed and ill-cared for, gnawed by hunger that saps their physical and mental capacities, without much prospect of productive and decently remunerated work, their real needs ignored by national development schemes. The great remaining problem is how to release the latent energies of those whom Gandhi called "the last, the least, the lowest and the lost."

Three decades of development experience suggest that a bureaucratic approach to the poor will have to be replaced by efforts to mobilize the internal motivation that self-organization can bring. The articulation of their own material, social, and spiritual aspirations is an essential precondition for the empowerment of the poor. At the same time, these aspirations will have to be related to the constraints as well as the opportunities—economic, social, and technological—of their situation.

This in itself constitutes a major learning process: the organization for new purposes, the adjustment of traditional institutions to serve these ends, and the continuous scanning for new technologies that might upgrade traditional capabilities. The role of nongovernmental organizations and civil volunteers, who straddle the modern world and traditional cultures, will be crucial in this endeavor.

The need to learn is not, however, limited to the poor. It is the essence of the development process in its entirety, requiring all segments and levels of society to meet new learning needs. Communities will have to learn new lessons in the management of community irrigation or forestry projects. Government bureaucracies and institutions will have to learn to adjust to such a system of self-management. The kinds of adjustments that today's development and social changes require involve learning beyond that which takes place in the formal education system; these adjustments will have to be made by all layers of society. In a period when change compounds change, mutual learning processes in social, political, and organizational innovation must be stimulated in an environment where there are no teachers and no students. It must involve governments as well as citizens, the poor as well as the rich, the planners and administrators as well as their targets. Many other adjustments will have to be made—but, for the moment, it may be best to look more generally at the other lessons of more than thirty years of development experience.

One obvious new learning need arises from the urgency of living with the fact of global economic interdependence. The phrase has become a cliché, but the reality behind it has not yet been assimilated into our thinking, actions, policies, or institutions. The setting of international interdependence within which development takes place adds to the difficulties of adjustment and creative response. The permeability of national boundaries to information flows from the outside world strengthens tendencies to respond to change in imitative rather than authentic and relevant ways. In addition, these transborder information flows make the process of continually self-defining a country's national identity even more difficult. At the same time, interdependence provides access to a wider variety of responses than might have come from a search in isolation. The need to integrate social change into one's own culture requires a constant effort to reinterpret indigenous basic values. This kind of effort in national self-reflection and dialogue is especially difficult in plural societies. Yet plural societies have a more varied repertoire of social response and adjustment, the most successful of which may be imitated by other groups, thus enhancing the overall learning of the nation as a whole. Pluralism can therefore also be a source of strength.

A positive approach to pluralism, however, cannot be imposed by authoritarian means. The skill of consensus building, the art of compromise, the habit of constructive criticism all take time to learn. This kind of social learning, in which the whole society must participate, is a particular challenge to emerging nations. In many of them, the development of civil society was arrested, even destroyed, by colonialism. Indigenous forms of participation, indigenous vehicles of consensus and conflict resolution, and indigenous sources of legitimacy have rarely survived or been restored; indeed, they have often been further suppressed by the modernizing bureaucratic state. Pluralism therefore also requires a commitment to the rule of law and equal access to legal redress for all segments of society.

The postwar development effort has taken place in a historical setting of war, revolution, and political upheaval. Something on the order of 150 wars have been fought since 1945, most of them in developing countries. Apart from outright war, many Third World societies have been rent by serious domestic conflicts along class, ethnic, religious, or ideological lines. Fear and obsession with national security have led to militarization; the rapid rise in arms purchases is only one manifestation of this.

The violence that has accompanied change in recent decades demonstrates that the development process is more convulsive than anyone had imagined. One thing that has become apparent is the need to concentrate on conflict resolution at the level of the village and the neighborhood. Changes resulting from development itself—for example, the upward mobility of certain social groups—have disturbed the social equilibrium and often led to conflict. The effects of worldwide recession have only exacerbated civil strife and violence.

One major feature of these recent decades has been the growing self-assertiveness of the traditionally powerless and those marginalized by development. In many different ways, the grassroots are shooting up—fertilized by an exposure to the sight but not the benefits of wealth. In some cases, groups of people have managed to move up the economic ladder, though many have met violent resistance on the way. And how does society deal with the violence of emerging groups themselves, which they sometimes resort to when the community is perceived as not willing to accommodate their aspirations? Heightened expectations and a refusal to accept a miserable lot have also contributed to massive population movements, involving migration within and across national boundaries and even across continents.

In Asia alone, accepting only the more conservative estimates, some 50 million people are involved in internal and external migration, and that number swells daily. On this one continent there is a veritable "nation of migrants" with a population larger than that of all but six Asian countries. Governments are simply incapable of dealing with these enormous, often inchoate, social and cultural forces; thus, other kinds of institutions and modes of organization must be considered that might help fashion the learning processes necessary to deal with these forces before they escape all control.

One problem is, of course, that no one really knows, through any sort of ordered, rational process, which institutions may prove to be most effective. History tells us of the rise of spontaneous, unexpected currents that have altered the course of human affairs; the Gandhian movement in India is one of the classic examples of this. Such forces for change and renewal, which arise outside the normal government structure, are bound to continue. Finding ways to encourage and facilitate these impulses will test the creative abilities of established structures— including governments.

Those involved in the political system must learn to adjust to new configurations of power without losing their bearings and must develop the ability to socialize hitherto marginalized groups, left out of the mainstream of national life, into the political system. This includes, in particular, the members of each new generation who, given the rapidity of social change and the bleakness of their prospects of finding jobs, are likely to have different perceptions and expectations of the political process—to the extent that they are not alienated from it altogether.

How does a country socialize its youth into the political system when unemployment is rampant? What adjustments must the political system make in order to be able to accommodate the young with their different visions of society and their different values? If they cannot be integrated into the political system as such, how can they at least be made to feel a part of the political culture? These are urgent questions with which political parties and political movements in the developing countries must wrestle.

Given these circumstances, those who control the machinery of the state cannot take the state itself or its continued viability for granted. Especially in the Third World, the nation-building effort is a never-ending, constantly changing task. Nation building has proved to be a much more complicated challenge than was anticipated—and its accomplishment is made all the more difficult in a time of growing interdependence and continuing economic crisis. Third World nations, furthermore, are forced to telescope the centuries-long and often bloody experience of war and oppression that Europe underwent before the concept of the nation-state was finally stabilized. They must also learn new political lessons that did not apply during the early period of European industrialization—those that arise from the rapidly changing context in which development now has to take place.

The old elites and the newly emerging elites will have to agree that the continued viability of the state is a worthy goal in itself— forcing them to try to reconcile their differences or at least keep them within manageable bounds. They will need to reconcile the centrifugal pulls with the centripetal tendencies in their societies. The penalty of not doing so is cynicism and corruption, the fragmentation of the political system, the weakening or paralysis of the state, and the likelihood that its parts will become the eternal victims of external power rivalries.

History has shown how difficult it is for any elite to learn how to share power with others and to realize that only a constantly expanding polity will ensure the continued viability of the state— to say nothing of the continuity of the elite's own privileged position. It further demonstrates that the resort to military power is often an admission of the elite's inability to handle certain problems. Historian Barbara Tuchman, reminding us of Lord Acton's dictum that power corrupts, notes in her recent study of the misuses of power that "we are less aware that it breeds folly; that the power to command frequently causes failure to think; that the responsibility of power often fades as its exercise augments."[2]

The lessons thus far seem to suggest that there are a host of insufficiently explored cultural factors that bear on a society's response to modernization. These touch upon such matters as the often alternating choices between isolation and openness, on the capacity to maintain national and social cohesiveness in the face of profound change, or the ability of a society to incorporate innovation, science, and technology in ways that are consonant with its own sense of moral purpose. If this moral sense is violated, manifestations such as the upsurge in religious fundamentalism can emerge. Cultures that can respond only dysfunctionally to change are doomed to stagnation, decay, or irrelevance. These are all matters that involve social learning but have been little recognized in development planning to date.

The pervasive influence of traditional notions of power and the role of the state in the development effort also need sustained study. Too often, supposedly new political and developmental institutions are simply new bottles for the old wine of traditional concepts of power.

Traditional factors have been instrumental in determining what is perceived as a proper relationship between the governing and the governed, between state and society. They explain a great deal about the difficulties in turning a colonial bureaucracy, dedicated primarily to preserving order and collecting revenue, into a developmental bureaucracy dedicated to public service. Modern training in development administration, with its emphasis on efficiency and technique, has unwittingly tended to strengthen deeply rooted colonial and precolonial paternalistic notions about the official's relationship to the public. It has further reinforced the elite's disinclination to accept the legitimacy and importance of people's participation, self-management, and self-reliance as essential vehicles for development.

Large programs of rural development mounted by international agencies have in some cases increased the power of the local bureaucracy and the police while stifling the potential for local leadership. Projects that were started in the name of development have produced other kinds of unanticipated consequences as well.

One final point needs to be made in considering the lessons from the development experience: Both the successes and failures of the development experience have shown that the organized pursuit of material improvement does not automatically bring in its wake freedom, human dignity, justice, and civility. These values have, in fact, often fallen victim to the development endeavor, even when the provision of basic services includes access to education and legal protection.

This has been true, it would seem, whether one started from the philosophy of growth—which motivated many of the earlier development strategies—or that of equity. The growth models tended to founder on the resistance of elites to sharing the new wealth that came to them with this approach. The pursuit of equity led to the bureaucratization of society without accompanying economic growth. Considerable accumulated experience in developing countries shows that neither growth nor equity follow each other automatically—whichever is taken as the starting point.

We need instead explicit strategies for democratic structural change that would enable people to liberate themselves from the oppressive social structures that perpetuate their dependency and their powerlessness. This could help build societies with the resilience and the capacity for autonomous creativity and continuous redefinition—the conditions essential for survival in a rapidly changing world.

In the efforts of these last three decades, development strategies have too often overlooked the immense political pressures that have built up as a result of the persistence of severe poverty or the destabilizing impact of the development process itself. An urban success story can prove to be an alluring—and dangerous—magnet. The more successful it is, the greater the influx of people from outside, further straining already overburdened city services while emptying the countryside of its most ambitious people. As a result, urban dwellers have often become the most important political constituency, to the neglect of the rural areas and agricultural production. The challenge that is raised is how to develop strong constituencies that will speak for the poor in the countryside and not be drowned out by the urban voice or the rural elite. We must recognize that it is no longer possible, in many countries, to respond to urban problems without some accompanying response to rural constituencies.

Fully representative constituencies with long-term viability can be developed only through democratic processes. This means giving rural residents free access to information—to let them learn and think for themselves—rather than urging them to do what is perceived as good for them by that unfortunate yet so often paired team of the insecure bureaucrat and the quick-fix technocrat.

The fruits of economic development are seldom spread evenly among all groups within a society. The shifts of relative positions can be deeply destabilizing, with violent resentment expressed by those who are the relative losers and an edgy defensiveness, which may also turn violent, on the part of an achieving minority. There are responsibilities on both sides of this unhappy equation: Upwardly mobile minorities must demonstrate their allegiance to the welfare of the whole society rather than to their own group exclusively, and others must recognize the right of the upwardly mobile to enjoy, in a nonexploitive manner, the fruits of their success. There is also a role for government: to protect the rights of even an unpopular minority but also to insist that they respect the law and to some extent the conventions of the society in which they live.

Such political problems all have to do with learning—the urgency of learning how to integrate politically different segments of society at different levels of advancement or sophistication. The assumption has been that development would automatically socialize people into the existing political system. We are now beginning to recognize—in the unceasing flare of violence and strife we see between recent achievers and those who feel left behind—that this assumption was incorrect. These tensions are, of course, all the more capable of erupting into murderous retaliation and counterretaliation when a regressive economy makes the gaps between rival groups all the more apparent and harder to close. Whatever the situation, however, this is a problem that has forcefully driven home the need for mutual tolerance in different religious and social groupings.

The enhancement of capacity for cohesiveness is an area that social science has generally neglected. In the past, social scientists concerned with social cohesion based their work on assumptions of convergence and increasing secularism. Now, however, they must contend with a far richer and more intricate brocade woven of religious and ethnic strands, each crying for equal visibility. New capabilities will have to be learned to attain cohesion in such a situation.

All the evidence we have accumulated from these past decades—during which the global community has evolved into some 160 nation-states beset by unstable configurations of power; rising ethnic, religious, and cultural tensions; and millions afoot who are fleeing fear and hunger in quest of a better life—should teach us just how complex the development effort is. Gone are our comfortable technocratic illusions that development success simply means achieving a kind of critical mass of skills, machinery, and capital.

We are realizing instead that the ultimate purpose of development is to make the population of a country—especially its weak and poor—not only more productive but also more socially effective and self-aware. Truly humane development also requires human growth in the sense of people becoming freer human beings, liberated from their own sense of powerlessness and dependency.

Poets have a way of capturing the essence of truth. Rabindranath Tagore wrote, "Man is a born child, his power is the power of growth." That power can lead to the emergence of people who feel capable of assuming responsibility for their own lives and those of their families and communities. Human growth means that the socially weak have the capacity to regain their sense of dignity and—armed with that inner security—to recognize the basic dignity and humanity of others.

There is thus a lengthy agenda of social, political, cultural, and organizational adjustments that emerges from our past development experience. In order to adjust successfully, we will have to learn to develop the will, the commitment to values, and the mechanisms needed to bring about a better society. Learning, here, means social innovation and inventiveness. The central need of many developing societies is learning how to deal with the challenge of poverty and the structural dualism underlying it. And make no mistake about it—until the problem of poverty is solved, all efforts at development will be of little lasting avail.

This agenda would be one-dimensional, however, if we did not simultaneously set in motion other learning processes to deal with the new array of concerns that the microprocessor, the communications satellite, the laser, and other accoutrements of the information age are now setting before us. Some might consider it enough to concentrate our efforts on what we have learned thus far from our mistakes. But new and powerful forces are already unleashed that will have great impact on the shape and texture of the future global society and on the place of developing countries in it. The next section turns to an examination of how those forces might be harnessed to the greater benefit of all.

New Learning Pathways to Development[3]

The experience of postwar development is full of discontinuities, which illustrate that development is a much more complex process than the early theories seemed to imply. Experience has shown that greater equity and justice do not necessarily follow economic growth. This conclusion now seems so obvious that it is hard to recall the naive faith in "trickle-down" that was once held even by people of goodwill. Indeed, economic growth does not necessarily bring in its wake even a better physical quality of life for the majority. If there is one lesson to be learned from the last few decades, it is that development cannot be equated with growth, nor with the sheer accumulation of wealth. Some of the wealthiest countries, in terms of natural resources, are the least developed, and the converse is also true.

If development is not growth, not resources, not wealth alone—what is it? It is, above all, learning. Certain kinds of learning embody development. New learning needs are emerging for the future that concern the ability to adjust to new technologies, new demographic patterns, new modes of production, new stages of political consciousness, and new and ever more deadly forms of weaponry.

There are many different kinds of learning—and it might be worthwhile to enumerate some of them. There is, first, the acquisition of knowledge: the accumulation of wisdom and lore from over the centuries that comes to us in many ways, both formally and informally. Other types of learning include learning the skills by which people acquire or produce the necessities of daily life and learning how to plan, organize, and manage the support systems that undergird the human endeavor. Formal education has its role in the learning process but is only part of it. The deliberate pace and structural rigidities often associated with formal schooling may even impede adjustment to rapidly changing conditions.

The form of learning that lies at the heart of development is the rather elusive process that might be called *social learning*. One observer described this as a learning form unique to the human species in that it presumes a learning environment characterized by interaction with other learning organisms.[4] It can be understood as a collective process by which neighborhoods, villages, communities—and ultimately nation-states—prepare themselves for living in the future. This world, on the doorstep of the twenty-first century, will begin that next century with another two billion people crowded into a shrinking global village already beset by violence, hunger, poverty, environmental deterioration, and constantly shifting, frequently bewildering rules of play.

Demographers make projections about our cities very easily: Bombay, for example, is projected to have 17 million people by the year 2000. It is an illusion, however, to assume that people know how to live in such conglomerations at the level of income that is likely to prevail in our societies. People will have to learn new ways of making urban communities function, concerning themselves not only with how these mega-cities can be assured of their food, energy, and housing needs but also with how human communities of such size and density can function effectively and with civility, avoiding violent conflict and retaining their creativity.

Demographic increase will bring about significant changes not only in the density of population but also in the distribution of age cohorts, particularly in the Third World. The numbers of elderly people will increase, but the median age will decline since the ranks of young people will swell even faster. This latter growth will have immense implications for the labor market. It has been estimated that work must be found for some 500 million new entrants to the global job market between now and the end of the century, with some 440 million of these new jobs needed in the Third World—and that is if one accepts what is truly an unacceptable unemployment rate of 15 percent in developing countries. In order to reduce unemployment to 6 percent, another 120 million new jobs will have to be found, bringing the total to well over half a billion.

The difficulty in creating new jobs is, of course, compounded by technological developments. Industrial research tends to focus on lowering production costs by improving the productivity of each worker; it is biased against the creation of new employment. This implies that the growth of employment is unlikely to keep pace with the growth of production, so that even an expanding economy may leave great numbers of new entrants to the labor force without jobs. Those affected are bound to put tremendous pressure on the political system, especially in countries where the welfare state cannot provide a safety net for the unemployed and their dependents.

Few governments have proved to be capable of dealing with such challenges. Life is changing in ways that have unsettled the sense of natural order and raised questions about the ultimate purpose of development. The changes have helped spark the rise of religious and moral objections to the very notion of development and modernization and, by implication, to the legitimacy of its official sponsors.

Despite the growth of mega-cities, for most developing countries the bulk of the population will continue to reside in the countryside. There, increasing rural density is driving people to exploit marginal lands more intensively. In many cases, rural communities have traditional ways of working productively within ecological limits. But the increase in human numbers is not being matched by an increase in the resources, techniques, or options available to the people who live off the land. For the sake of short-term survival, they are forced to violate ecological rules, even though in many cases they understand that to do so is to court disaster in the long run. The scientific basis of a more productive, sustainable way of life is already available for many kinds of ecological conditions. But the knowledge has not yet reached the people whose very survival depends on it—and their communities are not organized to use scientific knowledge even when it is available.

In both city and countryside, there is little question that increasingly sophisticated communications have sharply affected aspirations and life-styles and led to higher levels of political consciousness. They have brought on shifts in values so profound that, in many cases, one can speak in terms of generational quantum jumps.

It is worth reminding ourselves that when the postwar development experience began in about 1950, the modern communications age was just dawning. The transistor had been invented only a short while before, the first *Sputnik* was not yet launched, and the first communications satellite would be another five years beyond *Sputnik*. Microchips had not yet been devised; the typical computer was enormously expensive, very large, and accessible to only a handful of specialists.

But the new information and communications technologies proliferated at an astonishing speed. During the late 1950s and 1960s, according to United Nations Educational, Scientific, and Cultural Organization (UNESCO) statistics, radio ownership increased more than 100-fold in Latin America, more than 200-fold in Asia, and more than 500–fold in Africa. Television, with its even greater power to stir hopes and expectations, followed apace.

Today, new technologies for processing an ever-increasing volume of information are putting great pressure on cultures to somehow absorb new knowledge and information and weave them into the fabric of everyday life—and this is leading to dissonance. A recent conference on the sociocultural aspects of the information revolution concluded that the "ecology of knowledge" is outpacing cultural adjustment. New gaps between information haves and have-nots are developing and exacerbating existing disparities.

Inequality in access to information is a prime example of change in the context within which development is taking place. Exposure to new information triggers both increases in political consciousness and heightened expectations on the part of different social groups. The inevitable unevenness of the development process itself is thrown into high relief and often destabilizes and upsets traditional social equilibria.

Yet these dangers can be seen as hurdles to be overcome and not as reasons to forswear the use of new information technologies in Third World communities. We are now moving into an age of "the survival of the best informed" (to use Jeremy Rifkin's phrase[5]), and the developing countries dare not be left behind. A third industrial revolution is now taking place based on advances in biotechnology, materials technology, microelectronics, and information technology. If the countries of the South do not develop the capacity to participate in this revolution, they will become even more vulnerable and dependent on the North than they are now.

People in the developing countries cannot confine themselves to thinking in terms of closing a knowledge gap. Rather, we must attempt to leap over a whole generation of outmoded technologies and theories of organization. We do not have time to repeat the mistakes of the North or even to follow passively in its footsteps, picking up techniques that it has outgrown or discarded. We must cultivate the art of innovation or invent it in a form that is consonant with both the real needs of Third World societies and the new information "landscape" that is being shaped by advances in technology. Only in this way will we be able to benefit from the fruits of the information revolution in their totality—not merely the new technological aspects that appear so inviting, but also their potential ability to spur the growth of knowledge and the creative expression of values in our own countries.

The new information technologies intensify interdependence. Yet, paradoxically, they are also capable of powerfully reinforcing the independence of the individuals and associations that have access to them. They enlarge the universe of information available to the user and allow the user to make a selection without an intermediary filter. There is, in this, some danger of fragmentation; if all the members of the community are selecting different tailor-made information packages, their common ground of knowledge and mutual understanding may erode, and social cohesion may suffer. This process can already be observed; one of its most familiar manifestations is the generation gap. But on balance, provided the lines of communication are kept open between groups, this proliferation of information microenvironments is a healthy development.

Access to information is itself a kind of power, and the empowerment that independent access brings is multiplied when information can be exchanged as well as received. New information and communication technologies, ranging from those as simple as the cassette tape to those as complex as the communications satellite, hold out this promise. They can be organized in a way that not only permits people to choose information from a larger and more varied menu but also permits them to participate in programming, in reporting news relevant to themselves, and in sharing what they have learned with others.

The opportunity to organize and manage and profit from one's own endeavors creates a motivation to learn and, very often, a motivation to communicate one's acquired knowledge— in other words, to teach. Obviously, this kind of teaching is not something that takes place only in a classroom. It is the kind that takes place, when the circumstances encourage it, between neighbors, business associates, farmers in contiguous fields, and so forth. And it is the kind of teaching, and learning, that has transformed some voluntary associations into the most powerful development agencies operating in parts of the developing world. Mothers' clubs, traditional savings associations, funeral societies, irrigation or forestry cooperatives, mutual assistance housing pacts, marketing cooperatives, and so forth are all examples of the successful mobilization of local initiatives. It is important for governments to encourage and enable such initiatives, but governments have rarely been successful in creating them. Too often, political and bureaucratic institutions have been a source of obstruction rather than encouragement to local initiatives. Indeed, because they are outside the framework of bureaucratic programs, spontaneous movements that organize and share information independently are often seen as a threat to central control. They *are*, in some respects, a threat, so it takes a degree of courage for governments to encourage them wholeheartedly. However, the reward for relinquishing all-embracing control is worth considerable risk: It is the possibility of unleashing a kind of energy that is the most essential development resource.

In trying to characterize this kind of energy, a conversation with a Balinese painter comes to mind. The Hindu island of Bali is the home of a rather distinctive culture within Indonesia. It is a poor island, but the society is well integrated, dynamic, creative, and supremely adaptive—this painter seemed to embody all these qualities personally. Asked to explain what inspired him, he said that his life, like his culture, had three sources of inspiration. One was religion, which nourished the soul. The second was art, which nourished the heart and feelings. The third, he said, was the customary and ritual interactions of the community, which generated what he called "social energy." How can this precious resource, social energy, be mobilized, encouraged, and put to work on the scale required?

Part of the answer must be supplied by the poor themselves—which means that more privileged people must learn the art of listening and be willing to recognize past mistakes. Too often in the past, local bureaucrats, taking their cue from the national bureaucracy, have been averse to listening to ordinary citizens. Many of the projects created and managed by governments leave little decisionmaking to citizens and, thus, generate little popular participation and support. Frequently the best-intended "participative" development strategies falter because they rely on a bureaucracy that is unable to respond to community needs and unwilling to rely on community skills and problem-solving capacities. Yet it is just such resources that, time and again, have proved to be so rich. Various studies of development "success stories" demonstrate the importance of a learning process in which local residents, both male and female, and "experts" from outside share their knowledge and display a willingness to learn from mistakes and make adjustments accordingly.

In helping to create the information microenvironments in which cooperation between villager and project worker could flourish, one should explore a variety of ways to extend the learning process. The response of formal education systems has thus far been inadequate even in the conventional sense of education—and far from what is called for in this much broader learning process. In many places, a number of other institutions and organizations have gotten into the business of education, including corporations, labor unions, the military, governmental and private agencies, libraries, museums, and professional associations. In Japan, both newspapers and department stores run educational and cultural training programs. In the United States, the educational programs of the giant communications company AT&T enrolled nearly half a million people in 1979 before the company was broken up. This total exceeded that of the largest university system in the world, the State University of New York.[6]

Technological change and longer life expectancy give added urgency to the recognized need for continuous lifelong learning. Many people will want or need to prepare for second careers or seek retraining in order to keep abreast of new skills and job opportunities. But even the most innovative educational programs must be monitored carefully to ensure that they remain in tune with the changing contexts in which their participants have to operate. Training should cultivate the capacity for innovation, for improvisation, for recognition of emerging opportunities in new social and technological situations that cannot be precisely foreseen.

Local learning environments could be greatly stimulated through the establishment of decentralized radio stations and citizen-band systems through which farmers, for example, could exchange information on local crop prices, weather, and market conditions. Through the use of videotapes, it may be possible to revitalize oral traditions and bring even the illiterate into the information age. Markets have always been important loci of information. It is interesting to note that even in several countries where private capital is not accepted as a legitimate basis for economic activity, the mechanisms of the marketplace are increasingly valued for their information-clearing functions.

Similarly, in socialist and capitalist as well as mixed economies, innovation seems to be most at home in relatively small enterprises that are allowed to exercise initiative, take risks, gather and dispense information. The resilience of an economy depends, to a large extent, on such small enterprises. The problem, however, has been to organize the small entrepreneurial units into networks large enough to benefit from larger marketing systems, quality control methods, technological innovations, credit systems, and other possible economies of scale.

The role of planning cannot be overlooked, but planning should always be specific to the qualities of the enterprise, the region, and the cultural context. It requires sensitivity to and interaction with the people who are expected to carry out the plan. In other words, planning is also a learning process—at least, successful planning is.

There are working models of decentralized, participatory organizations that are well worth study. In the Prato area of Italy, for example, there are some 15,000 to 20,000 textile firms, most of them very small, employing only a few workers.[7] In these businesses, which provide work to 70,000 people directly and to another 20,000 in supporting services, traditional forms of production, social relations, and technologies survive side by side with very advanced production technologies and marketing systems; there is a blend of old and new technologies in an industry that is deeply rooted in the local historical tradition and social structures. The Prato experience—and similar experiences, such as in the Sakaki region in Japan—suggests possibilities for dispersed rural industrial production systems in developing countries that would be competitive with urban production centers. This would ensure that the urban areas would no longer monopolize new economic opportunities. This in turn might lead to new and more equitable urban-rural configurations, a central issue whose solution has so far escaped all development efforts aimed at poverty reduction. The prospects for this kind of rural industrialization hinge on a systematic effort to constantly modernize existing technologies and continuously integrate old and new technologies. It also depends on linking up traditional crafts and social infrastructures with modern, even computerized, quality control and marketing systems. One could think of a number of areas in the developing world where the preconditions for such an effort seem to exist.

To meet the learning needs of development, there obviously must be an unprecedented flow of information into the villages and urban neighborhoods that is capable of reaching the poorest residents as well as the traditional channels of communication such as the village headman, the extension services, and the school system. What is urgently called for is the transformation of the neighborhood from a traditional society to an "information community" that is capable of acting and responding creatively to the information reaching it and capable also of seeking out and generating that information.

The information environment in its totality—including every medium from wall posters and folk plays to television and computer data banks—must be shaped in such a way that it is accessible to all. Material that is comprehensible only to the more highly educated residents works to the relative disadvantage of less educated groups and serves to widen the income gap. Villagers and urbanites also need specific information about their rights as citizens. Ideally, this should be tied to information about where and how to obtain legal redress for injustices, but even basic information about individual and collective rights may encourage people to assert themselves. Above all, and this cannot be emphasized too strongly, the information channels must include new or improved mechanisms for dialogue and interaction—in short, for mutual learning.

The problem of equal access to information is by no means confined to the developing countries. One relevant critique of the American educational system by Clifton Wharton pointed out that the information revolution, and the educational system's response to it, is bringing about a new dualism in U.S. society—one that, like the old dualisms, breaks along lines of race, ethnicity, income, employment, and education. This arises from the fact that fields requiring the most sophisticated training generate the fewest jobs; the majority of job openings are in fields requiring little skill. Most of the desirable jobs go to members of the privileged social groups. With little variation, these same observations apply to many Third World nations. All levels of formal education have a responsibility to do what they can to combat what Wharton calls "technological feudalism."

Educational systems in the Third World, however, face a broader set of challenges. Four of them deserve emphasis:

The first is to move away from the common emphasis, in both schools and universities, on learning by rote. I would be the last to denigrate the importance of the study of history, philosophy, or classical writings from all cultures, but we simply cannot go on treating textbooks as if they were sacred texts. In such a fast-changing world as our own, positive knowledge is quickly outdated. The schools now need to take up the challenge of teaching the art of learning, preparing minds for an ongoing, lifelong process of education.

Second, Third World universities in particular must reconcile the conflicting pulls on them to be both at the cutting edge of modern science and technology and deeply engaged in the problems of poverty that continue to affect the majority of people in the Third World. Without the former emphasis on building capacities in the basic sciences, major new dependencies are likely to develop. Without the latter, the universities' work will have little relevance to the suffering communities in their countries.

A third challenge is for education to break out of the narrow disciplinary approaches that can so easily ignore the political, social, and cultural complexities of development problems. Responding to the explosion in scientific knowledge will mean building a much greater capacity for critical judgment, selectivity, and synthesis.

Fourth, there is the challenge posed by increasing pressure for higher enrollments at all levels of the educational system. This reflects a growing hunger for knowledge on the part of people at various levels of society as well as sheer population growth. Responding to this challenge will require innovative approaches to extend learning beyond the conventional classroom. These challenges cannot be met by the educational system alone. A number of other organizations and systems must also be enlisted to meet the new learning needs we face.

Government bureaucracies, for example, must make adjustments to enable civil servants to break ingrained habits that can stifle creativity, perhaps through such arrangements as sabbatical leaves similar to those in academia. Planners should be expected to work in the field on a regular basis in order to encourage a two-way flow of information. District administration offices could be the locale for expertise in conflict resolution, perhaps working through local ombudsmen who could train and call on volunteer mediators. India already has a legacy of enormous value in this respect, growing out of the Gandhian tradition. It is necessary, of course, to select listeners with a real interest in helping people. In this context, it will not suffice for the government merely to appoint someone without consulting the people; the major role of the government would be to provide services to aid the ombudsman in doing his or her job.

The central need, however, is for new policies to come to grips with structural impediments to change. The policies that have guided development to date—and perhaps *misguided* is a fairer description—have tended to create and reinforce powerful political constituencies among the urban elites and to neglect, relatively, the rural masses. Changing the balance between the urban and rural sectors in the developing world, and integrating into the national mainstream the previously disenfranchised and marginalized, will amount to a fundamental change in the distribution of economic and political power.

The foregoing may sound naive. It is undeniable that such changes entail grave political risks for any government brave enough to attempt them. Given the fragility of many governments in the developing world—despite the authoritarian character of a great number of them—their capacity to make a fundamental adjustment of this kind within a short period is limited. At the same time, the risks of continuing to ignore the problem may prove even more catastrophic. There is therefore a trade-off between present and future risks.

The specific nature of the challenges will be different for each society, shaped by its own distinctive culture, history, and aspirations. But five general qualities can be identified that, in all likelihood, will characterize the leaders and institutions of those societies that adapt successfully to the challenges of the future:

1. Both leaders and institutions must be flexible and innovative, not frozen in old rigidities, and must be prepared to take up new initiatives and directions.
2. They must possess a working familiarity with the latest achievements in science and technology.
3. They must be firmly rooted in the cultural soil of the society they seek to serve and able to relate society's goals to currents in the international scene.
4. They must approach their very difficult learning tasks in a spirit of humility, cognizant that human endeavor is as capable of folly as it is of wisdom.

5. The leaders and institutions of the future must be keenly aware that development is much more than a quick technological fix; it is driven, in very important ways, by the inner impulses of the human spirit, which are often reflected in religious or moral convictions.

It seems appropriate to end with a quotation from a great scientist who was also a great humanist—Albert Einstein. In 1937, Einstein said:

Our time is distinguished by wonderful achievements in the fields of scientific understanding and the technical application of those insights. Who would not be cheered by this? But let us not forget that knowledge and skills alone cannot lead humanity to a happy and dignified life. Humanity has every reason to place the proclaimers of high moral standards and values above the discoverers of objective truth. . . . What these blessed men have given us we must guard and try to keep alive with all our strength if humanity is not to lose its dignity, the security of its existence, and its joy in living.

4

....

The Challenge to Higher Education

Soedjatmoko was greatly concerned with the relevance and integrity of higher education, especially—though not exclusively—in the Third World. He saw that academic disciplines easily fall into rigidity and fragmentation of reality; they lose touch with the needs of the society they are supposed to inform. In the three speeches reproduced below, he examined the role of the humanities and social sciences and of universities in general. As ever, he focused on their roles in preparing people and societies to cope with rapid change. In the first selection, a 1986 speech to the Congress of the Indonesian Council of Sciences, he exploded the myth of the humanities' supposed irrelevance to development. The second selection was delivered to the Association of Asian Social Science Research Councils in 1985. Its discussion of the social sciences recognized their intrinsically antiauthoritarian nature; it also highlighted the importance of equipping people to engage in constructive social criticism on the basis of a respect for empirical fact and intellectual rigor. Finally, in a 1985 address to the International Association of Universities, he insisted that institutions of higher education must remain firmly rooted in their own cultures but also address themselves to global concerns.

The Humanities and Development[1]

The academic underpinnings of development are usually considered to be the "hard" sciences, with their technological applications, and the social sciences such as economics, political science, and sociology, which have direct policy implications. In contrast, history, philosophy, ethics, literature, and languages are often placed in the category of luxuries: pleasant to have but not really central to the basic needs of a society. No conception could be farther from reality. What follows will argue that the study of the humanities is central to the development process and that many of the distortions now apparent in development arise from the neglect of the humanities. The study of the humanities is becoming more, not less, important in this technological age.

History, philosophy, ethics, literature, and language are the core disciplines of the humanities. Other fields of study such as comparative religion, law, archaeology, and art history and criticism are also usually considered to be within this realm. Collectively, these fields provide a framework and a vocabulary for the study of human values, needs, aspirations, capacities, and flaws as expressed in human culture. The study of the humanities helps make sense of experience and provides ways of understanding the activities and purposes of one's own communities and those of others. As a chairperson of the U.S. National Endowment for the Humanities said, the humanities help in "developing a moral and imaginative framework for action."[2]

Obviously, to learn about the qualities of human beings requires going beyond the experimental and analytical methods of the natural and social sciences. Human needs, ambitions, frustrations, and so forth cannot be empirically observed; they cannot be reduced to equations. They can be grasped only by an effort of imaginative projection—and this is the capacity that is fostered by the study of the humanities.

The process of reading fiction or history automatically takes us outside our own immediate time and place. The fiction and poetry that are dignified with the name "literature" are those works that are successful in making us empathize with the characters they create, that make us understand their travails, their triumphs, and their tragic flaws. We recognize ourselves in others. Through the novel, the biography, or the play we experience vicariously the joys and sufferings of others. In the process, our universe is expanded beyond its mundane boundaries.

What does this have to do with development? The projection of our own imagination into the experience of others breeds an awareness of the commonality of human experience and aspirations. This is the beginning of empathy and tolerance. Empathy is the power of fully identifying with and thereby comprehending another being. It is the quality that binds parent to child, brother to brother, neighbor to neighbor, and citizen to citizen. It is the raw material of nation building. Tolerance is the recognition of the validity of difference and, as such, is the foundation of peaceful relations within and among communities and nations.

Few would deny that the humanities are and have been under pressure in most educational systems, marginalized by the supposed imperative to forge ahead with science and technology first and the more instrumental social sciences as a poor second. The usual defense of the humanities is two-pronged. It argues that the humanities *are* useful and that, in any case, learning should not be judged only according to its instrumental value. One may agree with the second of these arguments, but it seems to cast the humanities in the role of a luxury—an enrichment to the spiritual, aesthetic, and communal aspects of life. Many people might see these as the reward of a successful development experience rather than an essential component of it. A greater emphasis should be placed on the first argument: that the humanities perform functions in the education of the citizenry that go far beyond the personal enrichment of the individual mind.

One key role of the humanities has already been noted: the development of the capacity for empathy and tolerance. A further and related function is to foster the habit and the intellectual tools for independent analysis, judgment, and criticism. This is particularly important when it comes to questions of public or private morality. The humanities have a civic function that has long been acknowledged: to educate citizens for intelligent and responsible participation in civic life. Education for participation is usually understood as a process of equipping citizens to participate. It is equally—perhaps more—important that it equips them to accept the participation of others.

The humanities are the realm, along with the arts, of the most human aspects of human life: love, honor, and envy; courage, guilt, and revenge; liberty, justice, and rectitude. These are central to human motivation and achievement—and therefore central to development. But they are beyond the reach of the sciences, natural and social. How can people understand the processes of social change that are sweeping their societies if they cannot apprehend these fundamental forces that move people to behave as they do? The humanities are a window into the human heart.

At long last, development experts have begun to talk about the "cultural factors" in development. This implies an overdue recognition of the importance of the humanities in development. In the humanities, along with the arts, is embodied a people's cultural memory: the record not only of what they did as a people but of what they became, and how and why. In determining the development potential of a society, what people *are* is as important as what they can do. What they are and what they want to be determines what they actually do with the capabilities that science and technology put into their hands.

To know their own history is fundamental to a people's sense of identity, as is a familiarity with their own literature and philosophy and an articulation of their own aspirations. The study of the humanities within a specific cultural context is meant to endow people with a sense of historical perspective, of cultural identity, of the worldviews and values distinct to themselves. This is especially important for countries of great internal diversity, such as Indonesia. Indonesian culture is a mixture of the modern national culture and the various regional cultures of the archipelago. The national culture is still evolving. The regional cultures are changing under powerful internal and external influences. The relationship between the two is constantly shifting as both respond to opportunities and pressures.

Indonesia is a rich amalgamation of many cultures. Not only is the relationship among them a dynamic one, but they all operate in a rapidly changing international context. The instabilities of the international economic system, great-power politics, the impact of modern communications, and rapid developments in science and technology assure that the challenges facing its cultures will proliferate rather than diminish. Indonesia's greatest resource in facing these challenges is precisely the diversity of its cultural resources. This diversity is the cultural equivalent of nature's vast biological gene bank, an asset rather than an obstacle to national development.

One of the conditions for using this enormous wealth of cultural resources to collective advantage is that all Indonesians must come to regard the whole panoply of cultures within the nation as the collective heritage of all. It is through the humanities, taking as their subject this diverse heritage, that this may come about. The cultural treasures embedded in the various regional cultures must be made available to the whole nation. This implies the translation of regional classics into Indonesian as well as other regional languages. It also requires the systematic study and preservation of regional languages, literatures, and arts as well as serious research into regional histories. For Indonesia, cultural cohesion will come through the nationalization of regional cultures rather than through homogenization of all into a bland and generalized unity.

In young developing nations there is a constant temptation to impose from above a common culture on the nation. Sometimes this impulse is rooted in a particular perception of the need for national unity; sometimes simply in a lack of sensitivity to the inherently pluralistic nature of the society. The humanities are then expected to reinforce the values and goals considered appropriate for the whole nation. Rather than promoting the participatory civic virtues of judgment, criticism, tolerance, and empathy, the humanities are encouraged to celebrate and perpetuate the acceptable version of national culture. If they reduce themselves to this role, the humanities abdicate their positive role in developing an authentic and vibrant pluralistic culture.

The stress on pluralism does not negate the importance of a vigorous overarching culture that draws its strength from its inclusiveness. National culture should never be seen as a threat to or an opponent of regional cultures. Rather, national culture is a collective response to a changing world and an interface with modernity. Most importantly, it is the manifestation of shared values and the willingness to live together and take a place in the community of nations.

The humanities play their role in national development by addressing the larger questions that people must ask themselves amid the processes of social change. Who are we? What are the values that we hold most dear? From where do our values and aspirations come? What are the sources of our creativity and resilience? Is the development path that we are treading consistent with our collective vision of a desirable society? These are the questions that the humanities should help answer. They should help relate a people's past to their future, evaluate the present, and reinterpret experience continually in the light of the new influences and challenges of modern life.

The study of culture through the humanities should also make people more aware of their weaknesses. An Indonesian, for example, must ask: What are the roots of the patron-client relationship that is so pervasive throughout Indonesian culture? What were the weaknesses in the culture that made colonization so easy? Close examination of the past should not be pursued as an exercise in nostalgia or recrimination but as a platform for anticipatory learning.

The sources of social change are so many and complex, and the pace of change so rapid, that no government, group, or individual is fully in control. Many of the forces for change are global forces, external to any one culture or national boundary, but their impact is nonetheless inescapable. Rapid social change often gives rise to confusion, to alienation, and, in some instances, to reaction. The crucial question for the people of Indonesia, as for those of other emerging nations, is: How can we learn to live with rapid and accelerating change without losing our sense of self? The answer will never be a fixed, single answer, but rather lies in a process of continuous reflection and dialogue on the meaning and direction of our experience.

The scholarly pursuit of history, philosophy, literature, ethics, and the other branches of the humanities is a crucial part of this process of maintaining the integrity of our culture. However, cultural integrity must coexist with openness to external stimulus; otherwise, stagnation sets in. The defense of this balance requires determination and self-confidence but also inventiveness and creative imagination that pervade the whole society—not just the intelligentsia.

In the postwar period, all new nations embarked on a course of development, with varying degrees of success. But even where economic success has been achieved, the human dimension of development has been neglected, sometimes with very destructive effects on the people's quality of life, sense of identity, and clarity of purpose. The resulting resentment, confusion, and uncertainty have often promoted a tendency in people to fall back, uncritically, on narrow loyalties to family, region, or ethnic group, forsaking the broader ideal of the nation as a whole. The reversion to primary loyalties is not a bad thing in itself, but it is an inadequate response to the complexity of the interrelated problems we face.

The development theories that tended to hold sway in the past portrayed development as a mainly linear process. It was up to the policymakers to choose the destination and the experts to furnish the means of getting there. It has become apparent, however, that a top-down, linear development effort often leads to major errors and proceeds at the expense of the values and well-being of the poor, minority groups, and so forth. The task of nation building in a pluralistic society is a much more delicate and complex task than the old notions of development would suggest. The learned habits of empathy, tolerance, and ethical judgment fostered by the humanities are an asset that should not be underestimated.

Development has created its own problems of value change and value choice. Some of these arise from the discontinuities in life-styles that are almost inevitable companions of development. Others are the product of increased disparities among different segments of the community, as some groups move ahead more rapidly than others. There is a strong and widespread feeling that development has brought out the worst in people, emphasizing material affluence and consumerism out of all proportion, encouraging greed, envy, and corruption as a consequence.

Can development be humanized, and can the humanities help bring this about? The contribution that they have made so far does not match their potential. This is partly because they have become too fragmented into separate disciplines, so that a wider perspective on the whole culture has been difficult to achieve. Then too, the humanities as taught in educational systems at all levels in the Third World have been too quick to give precedence to the classics of Western cultures rather than their own. Although it is extremely important to know and understand other cultures, it is essential to do so on the firm basis of one's own. Without this, it is difficult to achieve the self-confidence and pride that are the sources of creativity. Indeed, cultural impoverishment has been the result in extreme cases where indigenous songs, stories, verbal skills, and so forth are neglected for a menu of standardized imports.

A third problem with the humanities is that they have allowed themselves to become too remote from the burning social and political issues of the day, feeding the "ivory tower" image that leads many people to question their relevance to development. The study of literature, for example, is not just a matter of aesthetics but a matter of understanding the message embodied in the writer's portrayal of a particular human dilemma or social setting. Works of fiction are commonly far more effective in elucidating moral issues than are journalistic reports or social science analyses. Similarly, the new social history—which concentrates on the daily actions of the common people or on suppressed groups such as women, indigenous people, or slaves, whose lives were largely missing from the history books—has provided new insights into historical social change. It has restored to suppressed people their voice, their past, and their sense of identity by recognizing the significance of their experience.

A closer relationship between the social sciences and the humanities would strengthen both. Ways of perceiving the meaning of life are embedded in myths, epic poems, the structure of languages, and traditional legal systems. These levels of meaning must be understood and articulated by the humanists and shared with the social scientists, the technologists, and the planners if development is to unfold in a way that is compatible with social values.

In order to fill this role, the humanities must reach an enhanced capacity to address contemporary issues, especially the moral issues posed by social, economic, and technological change. The choices that have to be made are often agonizingly difficult. Technology itself does not provide the answers, though the choice of a particular technology may well place limits on policy options. The humanities would challenge the experts to face moral and ethical questions rather than treating such issues as accidental by-products of development.

It is of the utmost importance to give a place to the humanities in the professional schools in order to sensitize professionals to human values both during their training and later, in the application of their expertise. The integration of the humanities with professional training will help develop social and cultural imagination as well as critical judgment; this could be an important step toward the humanization of development.

The more the human environment is shaped by technology, the more important it is for the humanities to relate to science, technology, and policymaking. Each new technology brings with it new questions of ethics and values, new dilemmas that every society must answer for itself according to its own spirit. Without the application of indigenous moral reasoning, it is likely that the evolution of our societies will be shaped more by external forces than by internal impulses and aspirations, leaving us spiritual strangers in our own land.

The humanities help instill the understanding that allows the human being to be the master of the machine rather than its dependent. Professor Elting Morison of the Massachusetts Institute of Technology wrote that "if you are concerned to understand almost any modern situation—one that may start from a dialyzer or a robot—you must know something about the machinery but you must also bring to bear in your investigation things you have learned about economics, politics, social organization and the needs, capacities and qualities of human beings."[3] His point highlights the importance of a closer integration of science, social science, and the humanities.

Though the stated purpose of development is to strengthen the nation and develop its human potential, experience has shown how easy it is for development to be dehumanized by an excessive preoccupation with economic factors, the application of narrow expertise to complex problems, and a disregard for the critical judgments of nonspecialists. Development depends on the liberation of the creative energies of a people. Overreliance on technique, or at least on technique that is uninformed by the spirit and values of a culture, is bound to stifle popular initiative and creativity.

If one accepts that the humanities do indeed have an important role in development, then one must proceed to a close examination of how they are taught in particular settings. The state of the humanities in Indonesia is illustrative of the kinds of issues faced by most developing nations. In this setting, the goals to which education in the humanities should aspire can be roughly summarized as follows:[4]

1. A thorough familiarity with Indonesian culture, including the national culture, the culture of one's own region, and the cultures of several other regions within the country.
2. Knowledge of Indonesian history and its relation to world history.
3. An effective command of written and spoken Indonesian and at least one of the regional languages.
4. An understanding of at least one foreign language and the culture in which it is used.
5. Enjoyment and informed judgment of the arts.
6. Ability to analyze and assess ethical problems, public policy issues, and questions of values (particularly those relating to science and technology).
7. The capacity for responsible criticism and debate.

The humanities at the university level in Indonesia have made significant though uneven strides. In the field of history, progress has been made in establishing the basic paradigms for the building of a national, regional, and maritime history that is genuinely based on the view from within the country and culture. A beginning has also been made with the study of the historical roots of contemporary problems and public issues. But more must be done. There is an urgent need, for example, to develop the study of the history of science and technology—Chinese and Islamic as well as Western science. A broader and more systematic effort in historical research would also contribute to the stock of relevant teaching materials. Ideally, teachers, students, and independent scholars will be involved in research, the development of teaching materials, the publication of results, and the design of curricula.

A vigorous language policy should help speed up the evolution of the Indonesian language not only as a language of wider common usage but also as a language of scientific communication. The establishment of a major scientific translation capacity will be essential for the latter purpose.

Improvement of writing skills in the Indonesian language should not be limited to formal writing classes but should be an integral responsibility of all faculties. Frequent paper writing should be routine, as it encourages clarity of thought and hones the skills of analysis and presentation of argument. The stimulation of debating skills is another essential requirement, especially in a culture that places a high value on conflict avoidance but has to stand its ground among more verbally assertive cultures.

The nurturing of regional languages, literatures, and historical studies is an important element in the maintenance of the diversity that is such an asset to Indonesia. Regional languages should be studied not only by people from the region to which they are indigenous but by Indonesians from other regions as well. The same holds true for the arts. The goal should be the establishment of centers for the study of regional culture, which would advance these cultures while avoiding the trap of parochialism. Faculties and student bodies at such centers should be multicultural, drawn from throughout the nation. Balinese studies are not just for the Balinese, nor Achenese studies just for the Achenese. It should become commonplace for each to study— and eventually, to teach—the literature, history, and arts of the other; for an Ambonese to become our foremost expert on Javanese philosophy and a person from Sulawesi a master of the West Sumatran *pantun*. In this way, the diverse cultures of this nation should become the property of all Indonesians and a source of strength and pride for all.

It is also important that Indonesians develop greater familiarity with the languages and cultures of those countries that are bound to have a major impact on the future of the nation. As a matter of urgency, the range of languages and literatures taught in Indonesian universities should expand to include Asian languages and others along with the Western languages that are already being taught. At present, even the command of Western languages is inadequate. This inadequacy commands a high price in terms of both international competitiveness and cultural enrichment.

The scholarly study of philosophy has a short history in Indonesia. At the universities where philosophy is taught, it is often limited to Western philosophy, overlooking the philosophical traditions of several indigenous cultures and religions. Other regional cultures carry worldviews embedded in their languages, customs, and rituals. These are important resources for collective self-reflection and for the further evolution of Indonesian culture. They should be brought into the mainstream of study of the humanities in Indonesia through a systematic effort, for their variety is an asset that increases our repertory of adaptive responses to change.

The humanities contribute to an informed awareness of national identity. That identity continues to evolve in response to changing conditions and new challenges. Free inquiry, critical self-examination, and lively debate are the means through which a people learn to know themselves and live cooperatively with others. Orthodoxy and bureaucratization in the humanities are capable of crippling this contribution to the development of a mature nation. Learning by directive and by rote is incapable of fostering the innovative, flexible attitudes of mind that are essential for modernization.

For the culture of Indonesia to survive and ensure the nation of its rightful place in the world, Indonesians as a nation and individually must learn to live in a situation of pervasive, accelerating change. The future is unpredictable; the challenge is to enter it without losing our civility, rationality, or deep sources of inspiration.

In the past, modernization was often seen as a process of catching up with the West, especially in material and technological terms. Now all nations, industrial as well as developing, powerful as well as weak, find themselves essentially unprepared for their common unpredictable future. All societies are vulnerable. All are thrown back upon their inner resources.

This new state of affairs reinforces a realization that began to dawn some time ago: that modernization should not be seen as opposed to tradition. It has become obvious in the experience of many developing countries that authentic modernization—which does not lead to a loss of identity, self-respect, and creativity—is possible only if tradition is recognized as a resource of great significance and power. Cultural continuity, in combination with rigorous self-criticism and constant reinterpretation, is therefore essential for the creative adjustment that modernization demands. Modernization that is fueled by outside forces or models is possible, at least for a time, but it leads to dependence rather than autonomy, to instability rather than social resilience.

Here lies the central significance of a strong capability in the humanities for developing countries. It is not a luxury but an essential faculty for ensuring that a nation moves forward in becoming the kind of society it wants to be.

The Social Sciences, Government, and Youth[5]

By virtually any measure, the youth of Asia face a disquieting and uncertain future. Their capacity for creativity and resourcefulness may very well be the hinge on which the future of this region turns. Their ability to assess their situation—its constraints and its opportunities—will depend on their capacity for healthy and responsible social criticism. Thus the social sciences have a great deal to offer the younger generation: the means to acquire the necessary tools and confidence to cope with the accelerating pace of change that is bound to be a constant factor in their lives. But to make such a contribution, the proper interaction between the social sciences, government, and society will have to be determined. It would be a denial of the very name of social science to attempt to carry out its work in a vacuum, unheeding of the realities of daily life.

In the vast process of change now under way everywhere in the world, young people are inevitably at the cutting edge—however much this might be masked by the inexperience of youth and their fascination with simple or radical ideas. Repressive action by governments against the frequently unsettling actions of youth only runs the risk of blunting this edge and stultifying the society's capacity for growth.

An important role for those who teach social science is to turn this youthful enthusiasm into constructive channels without squelching it. They must try to impart to the young a sense of history, a respect for empirical fact and intellectual rigor, and a solid notion of the needs, possibilities, and constraints of their own societies—now and in the future.

Social science is expected to serve two major functions, which may be somewhat contradictory. The first is to provide tools for social management—of the economy, of political systems, of international relations. These tools must be developed out of careful observation of the way things work or the reasons they do not work. The second function of the social scientist is to provide keys to societal self-understanding, based on analysis of the origins and means of change. The first of these two roles casts the social scientist very much in the role of scientist, with all its rather dangerous analogies to the objective, experimental observer of physical phenomena. Governments sometimes want to go further, casting the social scientist in the role of technician, with a bag of tricks that can smooth over wrinkles in the social fabric. The second function, that of providing keys to self-understanding, calls upon the social scientist to be what Robert Bellah calls a "public philosopher."

Social scientists can make significant contributions at various levels. One is at the level of policy sciences. However, it will no longer do to formulate policy recommendations that cannot be implemented because of the so-called absence of political will. So far, the effectiveness of the policy sciences has depended on the stability of power relations and specific assumptions about social and cultural environments. But stability of power relations does not generally exist in today's world, and the differing social and cultural settings in which particular policies must be implemented cannot be ignored. These elements will henceforth have to be included in the purview of policy science.

Social scientists should be able to say something about likely outcomes of policy, and they can contribute to the formulation of policy options. They are particularly suited to do so by virtue of being able to make use of wider horizons—derived from historical or comparative knowledge. In this manner, social scientists should be able to contribute to a reduction in the rate of policy errors. Social scientists can also bring out the broader social, cultural, and environmental implications of government policies and relate them to other objectives—such as equity, employment, or security. In this manner, they can make governments and the public at large aware of new structural changes in society, new demographic patterns, new modes of production, and new stages of political consciousness. These and other findings in the policy area will, of course, be of use to governments, opposition parties, and nongovernmental organizations.

Social scientists can also contribute to the process of evaluation of government policies over the longer term. Here, of course, the social scientist is being used basically as a technician; in a sense, it is a limited role. But even given these limitations, social scientists need to stress that there are a number of preconditions before they can play a truly useful evaluative role.

First, they must have adequate access to data and the freedom to use them. This will, in many instances, require overcoming bureaucratic resistance. Second, in many developing countries, they will have to develop an adequate data base. In many ways, this paucity of data constitutes the most immediate problem facing the social sciences in developing regions; it compels many Third World social scientists to devote themselves to "first-generation" problems of their disciplines—that is, basic descriptions and the production of baseline data. The collection of data must be an ongoing process before social scientists can play their other roles.

The broader concern of the social scientist is to help the government realize that the life and the direction of society go beyond the day-to-day cares of government. There are deep-rooted and long-term processes of change and discontinuity under way, and these processes cannot be repressed. Static theories are incapable of giving a satisfactory explanation of events of this nature. Much more dynamic approaches are needed in order to begin to understand the politics of instability and its relationship to power: the formation, the typology, the application, and the limits to applicability inherent in each type of power.

In this context, factors affecting the resilience of a society are of a greater concern than those affecting its stability. Conflict resolution, solidarity making, and community maintenance become even more important as the impact of modern communications erodes social cohesiveness.

In the Third World, most governments have a commitment to development and, in differing degrees, to development dictated by planning. Although there are variations in the approaches to and enthusiasms for planning, all imply the capacity for deliberate policy interventions. This has, in turn, meant the use of social scientists in the planning process—primarily economists, but increasingly people trained in the other social science disciplines.

This produces for the social scientist the problem of exaggerated expectations on the part of governments. Governments are interested in the social sciences chiefly for their perceived utilitarian value for government policy. They expect clear answers to policy questions and clear steps toward implementation of these answers. This is so because governments tend to perceive development efforts as mainly linear: It is up to the government to select the destination; the social scientists are expected to tell them and their agencies how to get there.

It has now become apparent, however, that a linear development effort from the top down often leads to major errors and proceeds at the expense of the values and well-being of particular groups—the poor, religious and linguistic minorities, and so forth. Thus other ideas about development have arisen, such as development from below or the notion of planning and development as a process of social learning. Nation building has proved to be a much more complicated challenge than was initially thought—particularly within the pluralistic societies characteristic of much of the Third World. It requires forging a single polity out of disparate ethnic groups brought together by the vagaries of colonial history. Making the process work tests the capacity for consensus building, the art of compromise, and the habit of constructive criticism—and these all take time to learn. They involve a kind of social learning in which the whole society must participate.

The key to development is the release of the potential energies and creativity of people at all levels of society. But energizing a society that, like many Third World societies, has been passive during centuries of feudalism and colonialism is an enormous task. How does one go about stimulating this development from below in a culture where, from generation to generation, the tradition of evasion and passivity has been handed down as the optimal way to respond to outside direction? When that energy is released, as we have seen in many parts of the world, it can destabilize social equilibria and cause concern to governments, which are inclined to see order and stability as a precondition for development. Thus the continuing search for alternative development strategies is part of the enduring tension between the social sciences and government; between those who would depoliticize development in the interests of order and stability and those who see development as an often untidy, frequently risky, but inevitable and desirable political process.

Part of the role of the social scientist is to explain to governments that these processes of change now under way are much more complex, much more ambiguous, and much more polyvalent than bureaucrats and politicians commonly perceive. Many other actors apart from government or its opposition are part of these processes. They are often autonomous or beyond the control of government. To be able to perform this role, however, social scientists will need to be engaged with far broader concerns than governments would ordinarily desire: with questions of freedom, autonomy, participation, cohesion, and social purpose, all of which are vitally important in a rapidly changing society.

We should have no illusions about the magnitude of the changes that are now under way. They are sweeping and very real. They have led to the fragmentation of states and, in some instances, to the collapse of political systems. They have triggered traumatic experiences in the transfer of power.

What is needed is a deeper understanding of the ongoing historic processes of change. What are the nature and scope of structural change now taking place? How does structural change become interwoven with cultural orientations and traditions? Who are the main carriers of the old and new institutional arrangements? Through what processes of interaction and struggle do these carriers influence events? How are these processes affected by events and forces on the domestic and international scenes?

The task for the social scientist is to help governments and society at large understand that social and political stability is not dependent on government action or policy alone. The family, the community, educational and religious institutions, political processes and institutions, the private sector—and, in this age of instant communications, even the committed individual—are all actors who contribute to or detract from stability.

It is natural for governments to be interested in maintaining law and order so that the process of development can proceed in the most orderly fashion. But in the end, order and justice are the responsibility of the polity as a whole. No government can impose stability by itself—and if it tries to do so, the inevitable result is oppression, violence, and bloodshed.

The role of social scientists in nation building—over and above their contribution to the development effort narrowly defined—inevitably brings them face-to-face with the social and political convulsions through which most developing societies have gone, including a high incidence of armed conflict. Development and security are very closely linked. It is therefore incumbent on the social sciences to provide a much clearer indication of these links as well as to evolve concepts of security that reinforce development and, conversely, concepts of development that reinforce security.

Nor can the social sciences escape their responsibility for studying the sources of conflict within and among states. This concern, in turn, leads to the most fundamental problems of society, which revolve around the issues of freedom, justice, and equity. It leads social scientists to concern themselves with oppression, the nature of the state, social knowledge, and social movements. This concern extends to the interrelationships among all these factors in a global context of growing vulnerabilities on the one hand and rising political consciousness on the other.

Many of the changes now under way escape the attention of governments in their preoccupation with the pursuit of short-term development goals, so it is important that these changes be identified independently by social scientists. There are changes that go on irrespective of government designs or policies. They include, for example, population increase, the growing sophistication of citizens exposed to the communications revolution and its accompanying rise in political consciousness, the impact of industrialization on culture and society, and the many forces that spill out of rising unemployment. Such rapid social changes often lead to confusion, to alienation, and, in some instances, to specific religious responses. Reactions of this kind are not very well understood and call for much greater attention from the social sciences.

There is much to be gained through improved understanding of indigenous conceptual systems—ranging from formal religious or philosophical creeds to unconscious linguistic structures. These are the basic instruments that define, order, and create meaning in individual and social perceptions. To increase our understanding of the workings of developing societies, social science, which was born in the West, needs to study more closely the undergirdings of indigenous cultures if it is to be more relevant to their concerns.

Social scientists have tended to define religion as something outside of their reality. But religion has deeply etched itself in Asian culture, and we now see that it has come to the fore as a major political force in Asia and in other parts of the world. To be honest, the social sciences have been caught unawares by these sudden swirling currents. Religion, however, offers a good example of how the social sciences should constantly try to relate to the larger issues of social reality and help articulate the intellectual framework for better understanding of different modes of being and living.

In this way, they could help pluralistic societies keep their bearings at a time when familiar institutions and moral certitudes are beginning to fall by the wayside. They could greatly enhance a society's capacity for conflict resolution. Modern history illustrates again and again how easily conflict can be triggered. It flares up as a result of both the failure and the success of development—either can make painfully clear the gap that separates different groups in pluralistic societies. This is why it is important to emphasize the need for resilience in our societies rather than stability, for we are dealing with forces that cannot be repressed. They must somehow be accommodated.

To the extent that social scientists have clear ideas about the future of their countries, the national goals that should be pursued, and the manner in which they can be pursued most effectively, they are inevitably drawn to political power as the means to translate their ideas into reality. But the slowness of social change, the inevitable compromises that go with administrative or executive responsibilities, the need to cater to popular prejudices, the unintended side effects of policy—all do violence to the clarity of the social scientist's vision.

Governments are generally concerned with the preservation of existing systems and the circumstances that brought them to power. New ideas and information often constitute a threat to the established order. Thus, although political leaders and bureaucrats may be well aware of the crucial contributions that social scientists can make to government, they may also maintain a level of distrust toward the qualities that make for successful social science: academic freedom, independence of thought, critical analysis, normative judgment. The social scientists see themselves as custodians of the tradition of free inquiry and intellectual curiosity, and the government administrators feel constrained by rules and regulations. The administrators have to obey a hierarchical structure of authority, and their options are blocked by decisions already made somewhere above them.

The delving of the social scientist may not always produce research findings that are convenient to governments. This can lead to loss of interest and funding, to suspicion or even hostility. Social scientists must therefore realize the possible costs and the possible dangers when attempting to serve their governments. They run the risk of losing their autonomy, their freedom to select and design their own research topics, when doing government contract work. There are pressures for secrecy that must be avoided; it is essential that the exchange of scientific information remain free. In secrecy, there is often no room for criticism or peer review, without which quality and credibility suffer. There is also the temptation of self-censorship in order to provide the buyer with a palatable result.

It should be realized that even by simply presenting objective facts, social scientists can run afoul of vested interests. As K. J. Ratnam pointed out, "Social science can become a radical force without being wedded to radical causes, simply by showing that society is not what it is commonly perceived to be." Like the child who cried, "The emperor has no clothes," the social scientist often challenges image with fact. Consider, for example, the revolution in women's consciousness that came about in part because social science research exploded the myth of the nuclear family. Social scientists revealed that women in large and increasing numbers were working outside the home, were raising families on their own, were making vital contributions to the economic survival and welfare of their families, and were being abandoned, mistreated, and discriminated against by the very men charged with their protection.

This then brings out dimensions of the work of the social scientist that go well beyond service to either the government of the day or the opposition. It defines a continuing, enduring role for the social scientist from which governments surely may benefit but, more importantly, from which the whole nation may benefit. Considering the many challenges open to the social scientist in interaction with government, it seems clear *why* the social scientist should take an interest in helping governments draw up, elucidate, and implement policy.

Before the social sciences can expect to play a truly constructive role, however, there is a need to look inward at their present weakness. Social scientists need, for example, to do something about the fragmentation and divisions that have arisen within their own disciplines. This has, in many cases, led to a disassociation of knowledge from social reality. In Third World countries in particular, there is an urgent need to pay more attention to the broad canvas of human affairs. This means greater attention to qualitative judgments and normative issues. The problems under study must be linked more closely with the moral concerns of the times and less with the selection of areas of research defined by the availability of quantifiable data.

In the accomplishment of this, one important step will be to move beyond present disciplinary boundaries into cooperation with a range of other disciplines in the natural sciences and the humanities. Indeed, a significant initial move would be closer linkages and dialogue among the social sciences themselves— chiefly across the bridge that seems to separate the economists and noneconomists.

It is also important that links between social science and science and technology be forged. There are a host of unexplored issues on the interface between science and technology and society, especially in the developing countries. The social sciences will have to address these issues and bring out the social and ethical implications of technology choice. Many of the most crucial development problems with which we are confronted lie at the intersection of biophysical, social, economic, and cultural factors, and we have not developed the concepts that allow us to deal with these problems.

Particularly important, in my view, are closer links between the social sciences and the humanities. The social sciences originally took shape in the West, in stable, secularized societies that helped mold many of their concepts and methodologies. It is now becoming clear that it will be necessary for the social sciences to look more deeply into the structure of ideas and perceptions that give meaning and direction to the lives of people in their own culture. Without this, much of social behavior and many social phenomena cannot be adequately explained. Through closer cooperation with the humanities, social scientists can enhance our understanding of the dynamics of change and the manner in which new factors can be integrated into our value systems. Therefore, when we speak about the so-called indigenization of the social sciences, we mean not only the setting of independent agendas by Asian social scientists. Woven into the indigenization process will have to be greater linkages and cross-fertilization with the humanities. It is only by paying careful attention to such dimensions that we will be able to develop a truly indigenous social science.

Having said this, it should be equally clear that in overcoming the Eurocentrism of so much existing social science, Third World scholars must not become prisoners of parochialism. The pathway to be charted is one that will ensure both the indigenization of the social sciences and the continued pursuit of universality—but one rooted in the pluralism of present-day global society.

In all this it is essential to keep in mind the importance of enhancing the general level of competence of social scientists. Greater attention must be paid to improving the scientific rigor of this discipline in many of our scholarly communities. One important way of enhancing rigor lies in greater openness to peer review and peer criticism. Many of the cultures of Asia, for example, are built on the principle of conflict avoidance, and there is a reluctance to criticize one another. But if they are to be intellectually respectable, social scientists of Asia must be ready to offer an honest critique one another's work.

As indicated, even the simple presentation of objective, quantitative data can bring social scientists into conflict with political, economic, and social vested interests—and even more so when the social scientists add to the role of scientific observer the normative roles of critic and moral philosopher. There are, of course, many others in society who play these latter roles, including members of the press, the clergy, the artistic community, and, of course, political opposition movements and social action groups. What distinguishes social scientists from these others is the academics' grounding in empirical observation and a professional commitment to and respect for empirical evidence. This means that dedicated professional social scientists will not permit their own prejudices or preferences to drive out the evidence that their profession has trained them to gather.

To say this is not to demand of social scientists an Olympian detachment from the subject of their research in the name of scientific objectivity. There is a growing recognition that pure objectivity in the face of human turmoil is a quality that is not attainable or even necessarily desirable. Every observer has a point of view, which is the product of a particular culture or mix of cultures.

This raises large questions that social scientists have to wrestle with, turning on changing ideas about the value-free character of social science disciplines, about objectivity and quantification. More and more, it is recognized that it is an illusion to think that the observer can be detached from the observed and thus escape social and moral responsibilities. Social science cannot be value-free—the researcher is part of the universe that he or she is researching, and the very act of investigation can change the character of that universe.

A change in the self-perception of social scientists flows not only from acceptance of the inseparability of the observer and the observed but also from recognition that the very interaction between the observer and the observed could be the source of a new creativity in the social sciences. This has led some scholars, as a matter of conscious choice, to identify with and commit themselves to various grassroots movements. They have come to consider it a professional and personal obligation, in their work, to illuminate such movements and the options for further advancement of them. Such engagement has raised profound questions, still being debated, about objectivity and ideology, universality and specificity, and methodological rigor.

These questions have particular sensitivities for Third World social scientists. It has been all too easy for them, in the absence of relevant theory, to become deeply radicalized and, in the process, lose something of their ability to contribute to a more comprehensive understanding of the enormous complexities of their societies.

The lives of Third World social scientists are not easy ones—torn between the tradition of intellectual detachment and objectivity that educated them and the reality of suffering and despair that surrounds them. Theirs is also a risky calling—squeezed as they are between their professional integrity and moral commitment on the one hand and political pressures on the other. The greater their moral commitment and scholarly honesty, the tougher and more agonizing their jobs become. The price that some have paid is loss of their freedom or even their lives.

The rewards of the social scientists' profession, however, can be large ones. Among the satisfactions is a role in enlarging society's choices—a major contribution to the evolution of their nations. They thus enlarge the space of freedom—without which rational and humane government is not possible.

Certainly not the least of these rewards is the opportunity to hold out some measure of hope to today's troubled and alienated youth. Hope always has its elements of irrationality, but it is, at the same time, an expression of the vitality of a society or of an individual. The role that social science can play is to provide youth with the intellectual wherewithal to build a reasoned hope so that the dreams of the young are not shattered by violence and hatred, but rather fuel the creativity and humaneness of future generations. Being one of the sources of such hope is a worthy legacy of social science as the world moves into the twenty-first century.

The International Dimension of Universities in an Interdependent World[6]

The great diversity among the world's universities makes it difficult to draw generalizations that are valid for all. Yet it is vital to seek common ground because of the reality of global interdependence. No country—and no country's system of education—can hope to overcome the problems they face in isolation simply on the basis of national solutions. Most internal problems such as inflation, unemployment, technological development, or security have international dimensions. Each nation—and each nation's educators—must respond to and try to shape the international environment in order to ensure the nation's survival in a framework consistent with its own people's basic values.

The problems educators face in the developing and industrial worlds are vastly different. In the North, institutions of higher learning have not responded adequately to the new educational needs and opportunities of their rapidly changing societies. As a result, many institutions and organizations other than the universities have entered the field of education. Corporations, labor unions, the military, governmental and private agencies, libraries, museums, and professional associations are now the competitors of universities in the North—for students and for faculty.

Such problems, however, seem far removed from the ones that Third World educators face, which include fundamental questions of quantity and quality. The brain drain siphons off some of their finest talent. There are simply too few institutions to accommodate the relentless growth of population. Those that exist are populated by many students whose primary aim is the pursuit of credentials rather than knowledge. A third challenge in the Third World—which is being addressed but is still not resolved—is to ensure that institutions of higher learning meet the specific needs of a developing society. Many universities continue to pattern their curricula and intellectual orientation on European models that are no longer relevant even in the West. A number of steps are needed to break this dependency, starting with the development of basic capabilities in the natural sciences and technology. A further step is that of building critical capacities to evaluate and relate creatively to the heretofore dominant streams of intellectual thought flowing out of Europe and its cultural offshoots in the United States and the Soviet Union. There is a need to revitalize and stimulate the scientific impulse and endogenous creativity in non-Western cultures, in the social sciences and the humanities, as well as in the natural and applied sciences. The universities of the Third World need to set their own research agendas and produce their own conceptual and analytical tools for understanding the societies in which they function.

To be sure, there are continuing efforts by some Third World universities to give greater attention to their local cultural roots, but many are still suffering from the Eurocentrism that is characteristic of the Western scientific establishment. The desire on the part of Third World scholars to be published in international publications at the major science centers rather than in the budding scientific journals of their own countries is indicative of the problem.

Undeniably, educators must answer to the communities they serve. It is vitally important that universities express, and be firmly rooted in, the essential tenets of their own cultures and that they respond to the needs of their societies. At the same time, they cannot allow parochial issues—however urgent or insistent—to eclipse their commitment to the world community. A healthy balance needs to be struck between legitimate absorption with one's own culture and community and an alert responsiveness to the international scene.

There is, of course, a tension between these two demands, but it is a creative tension. Often, it is through exposure to others that we learn to know ourselves, and better communication across cultural boundaries is a prerequisite for dealing adequately with global problems of survival, development, and welfare. How can universities, North and South, respond to the challenge of an interdependent world and enhance the commitment to and capacity for international cooperation?

Interdependence is an overworked word. But like it or not, it expresses the truth that we are all trapped together in a web of economic, ecological, and many other interlinkages. What happens on Wall Street, in Hong Kong, or on a Nicaraguan footpath affects us all. There are no sanctuaries from political, economic, and social instability—not in the most civilized cities or on the remotest farmlands.

Science and technology have an impact on every corner of the globe. An earlier naive faith in these fields is now tinged with distrust. We have seen how easily science and technology can be used for the oppression rather than the liberation of human beings. The satellites that warn us of tropical storms could also be used to target us for nuclear attack. And the same biological research designed to eliminate age-old diseases could create new forms of pestilence.

Above all, there is a new level of complexity in global problems today. The failure to cope effectively with them stems in part from a tendency to tackle each problem in isolation. We have tried to address the issue of structural poverty, for example, in purely economic terms without considering the tangle of factors—social, political, and cultural—that sustain the awful asymmetry between rich and poor. Famine in Africa is an example of the multidimensionality of contemporary crises. One-dimensional analyses, however intellectually elegant, fail to embrace the complex interlinkages of problems as they exist in reality.

This is the context in which we need to consider the international dimensions of the work that must be undertaken by universities today. Are they addressing the salient problems of an interdependent world? The list of these is long and daunting. It includes the imperatives of nation building; the forging of institutions for the management of interdependence; the stanching of the brain drain; the protection of academic freedom and free exchange of scientific information; the training of new leaders who are firmly rooted in the realities of their own societies but fully aware of the necessity of peaceful interaction with the rest of the global society; the acquisition of communications skills and the generation of the self-knowledge that helps make it possible for one culture to interact with others creatively and confidently instead of defensively and with hostility.

A particular challenge arises from the rapidly growing knowledge gap between the North and South, which is breeding new dependencies. The universities should strive to close such gaps and, in so doing, to facilitate the transformation of Third World societies into learning societies.

The brain drain is, fundamentally, a result of global disparities. Various solutions have been attempted. Some countries have tried to make it difficult for their scholars to leave. Others have introduced systems of high-paying, elite institutions to motivate their best brains to stay or even return home. Neither response is very satisfactory. The first merely builds discontent and frustration among scholars. The second is built on the sound proposition that merit should be rewarded, but imperfect selection systems all too often make the merit system one more instrument of elite self-perpetuation.

A more effective response is one to which the United Nations University has paid a great deal of attention—global networking of scholars. This allows the individual scholar, working in his or her own country, access to information from around the world. It permits her or him to work with other scholars who come from other cultures and perspectives. And in the process, it strengthens the scholar's own home institution, making it a more intellectually appealing base of operations.

The vitality of the international dimension of higher education depends a great deal on the vigor and the openness of international scientific and scholarly bodies. UNESCO and the various scientific advisory committees within the United Nations system help stimulate international activities at the university level. Organizations such as the International Council of Scientific Unions, the International Council for Social Science Research, and the Latin American Faculty of Social Sciences (FLACSO) also play a valuable role. The establishment of the Third World Academy is another response to the need for such mutual reinforcement. Increasingly, however, there is a need for institutional arrangements to supplement these. Problem-oriented international research institutions such as the International Federation of Institutes for Advanced Study, the International Institute for Applied Systems Analysis, and—in an even more open-ended way—the United Nations University are early responses to the need for more international, multidisciplinary, problem-oriented research.

Before we can speak of any truly equitable interdependence —rather than the skewed and lopsided state of affairs characterizing the present state of interdependence—developing countries must be able to generate scientific and technological innovation themselves. Without this capacity, the developing countries will remain ever-more-dependent consumers of technology.

As things stand at present, the divide between developed and developing country universities has three aspects:

1. The capacity for continual self-generated innovation in science and technology and the ability to apply them to the problems of one's own country.
2. The capacity to integrate scientific advances and new technologies with traditional infrastructures and technologies.
3. The capacity for creative adaptation and reinterpretation of one's own culture in response to new circumstances.

Helping the people and institutions of the Third World develop these capacities is one of the great challenges faced by universities in these nations.

In the coming decades, the universities must confront some serious intellectual, pedagogical, and institutional questions. Intellectually, the need is for a higher level of conceptualization, analysis, and integrative thinking to permit the transformation of avalanches of data into knowledge—and to make that knowledge usable.

The enormous diversity, complexity, and vulnerability of modern life create their own challenges. The intricate interlinkages among today's problems create in many minds a powerful longing for simple, reductionist explanations whose foundations in reality are so insecure that they have no capacity for tolerance of other approaches. This intellectual intolerance is one of the greatest dangers of our time. It is a source of conflict in itself—between competing religions or ideologies, for example—and it helps justify the expression of conflict through violent means. Intellectual intolerance is also linked to the erosion of commitment to multilateral institutions and undertakings, for it makes collaboration with other parties impossible except on one's own terms.

The responsibility of universities and those who work in them is to persist in the search for new syntheses to serve as the bases for cooperative action on present and emerging global problems. Where can this search begin and be maintained except in the universities? In a world so finely balanced on the brink of self-destruction, there is an urgency about the mobilization of intellectual resources on a global scale, with scholars addressing the pressing global issues of human survival, development, and welfare.

In addressing today's interwoven global concerns, the universities should consider two new dimensions in teaching the humanities: a recognition that the humanities can no longer be limited to a single cultural perspective, and a concern with the interaction of science, technology, and society. Every technological choice is, in the end, a choice among values.

Traditionally, the humanities have served to define a people's sense of cultural identity and to integrate new knowledge into the existing value system. The fast-breaking developments of both science and technology are rightly part of that integrative process. The value judgments mandated by scientific advances correctly belong in the province of the humanities. The knowledge explosion and the resulting increase in human power require a commensurate increase in human understanding, compassion, capacity for moral reasoning, and normative judgment. This humanistic filtering of technological development is an obligation on which the universities, both North and South, have largely defaulted.

The intellectual challenges facing universities today are matched by challenges on the pedagogical plane. In the future, it will be the capacity to learn that, more than any other single factor, will determine the viability, autonomy, and integrity of societies. This is a new kind of learning—one that will enable us to survive, in humane fashion, in a world undergoing profound transformation. We have to adjust to living in a world of 10 billion people, a world in which science and technology continue to trigger rapid social changes and in which configurations of values evolve at an accelerating rate.

How, in these circumstances, do we educate people to face an unpredictable future? By the time people complete their training for any specific vocation, that vocation may no longer exist. Today's longer life expectancies may require preparing people for two or three careers in a life span. Because of rapid changes in the labor market, universities need to become more responsive to the needs of the productive sectors of the economy without being co-opted by them.

Retraining could well be the key to the sustained productivity and growth of a society. How can this be built into systems of higher education? How can sufficient flexibility for our university graduates be guaranteed? Traditionally, the university has been engaged in a dual role. On the one hand, it has created knowledge and fostered the capacity to create knowledge— preparing scholars and scientists to work independently. But it has also served to enhance the general level of skills in a society. Lately, however, other institutions have begun to take up this traditional function of the university.

Corporations, in particular, are having a significant impact on higher education in the North. They compete with universities for teachers and promising graduates. The scope and scale of corporate educational programs are beginning to rival those of universities in some ways, having evolved from modest, in-house training programs designed to supplement formal education. The result is that there is no longer a clear-cut distinction between the activities of collegiate and corporate classrooms. The knowledge demanded of, and offered by, researchers on high-tech industrial projects rivals that offered by university faculty. Courses offered by some corporations have acquired academic respectability. By the mid-1980s, the cost of such corporate programs in the United States alone was estimated at more than $40 billion annually—approaching the combined yearly budgets of all American four-year and postgraduate colleges and universities. In Japan, the Hitachi Corporation spent $83 million a year on education—a sum equivalent to two-thirds of its advertising budget. And Nippon Telegraph and Telephone Company estimated that every year 240,000 of its 312,000 employees enroll in a company course. These figures provide an indication of the scale of corporate education. According to the *New Scientist* (March 21, 1985), Japanese industry funds 75 percent of the country's research and development. It has taken over this role from the universities and has revolutionized the way Japan manages pure science.

From a pedagogical standpoint, corporate education has proved its willingness to innovate and, in some cases, has taken the lead. It employs state-of-the-art equipment with the capacity to liberate learning from the spatial limitations of the traditional classroom and from the temporal limitations of a rigid schedule. But its pedagogical achievements are not confined to simple gadgetry. Industry-based educators are doing fundamental research into the learning process itself.

Though corporate involvement in higher education rivals the scale of university-based education, the two are quite different in philosophy and purpose. The goal of corporate education is, after all, the formation of a more productive employee. Some corporations take a very liberal view of the kind of personal and intellectual enrichment that encourages productivity, but the bottom line is an inescapable factor in business decisions about investment in education. University education is guided by other needs: the generation of new knowledge and understanding that may not have any short-term economic payoff; the formation of an enlightened citizenry; the development of the skills of responsible social criticism; the preservation and amplification of indigenous culture; the enhancement of knowledge and understanding of other societies; the training of independent leadership in all walks of life. These are essential but rather intangible needs that no society can afford to consign to the commercial sector.

However, if universities hope to meet the kinds of challenges posed by the corporate world, they will have to explore new ways of learning. They can begin by exploiting more fully the technology already available in, for example, radio, television, and satellite transmissions or video recorders. These techniques could be especially useful in the Third World, where the number of students exceeds the physical capacities of existing classrooms. But universities must also introduce other innovations—radical innovations—in the educational process.

Educators have been much too timid up to now in dealing with educational changes. They have merely been tinkering with marginal modifications of the traditional system. As the American academic George Keller noted in the journal *Change*, the major issues in higher education are largely ignored by educational researchers. Commenting on the narrow, limited focus of much educational research today, Keller observed, "If the research in higher education ended, it would scarcely be missed."[7] It is clear, therefore, that much more sweeping self-examination is required. This brings us to the third kind of challenge confronting universities today, the institutional challenge.

The interdependence of our world calls for a more integrative approach and demands interdisciplinary responses. It is time to reexamine the way in which knowledge is compartmentalized. In the past, traditional disciplines have served as the means for organizing knowledge in an orderly fashion. But those same academic pigeonholes have fragmented perceptions of the larger issues, which refuse to conform to limited dimensions. Some of the partitions between these academic compartments must be dismantled to permit development of a more flexible and dynamic educational structure that will foster, rather than impede, multidisciplinary approaches to global problems.

There was a time when the universities began to respond to this need by establishing multidisciplinary centers that integrated economic, political, and social perspectives, for example, within a broader framework. But many of these interdisciplinary centers have now been sacrificed to budgetary concerns. Universities have fallen back on traditional academic fields, which have the strongest constituencies. And this has occurred just when the need for integrative thinking is greater than ever.

There have been isolated experiments, especially among the younger universities, in broadening the graduate curriculum and preventing overspecialization. There are signs that the university world is changing, but not rapidly enough. For the most part, established universities continue to observe traditional distinctions as if they were set in concrete.

These, then, are some of the intellectual, pedagogical, and institutional challenges that higher education must face in order to maintain its relevance to our interdependent and pluralistic world. At the same time, the basic integrity of universities is being undermined by several serious trends.

One of these trends is a growing constriction of access to knowledge at the university level. The problem is most serious in those branches of study that are thought to have military or strategic utility. In the case of government funded research, secrecy is often a condition for sponsorship. But even in research programs that are not government funded, scientific symposia are increasingly closed to scientists from "unfriendly" countries, even if the subject under discussion has only remote strategic significance.

A second concern is the increasing commercialization of knowledge, particularly in fields with the potential for lucrative commercial applications such as biotechnology and information technology. Some companies are funding university research on the condition that they retain privileged access to the research results. The decision of the U.S. Supreme Court allowing certain advances in biotechnology to be patented has opened the door for such commercialization. This kind of arrangement contradicts the basic concept of a university, which evolved from the premise of free inquiry and the sharing of knowledge. The green revolution resulted from scientific information developed by a number of international research institutions funded primarily by philanthropic foundations. That information was free. We are now on the threshold of a second green revolution—a "gene revolution" based on the most advanced techniques of microbiology. But only those who can afford to pay for it will profit from this one. The Third World will have to purchase the information unless it can build up a capacity to develop it.

There are certain social and political preconditions for the pursuit of knowledge and the use of knowledge. Academic freedom is indispensable; without it the whole educational process shrivels, along with the nation's capacity for creativity and growth. Ways need to be found to keep political upheavals from destroying precious intellectual capacities. One partial solution could be a strengthening and broadening of the concept of asylum for intellectual refugees.

Third World scholars, like others, are confronted with a hierarchy of academic prestige that, for example, elevates nuclear physics above public health. They face a genuine dilemma. The excitement of working at the frontiers of knowledge, the prestige of being published in the leading academic journals, the seduction of fine equipment and facilities are entirely understandable. But these attractions should not blind scholars to the profound satisfactions of work that contributes to solving the problems of the majority of people in their own society: the problems of poverty, environmental deterioration, and disease as well as problems of freedom, participation, and equity. A commitment to these concerns may bring rewards that are less prestigious according to certain standards but are of greater service to society.

This is not to imply that Third World universities should devote their energies exclusively to domestic problems. But they do need to arrive at some working definition of where the line is drawn between legitimate preoccupation with national problems and an ostrich-like self-absorption. The reality of interdependence locates the line: There are real penalties to be paid for failing to perceive it accurately—the greatest penalty being irrelevance.

In the self-appraisals of education in the Western world, concern with the global community is conspicuous by its absence. There is little discussion of the contribution that universities might make to the global debate on the structures needed for a more just and equitable world.

There is a special need to develop teaching materials and modes of presentation that can sensitize students to the problems of global interdependence and to the fact that no country can live in isolation. The capacity of the educational system to do this will depend on the rebuilding of strong area and international studies at the university level, including the humanities.

One of the most effective methods of raising global consciousness is also one of the oldest: the international exchange of scholars. Even in the Middle Ages there were itinerant students who crisscrossed Europe and the Middle East in search of mentors. Knowledge has always been pursued across borders. In a sense, the scholarly exchange of both faculty and students is an extension of this itinerant tradition. How many lives have been profoundly modified by the enlarged perspective of living and learning in a foreign land? Student exchange is an investment that carries economic and political dividends, though not all governments accord it priority.

Charitable foundations play a valuable role in making these exchanges possible. But the nonprofit sector in many countries is underdeveloped. There is also a crucial need for more international research and training institutions in the Third World that are both rigorous and relevant to the problems of a particular region.

The concept of the university has changed over the ages. The medieval universities were primarily schools of divinity, devoted to the study of God and his creation. They were less concerned with developing new knowledge than with transmitting received knowledge. Until the nineteenth century, the *college*, with its orientation toward a single culture, was the model for institutions of higher learning, serving to educate national elites. The university as we know it today was greatly influenced by the ideas of Wilhelm von Humboldt, a contemporary of Goethe and Schiller, who proposed that the university should serve not only as a conduit for orthodox knowledge but also as a crucible for new knowledge. He saw academic freedom, underwritten by an endowment fund, as essential to this task. At the time, little more than a century ago, these were revolutionary ideas. Yet they are widely accepted today as premises of higher education.

The concept of the university, then, is a dynamic one. It is bound to undergo—it *must* undergo—even greater changes in the future. The emergence of the international university is one more stage in the process of educational evolution; the United Nations University may be seen as among the first of a new generation of institutions employing innovative concepts and methodologies to deal with the multidisciplinary and multidimensional aspects of global issues.

This global perspective should not be in the exclusive jurisdiction of the United Nations University. Our survival on this limited earth requires unprecedented levels of understanding and mutual tolerance. Higher education must commit itself wholeheartedly to these ends.

5

....

Violence and Nonviolence

The combination of rapid internal change and an unstable external environment makes the Third World a tinderbox for the ignition of violent conflict. One of Soedjatmoko's most urgent concerns was with the tremendous growth of destructive power and the ease with which it could be put to use by even relatively small groups of disaffected people. This fact gave great urgency, in his view, to the effort to understand the dynamics of violence and to seek nonviolent means of resolving conflict. In 1985, the Norwegian Nobel Institute asked him to analyze the patterns of armed conflict in the Third World for the prestigious Nobel Symposium on the Study of War and Peace, resulting in the paper reproduced here. In 1986, Soedjatmoko, like so many others around the world, was stunned by the assassination of Swedish Prime Minister Olof Palme, with whom he had worked closely on disarmament and security issues. He took on the sad task of delivering the memorial address for Palme before the Swedish Institute of Foreign Affairs; that address is reproduced as the second part of this chapter. It was the occasion for a moving reflection on nonviolence as an effective and courageous form of struggle against injustice.

Patterns of Armed Conflict in the Third World[1]

The urge to classify, to construct taxonomies, is a basic intellectual response to chaos. The record of armed conflict in the

The first part of this chapter is reprinted with the permission of Universitetsforlaget AS.

Third World since the end of World War II does, at first glance, give an impression of chaos. The vast majority of the more than 150 wars[2] that have been fought in the last forty years have been fought in the Third World, many with the direct or indirect participation of external powers.

There are at least three conclusions that might emerge out of an attempt to discern patterns in the apparent chaos. One is that armed conflicts in the Third World are a cluster of isolated instances, each unique in its causes, circumstances, and possible solutions. A second possible conclusion is that armed conflicts in the developing countries are expressions of a common condition and therefore require generalized approaches toward and on the part of the countries involved. The third possibility is that the interaction of Third World conditions with an unstable international environment implies a much more complex answer than either of the other two. The available evidence—and it is abundant—comes closest, in this writer's view, to supporting this third conclusion.

What do the diverse countries of the Third World have in common, apart from their location in Africa, Asia, or Latin America, that makes "Third World armed conflicts" an interesting category for consideration? Most developing countries share the experience of colonial domination, though its nature and duration vary tremendously among them. Most of them are poor. Perhaps most importantly, most are engulfed in a process of very profound social and economic transformation that, though a necessary condition for development, is in itself a source of instability.

There is also a psychological sense of belonging to the Third World, which arises from the recognition that the international system is dominated by and directed for the primary benefit of countries that exclude the Third World from decision making and a fair share of the benefits of interaction. The resulting sense of vulnerability and exclusion—and the often angry sense of injustice that accompanies it—is one factor that gives the countries of the Third World some sense of solidarity despite their great diversity and the considerable dissension among them.

The dislocations caused by rapid and extensive change make countries vulnerable to conflict arising from both internal and external sources. Adjustment to the developments of the late twentieth century is threatening enough to the equanimity of any society without the further challenge of trying to compress centuries of technological change and nation building into the span of a few decades.

It is important to keep in mind, however, that the process of social transformation is by no means confined to the Third World. All countries are in some measure caught up in sweeping value changes that respond to new technologies and modes of organization and to a pace and scale of change that are unprecedented in human experience. It is not only in the Third World that the reexamination of old and newer values has led to challenges to the state. The function, purpose, character, and structure of the state encounter challenges from neoconservatives and religious fundamentalists in the United States, from "green" parties in Europe, from minority nationalities in Eastern Europe, as well as from numerous social and political movements in the Third World.

Reference is often made, particularly in the context of the Islamic world, to a struggle between the twelfth and the twenty-first centuries—that is, between the Age of Faith and the Space Age. It may be more honest to acknowledge that this is a struggle that engages all countries to some extent. Many of today's conflicts are products of the inability to manage change. Others have their roots in contradictory perceptions of and beliefs about change.

No region has quite mastered the dislocations of the twentieth century, with its dizzying growth of populations and massive movements of people, its instant communications, alienating technologies, shrunken spaces, and horrifying destructive power—and so all remain vulnerable to conflict. The category "Third World" is therefore a fairly arbitrary one on any grounds except geography and psychology. It would be difficult, for example, to draw a clear distinction between the conflict in Northern Ireland and many of the ongoing conflicts in the Third World. Nonetheless, three of the widely shared qualities that have been mentioned—colonialism, poverty, and accelerated change—do give armed conflicts in the Third World some distinctive characteristics.

One further distinguishing characteristic should perhaps be mentioned: With the achievement of functional nuclear parity between the superpowers and the virtually uncontested recognition of spheres of influence dominated by one or the other in the North, the Third World became the only "safe" battleground in the Cold War. Neither side was willing to run the serious risk of direct nuclear confrontation implied by any armed conflict between them in the industrialized world. Thus the Third World became a theater, in both the military and the dramatic sense, of East-West competition. Of course, this competition has not been a factor in all armed conflicts in or among developing countries, but it has prolonged and intensified many of those in which it was not a prominent cause.

A Taxonomy of Conflict

Patterns of armed conflict in the Third World can be constructed in a number of ways—all of them, inevitably, somewhat arbitrary. Few, if any, disputes that erupt into sustained violence fall easily into a single category. However, a useful approach to the tracing of patterns begins with the identification of the kinds of issues that commonly give rise to armed conflict. The present attempt has arrived at five categories, all of which overlap considerably in the real world. They are (1) conflicts over national borders, (2) conflicts with or among minority groups, (3) conflicts involving questions of self-determination, (4) distributive disputes within or among states or regions, and (5) systemic conflicts. The examples chosen to illustrate these patterns are neither comprehensive nor unequivocal. They are merely illustrative.

The majority of boundary disputes in the Third World are the legacy of colonialism, and they are primarily of three kinds. The arbitrary drawing of lines on the map has balkanized some nationalities, leading to irredentist claims such as that of Somalia to the Somali-inhabited parts of Ethiopia and Kenya. It has artificially amalgamated others—often traditional enemies such as the Ndeles and the Shona in Zimbabwe; the Sara, the Arab clans, and the Toubou in Chad; the upland and lowland peoples of Burma and parts of Indochina—whose long-standing enmities were suppressed but not resolved under colonial rule. Very often, such ethnic divisions were compounded by religious divisions, such as that between the Muslim Fulani and the largely Christian Ibo in Nigeria. In these and many other such cases, hostility resurfaced after independence and burst into armed conflict.

A third and particularly tragic result of colonial division of territory has been the attempt to create homogeneous states out of ethnically diverse regions. This has contributed to some of the worst humanitarian disasters in the context of armed conflict in the postwar period—for example, the exchanges of population and blood between India and Pakistan at the time of partition and the interminable and complex aftermath of the creation of the state of Israel. There are, of course, border conflicts in the Third World that go beyond the problems of colonial mapmaking. The Sino-Indian war, for example, had more to do with the new accessibility and strategic importance of remote border regions that, in earlier times, were beyond control or concern.

Closely connected to the artificiality of boundaries are conflicts that arise from tensions between minority and majority groups or among minorities. The minorities involved in disputes that lead to armed conflict may be one of four types. The first that comes to the minds of most people is probably the oppressed minority that demands equal treatment or greater autonomy. In the case of the Tamils in Sri Lanka, the Miskitos in Nicaragua, the Muslims in the southern Philippines, and many indigenous peoples in Asia and Latin America, inertia or outright resistance to their demands leads some of them to accept violence as the only way to break the impasse. Once resorted to, violence enters an escalating spiral of repression, resistance, and reaction.

Second, armed conflict may also be the end result of disputes involving achieving minorities, as the situation of the Sikh community in India graphically demonstrates. Resentment against an achieving minority is particularly bitter in those cases in which the achieving group was preferred, or used and rewarded, by a former colonial ruler. The British philosophy of "divide and rule" left many minority groups in an exposed position—notably the groups of Asian expatriates who were introduced into colonies as far-flung as British Guyana, Malaya, and Uganda in order to function not only as laborers but also as commercial middlemen, minor bureaucrats, and, in some cases, professionals.

Similarly, the overseas Chinese communities throughout Southeast Asia were preferred to the native populations as commercial and financial collaborators with the colonizers. Unequal treatment gave certain indigenous or imported minority groups a toehold on the economic ladder, which some of them managed to parlay into lasting achievements through hard work and community solidarity. But their success carries with it a legacy of resentment that can easily become violent, especially in times of general economic difficulty.

Third, competing minorities may generate violent confrontation. The illegal entry of Salvadorans into Honduras in the
period leading up to the 1969 war between those two countries is
one example of competition for jobs, land, and resources leading to border tensions and finally to military engagement. There
have been repeated bloody clashes in the Indian state of Assam
between the native Assamese and land-hungry immigrants from
across the border in Bangladesh. Recently, relations between
Nigeria and Ghana have been severely strained by the forcible
expulsion of Ghanian workers, whose competition for jobs
became increasingly unwelcome as the slipping price of oil
caused Nigeria's economy to deteriorate. Fortunately, these two
countries have not shown any inclination to fight over the issue,
but it is clear that episodes of this kind can set the stage for
armed conflict. In the future, the pressure of rapidly growing
labor forces is likely to exacerbate the risk associated with this
source of tension.

Finally, there is the sort of armed conflict generated by an
oppressor minority's attempt to defend its position of privilege
against the majority's demands for social justice. The most familiar example of this is the South African white minority. Another
is the uprising of the Hutu majority against the dominant Tutsi
minority in Rwanda in the 1960s, which ultimately reduced the
Tutsi population of that country from 15 percent to only 9 percent of the total, through a combination of slaughter and mass
exodus.[3]

It is often difficult to make a clear distinction between minority issues and issues of self-determination and sovereignty, since
minority demands often develop into demands for self-determination in the form of regional autonomy or even independent
statehood. The separatist movements of the Moros, the Kurds,
and the Sikhs grew out of their dissatisfaction with their relations
with the state. Secessionist movements, however, often go beyond
this dissatisfaction to the conviction that, even if they are fairly
treated, a people such as the Eritreans want and have a right to
an independent state of their own. The clearest illustrations of
this sentiment are those arising from colonization, and out of
this clarity came the almost universal sympathy for the independence struggle of the people of Namibia, for example.

On the same principle, cases of postcolonial (or non-European)
imperialism should attract opprobrium for the empire builders

and sympathy for the victims of their ambitions, but these situations seldom generate such unanimity. The Organization of African Unity (OAU) has been deeply divided over the question of who should govern the western Sahara, and controversy continues about the establishment of Indonesian sovereignty over East Timor. Libya effectively annexed the Aouzou strip of northern Chad to the great consternation of its neighbors and the international community, and Vietnam's presence in Cambodia raised even greater alarms. In short, well past the supposed end of the colonial era, issues of self-determination remain one of the primary causes of armed conflict in the Third World.

Conflicts over the distribution of the wealth of a nation, or the fruits of development, are another major cause of conflict. Although these, too, often follow ethnic, religious, or racial lines, such factors are commonly intertwined with class, rural-urban, or regional divisions. They may have interstate dimensions as well, such as when the disputed resources require regional management or have special strategic significance. In early 1985, the then Egyptian Minister of State for Foreign Affairs, Dr. Butros Butros Ghali, was quoted as saying, "The next war in our region will be over the waters of the Nile, not politics."[4] Whether his prediction comes true or not, it illustrates the sensitivity that attaches to vital natural resources.

The distribution of land is one of the most ubiquitous and volatile of the issues that generate violence between communities and nations. In most of Central America, land reform is a prerequisite for an end to the threat or the fact of civil war. Officially sponsored settlement programs have provoked armed conflicts between settlers and tribal peoples in Bangladesh, Indonesia, and Brazil, among other countries. And in the poorest countries, the groundwork for conflict is being laid as rapidly growing populations press upon an agricultural base whose potential is, in some cases, actually declining through neglect or abuse.

Conflicts over the distribution of resources between states encompass many of the more traditional forms of interstate rivalry: boundary disputes; land grabs, such as the Zairian attempt to annex oil-rich Cabinda province from Angola; arguments over the distribution of river waters or aquifers; conflicts over fishing rights and other uses of territorial waters; and disputes concerning access to strategic minerals. Other intangible resources might also be mentioned here, including navigational rights (for example, the Suez and Panama canals and the Shatt al Arab waterway) and access to strategic positions (the Golan Heights, for example). All the preceding have contributed to the flare-up of armed conflicts.

Distributive disputes within and among states often veer toward the fifth pattern of armed conflict, which is of a systemic nature. In the case of internal conflicts, the search for solutions to basic problems of distribution may itself lead to armed conflict, as ideological contention over economic strategies degenerates into violent confrontation. This was clearly one element of the disputes between the governments and the armed opposition movements in El Salvador, Nicaragua, Angola, and Mozambique.

Interstate conflicts often take on a broader, systemic dimension when the disputed resource is seen as vital for the maintenance of one of the contending systems. The 1985 attempt by South African commandos to attack the oil refinery in Cabinda underscores how crucial that facility was believed to be for the economic viability of the Angolan state—a perception that is shared by both the supporters and the opponents of the state system in Angola. The retention of the West Bank and the Golan Heights is seen by Israeli decisionmakers as vital to the continuing existence of the state.

In general, systemic conflicts may be characterized as ideological (including religious ideology); as dedicated to the extension of certain regimes of force or of principle; or as defenses of an existing balance of power, sphere of influence, or alliance system. It is difficult to find pure examples of ideologically based armed conflict, though ideology is a factor in many cases, such as the ones in Central America and Africa mentioned above. Similarly, religious ideology was an important element in the war between Iran and Iraq and in Iran's involvement in other armed conflicts throughout the region—though it is only one part of the struggle for leadership taking place against the complex background of Middle Eastern radical politics.

The use of armed force to further either a political project or a moral cause is a category that may seem to combine very disparate elements, yet it is often a matter of judgment and perspective as to which pole of this classification is closer to a given conflict. The Cuban presence in Angola is presented by the Cuban government as a contribution to the historical process of self-determination and the defense of Angola's national sovereignty. It is portrayed by the U.S. government, however, as a simple extension of Soviet power in the region.

Libya's various attempts at coalition and conquest in North Africa are seen by some as crude expressions of hegemonical ambitions, but presumably by Colonel Qaddafi as attempts to realize the dream of a greater and purer Islamic Maghreb. The Tanzanian invasion of Uganda, the Vietnamese invasion of Cambodia, and the Indian invasion of East Pakistan are three examples of military action that put an end to situations of grave injustice and violation of accepted humanitarian norms. But in all cases, the regional political aspirations of the invading state were also served. The continuing conflicts of the frontline states with South Africa are less ambiguous; all pay a severe military and economic price for their efforts to put an end to the system of apartheid.

The third form of systemic conflict is that in which armed force is used to maintain, at the regional or global level, a balance of power, sphere of influence, or alliance system. The wars of the last thirty years in Indochina, though they contained elements from virtually every other category, were perhaps dominated by factors from this category: the effort to maintain the French colonial empire; the U.S. attempt to prevent the countries of the region from escaping the Western sphere of influence; and Vietnam's establishment of domination over Laos and Cambodia, which led it into confrontation with Thailand and China. U.S. involvement in Central America is another example of system maintenance as a motivation for armed conflict, as was the Soviet intervention in Afghanistan—though the two conflicts are quite different in scale, depth of involvement, and a number of other dimensions.

In general, systemic conflicts tend to be among the most bitter and intractable, since the parties involved often see themselves as fighting for their very existence—not only for their lives but also for the continuation of the principles, beliefs, and structures for which they have lived.

Uncertainty and Intervention: The Case for Restraint

The problem with classifications is that they are essentially static. The patterns of armed conflict in the Third World today are embedded in a historical process that exposes all emerging countries to tremendous turmoil. In many cases, the end of colonial rule was only the beginning of the struggle to establish representative government and participatory mechanisms. Access to positions of power in government has become a subject of fierce contention in many states among ethnic or religious groups or among regions—especially where the benefits of government activity and patronage are seen to be unfairly distributed. The tensions and inequalities generated by the development process itself make heavy demands on the government's capacity to mediate conflicting claims. Mediation, however, requires strong political, economic, and legal institutions, which are lacking in much of the developing world. All too often, therefore, states have failed in or abandoned their mediating roles and resorted to repression.

In many instances, Third World governments have compounded the error by inviting external military assistance to help them deal with the violent reactions engendered by developmental and distributive failures. Their opponents have, of course, responded in kind—or perhaps initiated the process to begin with. Thus, in many cases, Third World governments and opposition movements alike have lost control of the duration and intensity of their conflicts. The less successful they are in dealing with internal disputes through the exercise of persuasion, negotiation, and accommodation, the more vulnerable they become to external interference—often, ironically, by invitation.

The volatility of a world that is going through a period of fundamental transformation creates a tinderbox effect in which conflict cannot easily be avoided or contained. The range of combustible materials is vast. One of the flaws of modern political science is perhaps a tendency to reduce the causes of conflict to rather bloodless assessments of the interests or organizational imperatives of various actors. It is terribly difficult to capture in this kind of framework the tremendously powerful forces that underlie much of the armed conflict in the Third World. The passions that lead people to kill and to risk their own lives often spring from intangible attachments—a mother tongue, a religion, recognition of certain rights, recovery or establishment of identity. Such passions are not within the power of governments to control, though governments and opposition movements often attempt to manipulate them.

The frequency with which these passions are misread, misinterpreted, or simply overlooked tempts one to define a sixth class of armed conflict: war by miscalculation or underestimation. One can scarcely begin to count the number of armed conflicts that have been based on faulty perceptions of the monolithic nature of communism, the power of independent nationalism, or the depth of ethnic passions; on the overestimation of the pacifying power of prosperity or on the underestimation of religion as a motivating force in politics.

Two contemporary instances of armed conflict in the Indian subcontinent illustrate the ease with which deep currents of feeling are overlooked. The Indian Punjab has been cited repeatedly as one of the great success stories of the region for its great strides in agricultural productivity leading to remarkable economic growth. In a similar manner, Sri Lanka has been cited for its success in achieving a high quality of life and a relatively egalitarian distribution of income even under the constraints of poverty. Both were exemplary cases of the kind of developmental success that was widely believed to inoculate an area against violent conflict. Yet in the 1980s, both erupted in flames, for very complex reasons. The depth of Sikh and Tamil feelings of grievance was not reckoned on, nor was the powerful backlash of majority communities.

Perhaps the most spectacular recent example of this sort of failure to perceive the powerful currents of feeling that channel the course of history was the Islamic revolution in Iran. Waves of Islamic activism have flowed from its success to a number of different parts of the world.

These powerful currents that emanate from within the Third World play themselves out in the context of an unstable international system characterized by a number of dynamic currents. One is the progressive weakening or disintegration of less viable states such as pre-1972 Pakistan and perhaps, more recently, Lebanon or Chad. A second is the consolidation or attempted consolidation of new power configurations under regional hegemonic powers such as Libya in North Africa or India in the subcontinent. A third and related trend is the emergence of new economic and political centers of power, such as the newly industrialized countries of East Asia as well as, of course, China. In this setting, the demand for self-determination is sometimes an integrating and sometimes a disintegrating force.

East-West and North-South issues became even more inextricably intertwined as the superpowers symmetrically and strongly committed themselves to a global projection of force. The mere fact that one of the superpowers was arming and otherwise supporting one party to an armed conflict was reason enough for the other to back its opponent—though not without restraint. The Soviet Union, for example, was extremely circumspect about its material support for Nicaragua; in a similar way, the United States was careful about direct involvement with the Afghan resistance. In neither case was one power in any doubt about the desires of the other, but neither displayed an appetite for direct confrontation in the other's backyard. This was, of course, a profound relief, but its effect on armed conflicts in the Third World was, in many cases, to inject an element of proxyism that, as mentioned earlier, prolonged and intensified the conflict. It also made the position of former buffer states such as Cambodia and Afghanistan untenable and subjected them to a complete loss of autonomy.

The commitment to the projection of global force drew a number of Third World countries very close to the strategic networks of the superpowers because of the importance of forward basing areas for rapid deployment of forces, ports for blue-water navies, and air bases. It was thus all but impossible for armed conflicts over issues of modernization, national integration, and political succession in countries such as the Philippines and Afghanistan to be resolved according to a purely internal logic.

The volatility of alliances between Third World states and major powers has been amply demonstrated. In the Horn of Africa, for example, Somalia switched from Soviet to American patronage while Ethiopia made the opposite exchange. The self-interests of the major powers are consistently given priority over the interests of relatively weaker client states. Pressures from domestic and bureaucratic rivalries within the big powers may work for or against various parties to Third World conflicts, but the Third World's ability to influence the direction of such pressures is in most cases very limited.

The role of superpower's client, which was supposed to offer a strong degree of protection to the client, also carried with it a constant exposure to the risks of interference, external support for internal dissenters, and destabilization. It was this realization, presumably, that led peace researcher Johan Galtung to recommend, as three of the four central elements of a more effective and independent security policy, that countries decouple their vital interests from the superpowers, arm themselves with defensive weapons only, and cultivate friendly and productive relations with countries at all points on the political spectrum.[5]

Dr. Galtung's fourth recommendation was that countries do everything in their power to build up their "internal strength," a recognition that instability creates the opportunity for armed intervention by external powers.[6] This is not to suggest that countries that are subject to intervention always bring it on themselves by a failure to keep their own houses in order. It is nonetheless true that injustice, lack of participation, and a festering sense of unresolved grievance are breeding grounds for violence that may easily lead to armed conflict.

The foregoing may seem to be a truism, but it is frequently argued that the preservation of peace may require the acceptance of an unjust status quo.[7] The evils of armed conflict are weighed against the evils of the less-than-perfect reality and found heavier. So, for example, the member states of the OAU operate on the principle of respect for existing boundaries, though they themselves condemn the manner in which carelessly drawn boundaries violate the ethnic geography of the continent. Clinging to the status quo is seen as the only way to avoid bloody struggles in which no state or people could be sure of winning.

The idea that a flawed peace is preferable to almost any war is compelling in many circumstances, but there are two characteristics of contemporary armed struggle that rob the argument of its logic. One is the easy availability and vastly increased destructive power of modern weapons. The second is the willingness, discussed above, of external powers to supply and support armed resistance within states or armed conflict between states in pursuit of their own political or strategic objectives.

The increased sophistication and portability of weapons, the ease of manufacture of explosives, the eagerness of arms manufacturers in both the public and the private sectors to sell their wares all mean that even very small groups can inflict enormous damage—enough to keep a society in chaos and effectively derail its development efforts. In earlier times, it would hardly have made sense to speak of the activities of fifteen people as "armed conflict." Yet a cell of only fifteen rightists uncovered by the Argentine authorities in May 1985 was found to be equipped not only with small arms and military uniforms but also with high-powered explosives, sophisticated transmitting equipment, and napalm-carrying warheads.[8]

The effectiveness of small groups in armed conflict is illustrated by the history of mercenary involvement in successful and near-successful coups in Africa in the postcolonial period. The 1975 coup that installed Ali Solih as president of the Comoro Islands was accomplished by a total force of eight men. The coup that removed Solih from power in 1978 and reinstalled his predecessor was carried out by forty-five mercenaries under the same leader who directed the 1975 coup.[9] Very small states with weak military forces and highly centralized (often one person) power structures are particularly susceptible to a small mercenary strike force. The number of tempting targets for mercenary action is likely to grow with the importance of small states in politically volatile and strategically sensitive regions.

The ease with which serious violent disruption can be sustained by small groups if they are well armed, well financed, and well trained has reduced the cost of interference in the internal affairs of another country and raised its payoff. An adversary, or an adversary's client, can be kept off balance through the prolongation of armed conflict of the hit-and-run variety. This pattern is usually referred to as terrorism, though much of it is sporadic by virtue of limited means rather than a philosophy of unpredictability.

In order to operate successfully even at a fairly low level of intensity, armed groups need some base of local sympathy to conceal their activities and evade detection. Unresolved grievances and the persistence of an unjust status quo nurture the sympathy that the guerrilla and, to a lesser extent, the terrorist rely upon. The New People's Army of the Philippines is said even by the Philippine army to control or at least have friendly access to 20 percent of the villages in the country,[10] making it virtually indestructible by conventional military means. The spread of terrorism, and its growing sophistication as a means of political struggle, has also been encouraged by the failure to find solutions to protracted conflicts.

The function of the local base may be filled by the adjacent sanctuary if bordering states have populations or governments willing to harbor opposition forces. Sri Lankan negotiations with India in mid-1985 were a recognition of the fact that unless

Tamil separatists operating from bases in the Indian state of Tamil Nadu could be prevented from crossing into Sri Lanka, no military solution to the conflict could be attained.

Since any group with a grievance and a domestic power base can find potent means—from outside, if necessary—to disturb if not destroy the peace, it follows that the acceptance of unjust situations is not an alternative to armed conflict but a recipe for it. The only real alternative is political accommodation with the aggrieved groups. Obviously, this is easier to achieve before the resort to arms rather than after violent confrontation has heightened and polarized sentiments and weakened the will to compromise.

In a context that makes resort to violence so easy, the peaceful management of conflict requires a great capacity for political innovation. There is no formula that can be applied across the board, although there are many valuable examples, such as the 1984 internal peace treaty negotiated by the government of Colombia with the main domestic guerrilla movements and the unilateral amnesty declared in 1980 by Thailand toward domestic Communist insurgents who agreed to lay down their arms and reenter Thai society.[11] The regional conflict-resolution effort of the Contadora group was innovative in both its proposals and its methodology. The Contadora method involves all parties in thorough exploration of the issues and discussion of negotiable positions before the process of formal negotiation begins. The group's proposals in 1984–85 dealt with domestic political issues as well as international security issues of concern to the Central American states.[12]

Highly innovative and constructive proposals will not change the pattern of armed conflict in the Third World or elsewhere without some commitment to their implementation. Virtually every failed proposal for constructive change founders on this question of political will. Changing the current destructive patterns of armed conflict in the Third World does not require the wholesale adoption of new policies or negotiating formulas. It requires something that is perhaps a little easier to achieve: restraint.

The needed restraint has two major dimensions: one internal to the decisionmaking structures of parties to Third World conflicts, and one to be exercised by external powers. The first of these applies chiefly to the ways in which actors in the developing countries express and pursue the very real disputes among themselves. All have a stake in the peaceful resolution of conflicts, limits on the production and importation of arms, and the vigorous application and extension of humanitarian law.

Above all, it is in the interest of the developing countries to wean themselves from external military support and involvement, for two compelling reasons. One is that external involvement almost always increases the scale and destructiveness of conflicts by providing weapons that multiply the number of casualties (especially, in recent decades, civilian casualties) and do considerable damage to the social and economic infrastructure in the area of conflict. For example, U.S. military aid to El Salvador, which more than doubled from 1983 to 1984 to reach a level of $196.5 million, was invested in part in a dramatically increased capacity for aerial bombardment. U.S.-supplied combat helicopters increased from fifteen to as many as fifty from one year to the next; helicopter gunships and at least one C-47 airborne fire-support platform were also supplied. As a result, according to the Institute of Strategic Studies, "this caused such an increase in civilian casualties that widespread concern forced President Duarte in September to promise a tightening of the rules for bombing."[13]

When one party to a dispute turns to outsiders for support, its adversaries are encouraged to do the same, thereby subjecting the country or region to the expression of rivalries and antagonisms in which it has no direct stake. External military aid is often the trigger for regionwide arms races, which drain the resources and heighten the tension level of the countries involved. The external patron may discourage client governments or factions from entering into negotiations or from seriously pursuing any negotiations that do get started. It may prefer to continue an armed conflict that costs it relatively little but is an effective source of discomfiture to its rivals.

The second compelling reason to forgo external assistance is that such assistance undermines the autonomy of the recipient to such an extent that even the winner of a battle for control of a state may end up with a Pyrrhic victory. Measured against the loss of political independence and the danger of resubjugation to the interests of external powers, the political or ideological goals of the combatants must be reassessed. Furthermore, the acceptance of external aid often entails a serious sacrifice of legitimacy, as the U.S.-backed regimes in South Vietnam, the Soviet-backed regimes in Afghanistan, and the Vietnamese-backed regime in

Cambodia all discovered to their own and their patrons' frustration. The legitimacy of the rebel movements UNITA in Angola and FROLINAT in Chad are similarly tainted by South African and Libyan patronage, respectively.

For the sake of limiting the destructiveness and the duration of armed conflicts, as well as to protect claims to legitimacy, all parties to armed conflict in the Third World should use restraint in seeking external military assistance. But such a regime of self-restraint is unlikely to hold up without a symmetrical restraint on the part of the external powers themselves. In increasing numbers of armed conflicts in the Third World, the external intervenor is not a superpower or a former colonial power but one of the more powerful Third World states such as India, Libya, Vietnam, and Tanzania, to name just a few. Therefore, any code of conduct that might be devised to discourage interference in armed conflicts will have to be negotiated on an inclusive basis; regional organizations are often promising venues for initiating such discussions.

Restraint on the part of potential interventionist states has a powerful potential for limiting the scope of armed conflict in the Third World, given that few developing countries have sophisticated arms industries of their own. Only Brazil, China, India, Israel, South Africa, and Taiwan have a significant arms-manufacturing capacity. Few other developing countries even approach self-sufficiency, and although the arms imports of the Third World countries as a whole have increased dramatically in the last twenty years, many of the non-oil-exporting states are dependent on military aid or credit.

Lest a regime of restraint in supplying Third World countries with the weapons to cripple each other be thought utterly utopian, it is worth recalling the considerable progress that was made in the late 1970s in one effort to negotiate such an agreement in a strategically sensitive part of the world. The Conventional Arms Transfer (CAT) negotiations, which involved the major countries of Latin America as well as consultations with the United States, the Soviet Union, and other major arms-exporting countries, made substantial strides toward an agreement to lower the influx of weapons into that troubled region.[14] The deterioration of détente in the aftermath of the Soviet invasion of Afghanistan and the advent of a more conservative U.S. administration with little predilection for arms control were among the factors that derailed the CAT negotiations. But the progress made set a valuable precedent and may provide a model that can be applied in other regions and, one hopes, revived in the region where it began.

A more demanding form of restraint on the part of external parties requires a narrow interpretation of the kinds of political developments that constitute threats to their national interests. Demanding as this is, however, it is not the same as insisting that states subordinate their national interests to higher principles such as respect for self-determination—for this, the realist must admit, is not likely to be accepted by powerful states in the near future.

Restraint in defining one's legitimate national security interests requires making a distinction between developments that are threatening and those that are merely distasteful. The accession to power of a leftist regime in Nicaragua was certainly profoundly distasteful to the Reagan administration in the United States, but it is difficult to convince most of the community of nations that Nicaragua was a genuine threat to the security of the United States. Ironically, it became more of a threat the more it was forced to rely on the Soviet Union and its allies in order to protect its independence against U.S. intervention. Perhaps the most valuable immediate effect of the Contadora effort was to prevent the isolation of Nicaragua and the stark clientism that would almost certainly have been the result.

The United States shows a remarkable absence of restraint in defining threat in Central America—seeming to equate almost any degree of foreign policy independence or any social movement opposed to the social and economic status quo with a threat to U.S. interests. Yet the United States' relationship with Mexico amply demonstrates that an independent foreign policy can be pursued even by a close neighbor without compromising security.

A similar lack of restraint in perceiving threats may be seen in the Soviet decision to invade Afghanistan. In this case, the plausibility of the Soviet fear of domestic contagion from Islamic fundamentalism is difficult to assess, but the Soviet determination to consolidate its hold on a state it regarded as belonging to its own sphere of influence showed a grave lack of restraint. One extremely important aspect of restraint that is negatively illustrated here concerns the role of buffer states. What is needed is a mutually acceptable definition of what internal power configurations and external policies a buffer state can adopt and still be left alone by its more powerful neighbors.

Governments and nongovernmental actors are motivated to observe restraints either because they recognize a moral imperative shored up by the approbation of the international community or because they calculate the utilitarian value of reciprocal restraint on the part of adversaries. Any state that chooses to ignore restraints must calculate that its willingness to do so will inevitably encourage others to do the same; its calculations of self-interest must weigh the short-term advantages that might be gained in a particular conflict against the cost of achieving its objectives in an environment made more dangerous and difficult by a generalized lack of restraint.

The primary obstacle to restraint is desperation, and in that the Third World abounds. Reduction of the sources of armed conflict there, as in the North, will call upon the deepest reserves of political innovation that governments and other political actors can command. The task is obviously not one for the Third World alone, given how closely its turbulence is tied to that of the international system as a whole.

Nuclear Proliferation: The Most Dangerous Game

The patterns of armed conflict in the Third World are more like those of a kaleidoscope than a patchwork quilt: The patterns are constantly shifting. Unlike in a kaleidoscope, the variations are not predictable, and the elements of change are not contained within a finite system. The volatility of the interactions between the Third World and the international system and among the developing countries themselves cannot be overestimated. The foreign policy priorities of the great powers are unpredictable, particularly the future course of Chinese foreign policy and that of other emerging powers. The stability of alliance systems, regionally and globally, cannot be taken for granted. The precarious economic situation of many developing countries raises serious questions about their ability to achieve or maintain political stability.

In the light of this extremely unsettled context, the prospect of nuclear proliferation in the Third World is terrifying. Yet it is very likely that new and existing tensions will lead countries, and possibly even some nonstate actors, to an all-out effort to acquire nuclear weapons. The most powerful incentive for any nation to do so is the assumption that its opponents are planning to do the same or have actually embarked on the process. This vicious spiral has already been seen in action: between India and Pakistan, Brazil and Argentina, South Africa and the frontline states, Israel and Iraq. Many other states have the technical capability to develop nuclear weapons in a relatively short time.

Even more terrifying than the spread of nuclear weapons to potentially unstable or irresponsible nations is the prospect of nuclear weapons falling into the hands of nongovernmental groups, especially those that have already shown their willingness to use terrorist tactics and to sacrifice the lives of innocent civilians in the attempt to further a political aim. A few years ago, an undergraduate student at Princeton University in the United States published a credible blueprint for an atomic weapon. The increased sophistication, portability, and power of nuclear devices; the transparency of the basics of their design, and the increasing circulation of fissile materials break down any confidence that the nuclear monopoly can be retained for long. If an undergraduate student can design a textbook bomb, the nuclear suitcase bomb cannot be far behind. Already, government arsenals contain "backpack" bombs—tempting targets for theft if not imitation.

The growth of the nuclear power industry raises the risk of proliferation in two ways. The diversion of weapons-grade uranium and plutonium from conventional reactors has been constrained in large part by suppliers' and manufacturers' safeguards. However, the current economic crisis in the nuclear power industry has turned the reactor business into a buyers' market. There is a danger of a consequent bidding down of safeguards by countries that are in a position to buy reactors. Second, the spread of nuclear power is putting such quantities of plutonium into circulation that preventing the diversion of the tiny amount needed to construct a small weapon begins to seem a Herculean task. The development of the breeder reactor, even if it operates only in the industrial countries, promises to aggravate this problem.

If there has never before been a sufficiently compelling reason for nations to cooperate in managing conflicts and attempting to eradicate their causes, the prospect of one or two or half a dozen more Hiroshimas—to say nothing of the risk of larger conflagrations and the risk of general escalation—should be enough to encourage a reconsideration.

The Challenge of Nonviolence[15]

[This reflection on nonviolence begins with a personal memory about a quarrel Soedjatmoko had with his father when he was sixteen years old. "At the time, Indonesia was still a Dutch colony, and joining the Indonesian nationalist movement was a risky thing for a student. But I was very eager to join. My father forbade me to do so, saying that most wounding thing to a boy: that I was too young. I railed against him, and asked bitterly why had he taught me about the importance of freedom—both political freedom and inner freedom—if he would not allow me to act on the convictions he had worked to instill in me? He replied, 'I do want you to join in the independence struggle, but only when you have learned to fight without hatred.'"]

The assassination of Olof Palme left behind not only profound personal grief but also tremendous political shock. That such an act of violence could take place in Sweden, in this most rational and orderly society, was proof that there is no single corner of this world that can be considered immune from the plague of violence. It forces us to ask ourselves what kind of world we have created and what—if anything—can be done to restore, or achieve, a greater measure of civility in our relations as individuals, as communities, as states.

Violence has been a perpetual theme in the history of our species. But our era seems to be characterized by a breakdown of many of the restraints on violence that have been operative in the past. We can see this in the greater willingness to flout the laws of war that protect noncombatants; the increasing reliance on indiscriminate violence and terrorism as a routine method of striking an adversary or publicizing a cause or defending the status quo; the seeming rarity of negotiated ends to armed conflicts. What most distinguishes our times, however, is the power of the means of destruction human beings now have at their disposal, and the easy availability of many extremely powerful weapons to any group with cash or credit. We cannot dismiss the possibility that even nuclear weapons may eventually be bought, stolen, or fabricated from stolen materials by groups or governments willing to hold the whole world as hostage.

Despite the unprecedented power and availability of weapons, it must be said that the record of violence in achieving its objectives is, in recent years, a dismal one. Witness the intense and spreading destruction in the Middle East; the Iran-Iraq war, which produced only stalemate for all its carnage; the intransigence of the South African government in the face of armed attacks. In the latter case, nonviolent measures exerted more effective pressure for change, both domestically and internationally, than violence. Violent resistance, in fact, alienated supporters and gave the government an excuse for greater use of violence itself.

Any hope of minimizing violence depends on finding and developing alternative methods of struggle. A world free of violence would not be a world free of conflict. Today's world is beset with conflicts that stem from the denial of freedom, rights, needs, and self-expression. It must be clear that giving up violence does not mean giving up the fight against unjust and oppressive conditions.

A proven alternative mode of struggle is nonviolent action. Nonviolence is not just an idea, it is also a tactic or even a strategy. Its effectiveness as a strategy of the outgunned has been demonstrated repeatedly: in the Quit India movement; in the U.S. civil rights movement; and in the Philippines in the early 1980s, where the heavily armed Marcos government was unable to resist the massive demonstration of popular support for the opposition led by Corazon Aquino. Also, it should not be forgotten that for all its violent rhetoric and its subsequent record of violence, the Iranian revolution was a nonviolent revolution—a revolution of the popular demonstration, the sermon, the cassette—leading up to a massive withdrawal of support for the Shah's government.

Unlike brute force, nonviolence respects and draws upon the morality of the adversary. It does not depend upon hatred, aggression, or unthinking obedience to motivate its practitioners. Rather, it unifies the morality of means and ends and, in so doing, stimulates the development of the participants and increases support for its cause from the uncommitted. Nonviolence does not

suppress reason but frees it from inertia. In the process, it opens
the door to negotiation and builds up a more permanent system
of trust.

It may be, however, that the practical appeal rather than the
moral appeal of nonviolent struggle may provide the impetus for
reducing violence in the Third World. Nonviolence is often
described as the weapon of the weak. But this is true only in the
sense of comparative arsenals. Confronting a tank with only
one's body requires greater courage and entails greater risk than
confronting it with another tank. Nonviolent struggle is not easy,
it is not risk free, and it does not always work. But the physical
and psychological and moral costs of violence are so great that
an alternative form of political struggle must be given the most
serious consideration and trial.

Mahatma Gandhi thought that the absence of self-confidence
was the single most significant block to nonviolent action. Other
barriers include fear, despair that nothing can change, indifference, inconvenience, and the power of inertia that makes people
oblivious to the existence of choice and encourages them to be
submissive. Gandhi understood that the nonviolent society
begins with the restoration of dignity to the individual human
being and proceeded from there to the development of wider
societal resilience.

Resilience in society is the quality that permits people and
institutions to interact with one another without their conflicts
erupting into violence. Resilience allows a people to adapt to
change without losing their cultural identity. Resilience permits
faith in a system of justice to be maintained even in the face of
flaws in the system; a single travesty or even a series of them will
not bring about rejection of the system as a whole. The concept
of resilience is quite different from that of stability. Stability
under oppressive conditions means the perpetuation of violence.

Building social resilience is not a task for only the state,
though the state can play an important role. The quality of
resilience lies in the much broader sphere of civic culture. A collective commitment to the public good, to managing conflict
without violence, depends on community groups, nongovernmental organizations, religious institutions involving both clergy
and laity, volunteer groups, political parties, educational institutions, the media, and so forth—all of which have the responsibility and the capability to nurture a sense of civic responsibility.

The spontaneous actions of inspired individuals can also be extremely important at times when the resilience of a society is stretched to the breaking point. In the aftermath of the 1985 Mexican earthquake, the unorganized actions of citizens were far more effective in the early stages than official relief efforts both in rescuing and sustaining people and in preventing the development of an atmosphere in which looting and violence could have become widespread. Similarly, citizens intervened spontaneously in New Delhi after the assassination of Prime Minister Indira Gandhi to interrupt attacks on members of the Sikh minority. There are many such examples, and they underscore the importance of a public philosophy in which the citizens bear a sense of responsibility for the collective good.

Existing social institutions must become the vehicle for creating and expressing this sense of responsibility, but it may also be necessary to create new kinds of truly representative institutions at the national and local levels to cultivate the habit of thinking collectively but pluralistically about the public good. Political culture is nurtured by a broad approach to public affairs and civil and political action, which cuts across the divisions within the nation.

There is little doubt that violence will continue to mar the political and social landscape for the foreseeable future. Within many societies, the disparities are so great, the injustices so gross, and the privileged so fearful of and resistant to change that violence will be turned to as a last resort. The irony that history has so often taught us is that the use of violence, however justified, may demolish the very goals and ideals that were sought and create the mirror image of the injustice it sought to destroy.

Olof Palme understood very well, I believe, that nonviolence had, in his lifetime, gone from being a utopian dream to being a practical necessity. He remained committed to the fight for justice. He was vigorous in its pursuit, even militant—but he was never an advocate of violence. The memorial we can make for him is to continue that struggle, in peace with ourselves and one another.

6

....

The Governance of the
International System

Much of Soedjatmoko's work in the last few years of his life was addressed to questions of governance. By governance he meant the direction and management of the forces of change—not from above by any external authority but by internally generated, self-conscious cooperation and communication. Some of the most difficult problems of governance arise at the international level where there are few authoritative institutions that can coordinate policies for issues that extend across state boundaries and far into the future. On the occasion of receiving an honorary degree from Georgetown University in 1987, Soedjatmoko addressed this complex subject in the Oscar Iden Lecture to the School of Foreign Service. It is the first paper presented in this chapter. He had raised some related issues in an earlier speech to a forum of young leaders from around the world convened by the Center for Strategic and International Studies. The second paper looks at the impact of changes in values on governance and specifically at the effect that a prolonged period of economic stagnation may have on public attitudes toward economic and political systems. In this piece we find his fullest exposition

The first part of this chapter was originally presented as the Oscar Iden Lecture at Georgetown University on October 9, 1987, and published in 1988 by the Institute for the Study of Diplomacy, Georgetown University, Washington, D.C. The second part was originally published by MIT Press as "Values in Transition," *The Washington Quarterly* 9(4): 67–72 (1986). Reprinted with permission.

of the idea of social resilience, which he thought was a quality that enabled people and societies to adapt to change while maintaining civility. The third section of this chapter is a sweeping catalogue of the problems the rising generation will face in the next century; it was commissioned by the Japanese newspaper *Asahi Shimbun* for its 1984 International Symposium.

International Governance[1]

The governance of the international system resides, in formal terms, in a collection of agreements and institutions entered into by the governments of nation-states. Some see the proliferation of such agreements and institutions slowly chipping away at the prevailing anarchy of the system, perhaps leading to the emergence of some kind of world government. It is therefore important to make clear at the outset that international governance, in the sense in which the term is used here, is not international government. Indeed, one of the elements of the argument that follows is that national governments as such are capable of performing only a limited role in the governance of the international system.

The term *governance* encompasses the aggregate of forces, systems, institutions, movements, conflicts, and accommodations by which human beings cooperate and compete. Frameworks of human interaction as diverse as financial markets, armed conflicts, transnational corporations, international organizations, mass migration, drug trafficking, resource regimes, religious movements, and intergovernmental negotiations all fall within the realm of governance.

The institutions and arrangements through which national governments attempt to manage such complex phenomena were devised, for the most part, in the immediate aftermath of World War II. The world today is so fundamentally different from the world of 1945 that the obsolescence of the postwar institutions can scarcely come as a surprise. The population of the globe has more than doubled, with by far the largest share of growth occurring in the Southern Hemisphere. The achievement of decolonization has rewritten the political map, multiplied the number of actors in the state system, and opened a channel for the expression of the aspirations of the Third World. There has been a revolution of mobility and communication, so that the problems and conflicts of one group of people can no longer be confined to one corner of the globe. The international division of labor has changed radically and disruptively, but in the process of doing so it has contributed to an explosion of human productivity that has put undreamed of affluence within the reach of hundreds of millions of people. The new affluence has heightened the awareness and the insupportability of absolute poverty, which has also grown with human numbers.

The rise in production to meet human needs and desires has created problems of waste, pollution, and resource abuse on a global scale. The extension of humankind's prowess in penetrating hitherto inaccessible realms—the deep seas, outer space, the most hostile deserts, mountains, and frozen wastes—has removed buffers and neutral areas that once served to cushion and dissipate hostilities. The exponential growth of destructive power has magnified the difficulties of keeping the peace—especially the development of weapons systems that are small, powerful, portable, and easily obtainable. The construction of two vast arsenals of nuclear weapons has not only given the superpowers the ability to eradicate human civilization but also fundamentally changed the nature of international politics; the possession of nuclear weapons has come to be seen as the entry card to great power status.

The current pace of demographic, economic, and technological change is such that the next forty years promise to be as volatile as the last, if not more so. Any new institutions or arrangements for international governance that are devised now may also be seen as obsolete in forty years—or even by the time they are in place. No single group of policymakers has the capacity to marshal all the facts, understand all the alternatives, and predict all the reactions to or anticipate all the interpretations of an action. This fact argues for maximum flexibility, the widest possible consultation, and a large degree of humility in framing new instruments of governance.

Limitations of the Nation-State

Apart from its volatility, the major characteristic of the international system is its complexity. Reaction to this complexity is very often a tendency toward reductionism—one of the most serious manifestations of which is the fiction that the only actors of consequence in the international system are governments of nation-states. Even the term *international* reveals this bias. It would be more accurate to use the term global or transnational to describe the forces that drive individual and collective human interaction.

Today, there are a multiplicity of actors capable of making their presence felt in international relations. These actors exist at both lower and higher levels of aggregation than the nation-state. It has been amply demonstrated in recent years how powerful an impact can be made at the regional and even global level by very small groups of people accountable to no one but themselves—for example, terrorists, arms dealers, or drug smugglers operating on the margin of the state system, but also currency speculators and dealers in financial futures. Unorganized masses of people acting unconsciously in concert have similarly profound effects on the ecosystem and economies they inhabit. Individual decisions, such as whether to have a child, cut down a tree, open an overseas bank account, or move from the country to the city, aggregate themselves into major social trends.

At the other end of the spectrum, the freedom of action of national governments is constrained by the decisions and requirements of supranational institutions and forces. These include institutions such as the International Monetary Fund, organizations such as the European Economic Community and the United Nations, and corporations such as Toshiba, Fiat, and Citibank. Governments are also constrained by more diffuse forces such as currency and commodity markets, religious movements, the international communications media, and expatriate populations. The governments of individual countries, clearly, have very limited control—though they often have considerable influence—over either subnational or transnational processes. Governmental freedom of action is also inhibited by an ever-tightening noose of environmental phenomena such as air and water pollution, climatic change, soil erosion, and geological instability.

The bedrock of the contemporary international system is the principle of state sovereignty. Increasingly, however, state sovereignty is being revealed as a myth. Of course, it has always been true that, as George Orwell might have put it, some states are more sovereign than others. But the myth of sovereignty has been, until fairly recently, a useful one, deliberately adopted to blunt the edge of brute force and constrain the exercise of coercive power. Certainly for the new nations in the Third World, sovereignty is the expression of their right to self-determination and identity and their most powerful instrument for the protection of their rights and security. Sovereignty, therefore, still has a valuable and necessary function.

The myth of state sovereignty, however, also encourages a tendency toward unilateralism, an unrealistic belief that the problems confronting a country can and perhaps should be dealt with by the government of that country acting independently. This fosters an illusion—at best futile and at worst dangerous—that certain values that are in fact indivisible can be divided up into pieces corresponding to the size and shape of particular nation-states. Security, prosperity, and the integrity of the environment are no longer within the grasp of any single state, even the most powerful. Each nation is intimately bound to its adversaries as well as to its friends by a common vulnerability.

Our Common Vulnerability

A common vulnerability is something new in our era. The restrictions that it imposes on the behavior of governments and other actors set the parameters of international governance. The three spheres mentioned above—security, the economy, and the environment—provide some of the clearest illustrations.

War between the most powerful nuclear-armed states has utterly lost its usefulness as a way of resolving disputes or achieving policy objectives. It can be expected to lead only to mutual annihilation. Geopolitics has been changed, radically and permanently, not only by the technology of nuclear explosives but by what political scientist Daniel Deudney called the "transparency revolution": the advances in communications and transportation technologies that have abolished the geographical front line or rear guard as meaningful military concepts. Today, the global commons—the oceans and the atmosphere—are thoroughly militarized. Rather than serving as protective barriers or buffers, they are the fluid suspension media for a global war-making capacity against which there is no realistic defense. Security for the powerful is no longer divisible, and it rests on the ability to avoid war rather than the ability to defend against attack. The nonsuperpowers are also implicated in this imperative, since they would suffer equally from the destruction of civilization and possibly permanent damage to the planet's ability to support life.

It is relatively easy to make the argument for common security in the nuclear sphere, though it is by no means universally acknowledged. But conventional war, too, has lost much of its effectiveness and its legitimacy as a method of pursuing national interests. The spoils of war are no longer seen as the just deserts of the victor. For example, the Israeli annexation of the West Bank and Gaza Strip after its victory in 1967 (in a war it did not start) is not recognized as legitimate even after more than twenty years. Libya has twice won the Aouzou strip from Chad but is still not its acknowledged master. Vietnam's conquest of Cambodia was a subject of major controversy even though much of the world was relieved to see the Khmer Rouge dislodged from power.

The reluctance of the international community to accept a military victory as the decisive outcome of a conflict has reduced the effectiveness of war as an instrument of policy. Developments in military technology have had the same effect. Highly sophisticated, powerful, portable weapons are easily available on the open market, making it extremely difficult to put an end to resistance by military means. It takes only a handful of people to do great damage to a nation's infrastructure and tranquility, and only a modest amount of money from an interested bystander to equip them. The agonizingly protracted conflicts in Angola, Mozambique, Afghanistan, the Philippines, Sri Lanka, Central America, and the Middle East all bear witness to this. Not only is it easy and cheap to keep a conflict going; it is also easy for a small but determined force to inflict disproportionate damage on conventional military forces, which tend to present large and concentrated targets that are vulnerable to even unsophisticated weapons such as a mine or a car bomb. During the Iran-Iraq War, the picture of the mightiest navies in the world drawn into the Persian Gulf and then thrown into disarray by small units of speedboats laying mines by hand and firing machine guns or shoulder-launched rockets was a sobering one for military strategists.

The declining utility of armed force as a method of attaining security impels us to look for alternative methods. An end to conflict among nations and peoples is no more than a dream. Competition and conflict are normal states of affairs among states, among corporations, or indeed among members of a family. What is needed is greater reliance on methods of resolving or at least managing conflicts that are less destructive of the interests of the parties involved and the interests of bystanders.

It is, in other words, time to reverse the classic formulation that "war is diplomacy by other means" and resuscitate the art of diplomacy. It might be more precise to say that we need to reinvent the art of diplomacy, for the issues, instrumentalities, and dynamics of foreign policy have changed so thoroughly that time-honored traditions of diplomacy may require major overhauls. Certainly, the attempt to counter threats to security through the application of sheer physical power has shown itself to be costly, frustrating, and frequently self-defeating.

Economic security is perhaps even more elusive than military security. The global economy today functions as a single unit. Small and middle-sized countries especially are subject to economic forces over which they can exert little or no control and that play themselves out in distant, anonymous financial centers. The collapse of commodity prices from the mid-1970s onward was in large part the result of recession in the industrialized countries. It was compounded by advances in synthetic materials and technology and, ironically, by overproduction—as Third World countries desperate for foreign exchange tried to export more and more in order to make up for falling prices.

International capital markets shift huge sums of money around the world on electronic impulse, affecting the exchange rates, creditworthiness, and interest payments of sovereign borrowers. The governments of the largest market economies, such as the Group of Seven or the Group of Ten, have been compelled to cooperate in order to moderate the violent fluctuations in some capital and currency markets. But their policy coordination remains fairly superficial. They have not yet come to terms with the need for deep intrusion into domestic economic prerogatives. Nor have other actors, such as banks, corporations, and members of stock exchanges, accepted the need for self-regulation in the interest of the stability and prosperity of the system as a whole. Until they do so, they invite the intervention of the state, however limited and imperfect its power to control may be.

The domestic impact of global economic forces may contribute to the erosion of the perceived legitimacy of the state. The state is expected to defend and advance the material well-being of its citizens. When it is seen to fail in this task, the state comes under criticism or even attack from the growing masses of people who are progressively alienated from a state that is unable —or unwilling—to provide them with opportunities to sustain or better their economic condition. In some countries, a pattern of instability has been established as successive governments, equally powerless to control the economy, fall. Opposition may well turn to violence, or provoke it, as a particular regime clings to power in the face of economic failure.

Our common vulnerability is perhaps most graphically illustrated on a daily basis in our physical surroundings—the global environment. We are learning, as the science of ecology develops, to regard our planet as an organism and to understand how delicately balanced some of its resource systems are. We know that the origin of acid rain, which has reduced lakes in Northern Europe and the northern United States to crystal-clear deserts, lies in the burning of fossil fuels. We are fairly certain that the use of fluorocarbons threatens the ozone layer. We have good reason to suspect that the buildup of carbon dioxide from combustion of organic and fossil fuels may warm the atmosphere enough to melt the polar icecaps sufficiently to flood many heavily populated, low-lying areas. We understand much less about the general dynamics of the global climate and the way it may be affected by, for example, deforestation and desertification—but we know enough to realize that we may be approaching certain points of irreversibility.

The fate of the global environment and the disposition of resources lie not only in the hands of governments, international organizations, and corporations but also in the hands of hundreds of millions of people who face constraints in their daily lives that more fortunate people probably find difficult even to imagine. These are the poor peasants whose land-use decisions, made under the most cruelly limiting circumstances, will determine the future of forests and watersheds and thereby the productive potential of entire regions. These hundreds of millions are decisionmakers as surely as are the timber barons or cattle ranchers, though the latter are both more destructive and less constrained in the choices they make.

Long-Term and Nonterritorial Issues

The kinds of problems encountered in the spheres of security, the economy, and the environment illustrate the problems of international governance, that is, the governance of complex systems characterized by lack of control, lack of accountability, and great uncertainty about outcomes. Near the end of his life, Aurelio Peccei, the founder of the Club of Rome, lamented "the absolute ungovernability of society as presently organized. . . . Despite the system-like nature of humankind's global body, no political philosophy or institutions have been evolved to ensure its governance."

The problems of international governance—seen as a systemic need as opposed to the simpler notion of governing relations between national governments—are especially difficult when it comes to dealing with long-term issues and nonterritorial issues. There is no constituency for the future, particularly the more distant future beyond the lives of our own children or grandchildren. Today, we build nothing that is the equivalent of the medieval cathedrals, built to last for a thousand years and more. Short-run considerations—generally as short as a term of office—dominate national political considerations. And domestic political cycles are generally out of phase with global needs such as a consistent approach to multilateral negotiations, a decades-long plan for environmental recovery, or a gradual phasing out of nuclear weapons.

If constituencies for long-term issues are weak, so are constituencies for concerns beyond national borders. This is true despite the realities of interdependence, which have blurred the demarcation between domestic and foreign policy issues. One increasingly important example (out of many) of the interpenetration of domestic and international problems is that posed by the growing scale of population movements between countries. These are the result of continued and ever-worsening disparities in living standards and economic growth rates, deterioration of the environment, the quest for heightened physical security, and gross disparities in rates of population growth.

Mass movements of people confront many of the affluent industrialized countries with three options. One is to revive the flagging international development effort. The second is to allow the free movement of people across national boundaries, as is already the case, in large measure, with the free movement of capital. The third option is to accept the inevitability of multiethnic societies and to develop calibrated policies relating the scale of intake to improved absorption and integration policies that would help reduce the likelihood of racial or ethnic conflicts. The urgency of choice is obvious. Equally obvious, however, are the absence of political will, the weakness of national and international constituencies, and the lack of an agreed analysis that could form the basis for a collective approach.

The problems of policy making on a global scale for long-term and nonterritorial issues are not just political. There is genuine scientific uncertainty about the consequences of decisions made and implemented today and disagreement about the implications of that uncertainty. To take one example, many people believe that the probability of serious accidents at nuclear power plants is great and that it outweighs any possible advantage, given the availability of safer alternatives. Others believe that the probability is low enough to justify the benefits and doubt the viability of the alternatives on either technical or economic grounds.

In addition, many of the issues that have to be addressed lie at the intersection of traditional disciplines and fields of study: security and development; environment and human settlement; hunger and poverty; climate and human modification of the environment; interdependence and autonomy; science, technology, economic growth, employment, and culture. As these interfaces are approached, it becomes obvious that the basic conceptual tools for dealing with them are often inadequate.

The work that needs to be done will have to go beyond sectoral approaches, area studies, and even interdisciplinary means to find new modes of analysis for dealing with complex realities. This holds true for scholars as well as policymakers if we are to develop an understanding—and act upon it—of the complexities of simultaneous social, economic, political, technological, and cultural changes in each of our countries and their reflection in the international system. The turbulence in the international system cannot be separated from these profound and rapid changes at the national level.

Conclusions

What lessons can be drawn from this necessarily cursory sketch? For the governance of interdependence there is an obvious need for institutions at national and international levels that are capable of mediating among dissonant needs and values. For example, long-term imperatives often conflict with those resulting from the shorter-run cycles of domestic politics. Interests as they are perceived in the present need to be reconciled with the unexpressed interests of future generations—or even adjudicated. National interests and those of the human community as a whole also present many dilemmas.

A further lesson is that a crowded, diverse, competitive, and interdependent world community, itself undergoing rapid change, cannot afford to depend on a single system for global governance. It will have to rely on a plethora of intergovernmental as well as nongovernmental institutions and regimes as well as formal and not so formal arrangements. The growing awareness of this need is reflected in the rapid increase in the number of both intergovernmental and nongovernmental organizations within and outside the UN family.

At the domestic level, it is not primarily the national government that determines the resilience of a society but rather the vigor of its civic and religious institutions. Similarly, at the international level, dynamism of the transnational nongovernmental organizations determines the strength and cohesion of the world community and its commitment to the values of human solidarity and human rights.

In addition, the fact that many processes of change and many actors lie outside the control of governments inevitably puts limits on the effectiveness of intergovernmental organizations. The creation of nongovernmental organizations that are capable of policing themselves is therefore indispensable for effective multilateral action in those areas where governments have only limited influence. This includes professional organizations and institutions, commercial and financial associations, civic groups, and independent study groups or commissions. New institutional approaches to the need for increased participation, representation, coordination, and accountability are also needed.

Many of the developments described above are already in motion, but they are not moving at the pace or with the determination required by the urgency of pressing global problems. Transnational institutions that can hold governments in some way accountable for their actions or failures to act on global and regional issues are in their infancy. The European Parliament may well prove to be a useful prototype of regional and perhaps eventually functional parliaments. Such institutions may develop the ability to pass judgment on humanitarian and other kinds of issues and on the intergovernmental and nongovernmental policies designed to deal with them.

From these speculative assertions it should be quite clear that there are no ready-made formulas to meet the new needs for governance of the unstable, complex systems that together constitute what we loosely call the global community. It is obvious that the human community is at the beginning of a new era of collective learning, in which innovation and inventiveness are at a premium—not only in terms of policies and institutions but also in terms of basic forms of organization.

It may transpire that the most responsive and effective organizations in a rapidly changing global information society will not be hierarchical in structure but decentralized and "co-archical." They may be composed of networks with some strong nodal points. A dense multidirectional flow of information within the organization will allow for effective participation, dispersed autonomy, and effective coordination. Such organizations would be equally sensitive to signals coming from their changing environment. Social learning, creativity, initiative, and self-organization might well be the important properties in such a setting.

Much will depend on individual and social inventiveness as well as on what might be called the learning capacity of societies, of their component elements, and of the international community. The learning experience we are just beginning to embark upon will not be limited to the development of new organizational forms and concepts. It will also include an extension of social and moral sensibility—a willingness to assume responsibility for problems that go beyond our conventional definition of the national interest toward an extended concept of the public good.

To try to do this at a time when the complexity and intractability of so many global problems have led to reductionism, unilateralism, intolerance, and privatism will continue to be the major challenge of our time. It may well be the test by which history will measure us all.

Values in Transition[2]

A particularly urgent preoccupation of recent recession-bound decades is the effect of slow and uneven economic growth on attitudes toward political and economic systems and toward the values that animate international affairs. Slow and uneven growth has three major kinds of effects on people's attitudes toward political and economic systems. First, it throws the spotlight of public attention on distributive issues. These are among the most passionately contentious issues in any polity, resting as they do on fundamental moral relations and obligations among members of the community. Such issues are often submerged when a rising economic tide is raising all boats. But when growth slows or halts, the despair, frustrations, and rage of the have-nots clash with the fear, reluctance, or intransigence of the haves and may tear a society apart.

A second effect of slow growth is to accelerate the process of questioning material affluence as a value in its own right. When an economy is racing ahead, it is considered unfashionable or even unpatriotic to ask where is this leading us? or what other values are being sacrificed to the pursuit of affluence? When the process of economic expansion shows itself to be flawed and limited, it is easier to pose the above questions in retrospect and to express the moral revulsion that many people feel at the greed, corruption, and shortsightedness that often accompany a boom.

A third effect of slow and uneven growth is the erosion of the perceived legitimacy of the state, which is expected to defend and advance the material well-being of the people. When it is seen to fail in this task, the state comes under criticism or even attack from minimalists, theocrats, ideologues, and others—as well as from the growing masses of people who are progressively alienated from a system that is unable or unwilling to provide them opportunities to sustain or better their condition. It is this shift in values that most affects international relations.

It is perhaps not quite accurate to speak of a "value transition" in contemporary society. Transition implies movement in one direction from a given state toward another. But today, multiple changes in values are occurring simultaneously in disparate and sometimes contradictory directions. The result is not necessarily an array of new values but a different configuration of values that have long been held.

Social transformation is a complex, messy, uneven, and diverse process in which the interplay of local, national, and international forces obscures any unitary sense of direction. The perspective of the international statesman, or even the national policymaker, typically takes in only a fraction of what is really going on in this process. It is particularly easy for policymakers to overlook the nonmaterial facets of people's aspirations and discontents. Yet in a great many cases, governments have been rocked or even toppled by the passion for intangible but fundamental human values—a sense of cultural identity, demand for participation, a respect for religion, an insistence on human rights and justice.

A new kind of political spectrum can be discerned. At one end are the superpowers, with their tremendous nuclear and conventional arsenals, along with many middle and smaller powers in which power is increasingly concentrated in the central government. At the other end of the spectrum, in weaker states, we find a dissipation and leakage of real power despite formal centralization. This process is often accompanied by the fragmentation of the polity, the decline of political cohesion, and the emergence of grassroots groups and movements that are alienated from the political system. Many of them lack clear leadership or clearly defined purposes beyond the narrow and immediate goals that have brought them into being, and thus are beyond the reach of the usual forms of political manipulation.

People's movements, organized or unorganized, positive or negative, are significant forces in both the North and the South. Some display a grand generosity of spirit, such as the "Band Aid" fund-raising concerts for Africa in the mid-1980s and their many spin-offs that have raised money for people in distress—refugees, financially embattled farmers, the homeless, and so forth. In stark contrast to these are the quasi-fascist movements that have revived racism, xenophobia, and anti-immigrant sentiments in the industrialized countries.

People's movements have been in the forefront of efforts in Argentina and the Philippines to hold government officials accountable for abuses of human rights and for corruption and mismanagement. But they have also been in the forefront of mass violence against rival ethnic groups in India and Sri Lanka. The women's movement, the environmental protection movement, many human rights campaigns, and the most important peace movements have sprung from the grassroots. They have both led and responded to changes in values.

Popular movements engage themselves not only with concrete issues but also with questions of morality in public life

—questions that governments have found very difficult even to raise, much less resolve. Many governments find popular movements difficult to deal with precisely because they present a fundamental challenge to the received wisdom of so-called experts and insist on the primacy of intangible values.

The tendency to define problems and seek solutions to them in exclusively materialistic terms appears increasingly anachronistic. We are beginning to see now a reassertion of moral and spiritual values. The Catholic bishops in the United States brought that dimension to their statements on the national economy and on nuclear weapons in the mid-1980s. The Archbishop of Canterbury has been similarly vocal on behalf of the Church of England. The insistence of the Islamic clergy in a number of countries that Islamic values be explicitly woven into public policy and the social fabric is a political factor of major importance in those countries and in international relations.

The impression grows that we are at the end of a long period of secularization. People are beginning to assert that it is impossible for them to realize their full humanity in a totally secularized world where no value is assigned to immeasurable qualities such as rectitude, sharing, mutual obligation, inner peace, harmony with nature, and so forth. The resurgence of fundamentalism is only one manifestation of this process, and it is not in all cases a reactionary impulse. The morality of social and political structures is now being challenged from many other quarters as well.

The progression toward individualism also seems to be reaching a point of diminishing returns. The process of individualization, so successful in releasing enormous creative power, at some point begins to erode the bonds between people. It weakens the nation, the community, and even the family. It has also, at the national level, eroded the commitment to multilateral cooperation in dealing with pressing global issues. Instead we see increasing evidence of regional and global unilateralism.

It is often simply impossible to know which movements, trends, or practices may prove to be significant in the long term. Spontaneous currents arise unexpectedly to alter the course of history—the Gandhian movement in India is one example. Recent decades have been characterized by profound shifts in the values held by significant groups of people. These shifts, which are both a result and a source of social change, occur simultaneously in disparate and sometimes conflicting directions. Some look back to a revival of traditional values; others look to other cultural traditions or attempt to define an entirely new configuration of values.

Whether it is the result of improved communications, heightened expectations, or simply too many years of disappointed hopes, the impoverished masses no longer seem willing to accept deprivation and exploitation passively. Such widespread dissatisfaction with the state or the government is easily manipulated by those—either within or outside the state structure—who proffer simplistic solutions or diversions such as military adventurism, scapegoating, or public disturbances. Disaffection that takes the forms of political opposition often provokes defensive reaction on the part of the state apparatus. It may respond to protest with censorship, repression, and even murder, thus accelerating a downward spiral of alienation.

However, the alienation resulting from economic stagnation may have positive effects in some situations. It may persuade people to throw their support behind an opposition that offers a positive alternative, even if it is an unpalatable one in the short run. It may, in particular, persuade the professional and middle classes, who often have a bias for the status quo, that their interests lie with change, in common cause with the poorer sections of society. Redemocratization in Southern Europe, Latin America, and the Philippines was clearly given impetus by the economic failures of authoritarian regimes. Whether the political reformers will be able to better the economic record of their predecessors remains, in several cases, to be seen. Even the highest standards of economic management will not protect newly democratized countries—or any others—from the depredations of low export prices for commodities, high interest rates, the drying up of commercial lending, protectionism in the major importing countries, and speculative transfers of potential investment funds.

What conclusions can be drawn from the foregoing analysis? The cohesiveness of a society does not depend exclusively, or even primarily, on its laws. Cohesion depends much more on the existence of a general social consensus that the institutions of society are reasonably fair, just, and accessible. Without this basic consensus, the rule of law becomes entirely dependent on enforcement, with the police and the army functioning as an occupying force within their own countries. The consent of the governed is not just a morally desirable quality but a practical necessity.

A society that has achieved a workable consensus is not necessarily a society without conflict. It is questionable whether such a society exists anywhere—it certainly does not exist in the developing countries that are caught up in the tumultuous processes of economic development and nation building. The crucial question is how to reduce the human cost of the necessary and in many cases desirable convulsions associated with social change.

How can the need for change be reconciled with the need for order and the need for justice? The dynamic equilibrium among these three—change, order, justice—defines the scope for freedom and for the realization of both collective and individual aspirations.

A lack of social resilience in any of the three dimensions creates the conditions for violence. Change without resilience leads to alienation and loss of identity. A system of justice without resilience turns predictable human failures into catalysts for polarization. Order without resilience leads to oppression and a corresponding resistance.

There is no doubt that steady, evenly distributed economic growth is conducive to the development of social resilience. Rapid growth creates strains that many societies have had trouble adjusting to, even when the benefits of growth are fairly well distributed. Uneven growth is probably more damaging to resilience than slow growth. There are limits to the level of disparity that any polity can tolerate without coming apart at the seams. Finally, extremely rapid growth with increasingly unequal distribution is the combination most likely to undermine traditional values and impede the construction of a new social consensus on the basis of which the forward movement of a whole society can proceed.

The greatest obstacle to the achievement of social resilience based on an inclusive sense of shared values is the widening gulf between the rich and the poor. The satellite dish, the video recorder, and the color television allow the rich to envelop themselves in a cocoon of privilege, which insulates them from the harsh realities of the struggle for survival in which most of their fellow citizens are involved.

For the nonaffluent in poor countries, the images of privilege conveyed in the mass media have raised material expectations far beyond the developing economies' capacity to deliver within any remotely equitable framework. These dreams of affluence can come true in the short run for only a tiny minority, and for them only at the expense of equity. Perhaps the most pernicious effect such dreams have is on the nature of individual values and aspirations. Nurtured on the images of privilege, the ambitions of many poor youths turn to escape from, rather than commitment to, their own villages or neighborhoods. Frustration at the inability of the national economy to deliver general prosperity, along with heightened awareness of inequality within the nation, fuels the anger that is behind so much of the turmoil in the developing world. A failure to deal with these root causes of conflict is a major threat—perhaps *the* major threat—to the realization of commonly held values.

Lessons for the Twenty-first Century[3]

What message do we, the survivors of the twentieth century, wish to pass on to our children and our children's children who will inhabit and must manage this globe in the next century? Specifically, what lessons have we learned about freedom and oppression that might help human freedom survive and flourish? The inevitably competing requirements of change, stability, and justice will mark humanity's passage into the twenty-first century.

In the search for such lessons, history offers us some useful parallels. Nineteenth-century Europe, in post-Napoleonic times, witnessed a widespread surge for freedom that culminated in the emergence of a number of nation-states. Later in the nineteenth century and into the early twentieth, the struggle for equality in these new nation-states began—and a central dilemma of our time emerged: How is it possible to balance the demands for equity and freedom? The liberal welfare state evolved as one of a number of responses to that quest. Today the welfare state is in the throes of crisis, and we are forced to redefine an even more complex balance between freedom, equity, economic growth, and technological advance.

In the twentieth century, the years after World War II witnessed another great surge toward freedom, but on a worldwide scale. Nation after nation gained independence from colonial bonds. As the century comes to a close, we are engaged in a new struggle for equality, now on a global scale, within and among nations. The struggle is unresolved—indeed, our failure to overcome the profound structural dualism in the world is one of this generation's most tragic legacies to the twenty-first century. It must somehow be solved or the precious freedom gained through independence will be lost. Within this general context, we must seek lessons to pass on to succeeding generations.

The earlier struggles for equality in Europe and North America were bound up in the great ideologies. Here again, history can be instructive, for it demonstrates that in the twentieth century these ideologies have run their course. One important lesson of this century is that freedom is not the product of any one specific ideological construct. We have also found that no ideology can sustain itself as a motive force for more than one or two generations. Ideology has many functions, one of which is to provide the drive toward specific perceptions of a more desirable society. But the grandsons and granddaughters of any revolution simply see things differently. As a result, they act differently. The complexity of real life turns out to be too weighty for any ideological scaffolding to uphold. Moreover, the rapidity and scale of change in this era lead to profound and qualitative generational jumps.

The lesson in this is the need for a considerable humility of mind in the face of these enormous complexities of life. We must learn to leave room for the unexpected. We began this century confident of our capacity to uncover the certainties of the laws of nature and society. We are ending it in growing recognition that, beyond a few limited truisms, there are no certainties. Complexity, vulnerability, and unpredictability are inevitable companions of modern life.

New ideologies will undoubtedly continue to emerge as part of the yearning for a sense of direction and the search for understanding of the unfathomable. But we must recognize the limitations of ideologies. Life is vastly more intricate and richer in its complexity, both more terrible and more beautiful, than any preconstructed scenario.

The lesson for each human being from this age of uncertainty is that it is profoundly important to retain a sense of self. Inner life is the human being's ultimate sanctuary where each can find a true self and center. It can be the final refuge from adversity

and oppression and from the pressures of an increasingly populated world buffeted by change.

Inner freedom, we have learned, can survive even in the
midst of oppression—as we have seen in the case of political prisoners or others who have decided not to relate to their political
environments except when it is absolutely necessary to sustain
their right to life. To be sure, the inner life can also be an escape
from social responsibility. But at its most sublime, we have witnessed the power of the concept of inner exile—a notion that
lies at the heart of the civil disobedience that inspired Gandhi
and others and changed so many lives in this century as part of
the struggle for freedom.

Our world today, particularly in consumer-oriented societies,
is one in which many forces and distractions work to dissipate
the strength of our inner selves. We are caught up in an unending stream of trivial entertainment packaged by sophisticated
and cynical experts. Through the power of the media, vicarious
and real-life experiences are reduced to images. The overall
impact is disassociation, noninvolvement, a numbing of the senses
and of judgment.

Similarly, the political process is distorted and alienated from
the people by the impact of packaged political messages and syn-
thesized political personalities. If we want to reduce the chances
of greater oppression in the twenty-first century, society must
learn to develop unadulterated and less manipulative channels
for political information, participation, and action.

Ours is an age in which ever-larger organizations—whether
bureaucracies, political parties, trade unions, or corporations—
have tended to dehumanize actions and concerns. Participatory
social and political organizations have been correspondingly
eroded. What is needed are organizations more commensurate
with the human scale. That is the scale at which people can be
fully engaged as human beings in public affairs and can relate to
problems with understanding, empathy, and compassion. The
implications for political organizations, political processes, and
the role of the media are considerable. More meaningful mechanisms are required, capable of mediating between large-scale
problems and the human scale of daily life. This is essentially a
problem of governance. It tests our capacity to make crucial
decisions and choices that will determine the shape of human
society in the twenty-first century.

The problems that we will face in the future—such as increased population pressure, long-term structural unemployment, and, above all, continuing and expanding poverty—will challenge our ability to put science and technology to better use. In principle, science and technology have made possible the elimination of poverty; the fact that so many more people are better fed and housed and in better health than in the past demonstrates this potential. Yet poverty persists. It lies at the root of so many of the world's problems, and it is increasing. Poverty is the prime generator of today's huge migrations, which are bound to change the ethnic and cultural geography of the globe as hundreds of millions of people leave their villages and homelands in search of jobs, food, freedom, and security.

An important and sobering lesson from this century is that technology can be used just as easily to enslave as to liberate humankind. The seeds for more democratic and compassionate use of science and technology are there. But the danger is that these powerful tools will be employed to enlarge the political control by the few rather than to increase participation by the many.

Advances in science and technology raise yet another caution for future generations: How do we avoid the rule of experts? The logic of experts brought us the arms race. Scientific logic and military expertise were used to increase and accelerate the development of more and more destructive weapons. Only an act of political will can provide a counterweight to the closed, internally consistent, and partial worldviews of experts.

Reliance on military force as the way to solve our problems has led to the militarization of whole societies—despite the overwhelming evidence that military solutions generally prove to be limited if not counterproductive. We must devise better ways of settling conflict more peacefully in this crowded and competitive world.

While military oppression is open in its resort to naked violence, another form of subjugation is structural in nature and invisible—the oppression of women; of minority groups; of various castes, sects, and tribes passed over by history. Particularly troubling in today's pluralistic world is the tyranny that the majority can impose on those who are different and weak. It is well to emphasize that freedom and oppression are not necessarily polar opposites, unable to exist in each other's presence. One person's pursuit of happiness may easily trample upon another person's life and liberty.

In far too many places in the Third World, it is the majority who are the oppressed and the marginalized: the vast numbers of the rural and urban poor whose needs and aspirations are ignored by the urban elites bent on the pursuit of affluent life-styles. Increasingly, the poor are displaying a new assertiveness and demanding to be heard. They are no longer willing to accept a daily life of squalor, misery, and injustice. Ways will have to be found to integrate them fully into the national life of their societies, before violence and oppression become inevitable. This will be one of the great challenges confronting the twenty-first century.

The road to freedom has been a long and difficult one marked by war and revolution. Freedom has come within reach of many segments of society only within this century. The process is still unfinished, especially in the Third World. The more than 130 wars that have been fought in the developing countries since the end of the World War II need to be seen as an expression of the tremendous and profound social change occurring there. They demonstrate just how fragile social structures are in the face of change.

We live in an economy that has become a single world economy. The interdependence of the globe's politics and security means that any small war can turn into a major conflict. How are we to make sense of this swift process of chaotic global transformation? How can we emerge in freedom and justice? These are the central problems of our age.

With many countries still experiencing high birth rates, population pressures will intensify well into the twenty-first century. Before these pressures become too great, thereby complicating all other problems, we will need to come to terms with the urgency of liberating and empowering the many still marginalized groups.

Faced with the record of the twentieth century thus far, and in light of the unprecedentedly rapid change we are now undergoing, many futurologists assume that some kind of worldwide authoritarian rule will be unavoidable if the human race is to survive. We need to keep two tough questions constantly in front of us: Is a democratic scenario of the future possible? What must we do to make it possible?

The matter takes on particular urgency in light of growing and intensified political assertiveness from outside the mainstream. The conventional structures and organizations of democracy may not be able to take into account the varied manifestations of the democratic impulse in the densely populated nations of the Third World. How does one manage freedom on a scale of one billion people? The search for democratic government, under different demographic configurations, may take forms and go through stages other than those with which we are now familiar. The search may take place in a different civilizational context, during the course of which we may hope to witness the emergence of reinvigorated, democratic, non-Western civilizations that will insist on taking their rightful place alongside Western societies. The lesson to be taken here is that the shape of freedom is always changing. It is never static or inflexible.

A further question concerns the relationship between freedom and the rule of law. The present international legal system has been called into question by the emergence of new actors who did not participate in forming the consensus on which that system was constructed. A new consensus is needed involving all the relevant actors that could form the basis for a new global system of international law.

One of the most important lessons of this century has been the recognition of the limits of this planet. We began the twentieth century with a sense of power and a certainty bordering on arrogance that the earth was ours to exploit and that human beings were the measure of all things. But the state of our resource base—even when balanced against human creativity and innovation—tells us that nature is not at the command of the human race. Rather the human race is part of nature and must respect it.

It is beginning to dawn on us that it is wrong to attempt to define our problems and their solutions only in material terms; that is a dead-end street. We must take into account the moral dimensions to human problems and face them squarely. This will demand from each individual a redefinition of his or her own humanity as a moral being. We are coming to recognize the importance of religion and spirituality. In this century, the long historical process of secularization seems to have come to an end. It is becoming increasingly clear that men and women cannot live in a totally secularized world; they need some meaning to life that reaches beyond themselves. This realization is part of the "return of the sacred" of which sociologist Daniel Bell has written.

The sense of the transcendental can express itself in many ways. One way is through art. The appreciation of beauty can be a pointer to other dimensions of life, leading us to those inner spaces where the human spirit can find solace, shelter, and strength.

We have seen in this century that when disparities between rich and poor within a country grow too great, democratic government becomes impossible. The search for equity is now worldwide and must confront the fact of structural dualism rooted in the international system itself. This is the biggest unresolved problem that the twenty-first century faces: How can humankind organize and manage an interdependent, fragile, and competitive world in which there are such enormous gaps between rich and poor? How can we overcome the danger that science and technology will simply continue to perpetuate and widen those gaps? How do we devise a democratic international system that respects pluralism and is not under the control of the powerful few?

Such a system will have to work to reduce disparities, not increase them. It will need to manage the global economy in a more rational fashion. It will, as a matter of urgency, have to give better care to the global commons—our seas and skies and those other parts of the planet where humankind has a common heritage.

Beyond its enormous practical tasks, such a system must allow freedom to flourish. Freedom is fragile. It has many predators and needs constant tending. Progress toward it is still all too easily reversible. We have seen how quickly newly independent countries, after gaining their freedom from external oppressors, have slipped into internal authoritarianism and repression. Freedom is based on the strength of institutions, but it is also rooted in the attitudes and hearts of people. Its maintenance will be based on the human capacity for reason, love, compassion, empathy, and respect for the freedom of others—even our adversaries. We must therefore develop a new consensus on an international morality on which, despite all our differences, new systems of international governance can be based.

As for the present international organizations, let us be candid: They have not been able to cope very well with the enormously complex problems of our modern world. What is called for is a second generation of international organizations—where national governments can be held accountable for their international acts of commission or omission by the peoples of this pluralistic global society.

Finally, it should be realized that this new international system that is so badly needed will have to be built not by us who have lived our lives in this century but by those who must manage the next: the young. These lessons, therefore, need to be addressed to them.

To be sure, youth today is in large part disaffected and disillusioned with grandiose schemes. Many of the young have not been socialized into the political process—and who can really blame them for their lack of interest when so many of them, in the North as well as the South, are without jobs or any real prospect of a better life? In the Third World alone, some one billion new jobs will be needed by the year 2000 to employ new entrants to the work force. In the jargon of the young, that figure is mind-blowing—and whose mind would not be blown apart at the prospect of a life without any regular work, emptied of all inspiration by daily misery and poverty, and without the certainty of living out a normal life span in a world poised on the brink of nuclear self-destruction?

Our children do not have a great deal to thank us for. Perhaps our best hope is that they will determine for themselves how to build a better world. Having failed to do it ourselves, we cannot presume to tell them how. But we owe them at least an honest assessment of our mistakes.

7

....

Religion and Progress

Soedjatmoko stands apart from many writers on social issues because of the high importance he gave to the spiritual dimensions of development and change. He was acutely aware that human longings could not be satisfied by economic advancement alone, and that material enrichment could easily be accompanied by spiritual impoverishment. The scholar and the mystic in him were not at odds; both held the search for truth as the highest value. He realized that religion could be reactionary and obstructive of human progress, but he also knew that it could provide the ethical steering mechanism for social endeavor and a sense of higher purpose. He returned to these themes repeatedly. The first piece presented here—a speech to a seminar on "The Future of Mankind and Cooperation among Religions," which was held in Tokyo in 1987 under the auspices of the United Nations University (UNU) and the World Conference on Religion and Peace—explores the relationship between religious intensity and tolerance in a pluralistic world. Within a month of this speech, Soedjatmoko spoke in Tokyo again about the relationship between religion and science to the symposium on Science, Technology, and Spiritual Values. That speech is this

The last part of this chapter originally appeared as "Religion in the Politics of Economic Development, Parts III–V," *The Stanford Journal of International Studies* 6 (Spring 1971). Reprinted with permission.

159

chapter's second part. The third selection is a 1984 paper for a UNU project, "Religious Perceptions of Desirable Societies," in which he specifically considered responses to contemporary social issues from within Islam. Finally, we return to an earlier paper on religion and the development process in Asia for a reminder of the importance of religion as both an earthly and a transcendental source of motivation. The paper from which this section is taken was written for the Asian Ecumenical Conference for Development in 1970.

Between Transcendence and History[1]

The French philosopher and statesman André Malraux predicted that the twenty-first century would be a religious century—or that humankind would not survive to witness the twenty-first century. Without necessarily sharing his apocalyptic vision, I would surely agree that few factors could be more important in shaping the future of humankind. Religion has been somewhat pushed aside in the first part of the twentieth century by the ascendancy of humanism, so-called rationalism, science, and the great secular ideologies of this era. But religion is rapidly recovering the place it held in centuries past, recognized as one of the great motive forces in human history.

In many parts of the world today, a heightening of religious intensity can be observed. This is in part a reaction to the exclusively materialistic orientation of the major competing ideologies of the twentieth century—a reaction to both the aspiration and the fruits of developmentalism. Our societies are afflicted by economic inequity and instability, ecological deterioration, the continuation of violent conflict, and the dread of nuclear annihilation. The fact that these ills, as well as a deep spiritual malaise, beset even the most affluent, industrially and technologically advanced societies demonstrates that material prosperity does not necessarily lead to a satisfactory state of being. Is it not the responsibility of religion to articulate humankind's longing for a sense of meaning and higher purpose, and to point out alternative pathways toward the satisfaction of this longing?

The separation of religion and government is one tenet of political democracy that has taken hold in many parts of the world—especially in multiethnic countries where adherents of different religions must coexist. Of course, there are also religiously based states, and especially in the Islamic world the idea of the religious state has passionate adherents. Some part of the resurgence of religious intensity in the political sphere springs from the perception that the separation of religion and government has led to a banishment of religiously based values from the operation of the state, often leading to a divorce between ethics and policy.

A most pressing question, therefore, is this: How, in a period of growing religious intensity, can religions heal the breach between ethics and policy without opening the door to the abuse of religion for political purposes? How can they do so without introducing dogmatism, zealotry, and intolerance into a social fabric already rent with conflict? How is it possible for religions to cooperate in the effort to achieve a more moral and satisfying society while each tries to deepen and pursue its own vision of the ultimate good?

In examining these questions, it is important first of all to recognize that a religion is many things. A religion is a path toward individual salvation, redemption, or enlightenment; a vehicle to carry the believer toward transcendent truth. Almost by definition, a religion is a kind of cosmology, a carrier of notions of order and rectitude. At the same time, it is a major element of the cultural identity of a people. In many societies, a religion is also a mighty establishment, closely tied to the other political, economic, and social institutions of society. A religion may be an agent of change and mobilization—or immobilization—among communities of people. At both the societal and the individual levels, religion is a source of moral and ethical values, a guide to doing what is right. Among these dimensions, it is important to identify those in which cooperation among religions is necessary, desirable, and possible.

Communication among religions is the most important step toward cooperation. The adherents of each religion may deepen their own reflection on the nature of transcendent truth by exposure to the beliefs of others. The realization that there are multiple ways of seeing and expressing truth is often the starting point of tolerance as well as humility. Much the same might be said of religions as major elements of cultural identity. Communication within a framework of mutual tolerance permits a flowering of spirituality such as is envisioned in the Qur'an, which says that the purpose of diversity is to stimulate people to "compete in goodness."

It is religion in its more worldly aspects—as an establishment, a source of values, and a mobilizing force—that has repeatedly led men and women to violent conflict throughout history and continues to do so today. Cooperation among religions in these spheres may indeed be a prerequisite to the survival of humankind. We might add to this cooperation within religions as well, for the multiple roles and manifestations of a single religion are often in conflict with one another: the established church and the liberation theologian, for example; the Sunni and the Shia; the mystic who longs for transcendence and the social worker who is determined to correct injustice in this life.

As claimants to ultimate truth, religions have a dominant concern that in part stands outside of history; our perceptions and understanding may change with time, but truth is eternal. God is unchanging, by whatever name or names God may be called. However, although truth is eternal, religion is also historical, embedded in the turmoils and imperfections of human events. Religion does not simply coexist with history. It challenges and shapes history. It often tries to bend history to its own precepts. It fires passions, and sometimes guns, in pursuit of secular power as well as power over the souls of men and women. This relationship between the ahistorical and historical roles of religion, between the transcendent and the mundane in human life, is of great concern.

Rapid change, which is perhaps the central feature of our times, aggravates the tension between the transcendental and the societal concerns of religion. Rapid change leads to a sharp increase in the number of challenges to standards of moral behavior and conduct that have, over time, grown up around established religion in particular historical settings. The identification of religion with the standards of a particular time may strengthen the inclination to see the problems associated with social change as simple moral problems—or even to see change itself as immoral. The danger of conflict, violence, and reaction rises when a religion loses its ability to respond creatively to change and to express its unchanging transcendent truth in an idiom that is meaningful in the contemporary setting. Religious believers are compelled to ponder the meaning of the changes they experience and their own conduct in new situations from the perspectives of their faith. A religion fails its believers when it speaks to them in terms that are relevant only to the past. Worse, it may leave them mired in bewilderment. The resulting frustration and despair may lead them to reactionary traditionalism, to violence, or it may alienate them from their religion altogether. In other words, the difficulties of coping with rapid social change may result in a religion's losing influence and becoming irrelevant, or to serious social rigidities that compound the already complex process of social transformation. Religion, however, contains within itself the authority to reinterpret and reorder values and goals, to rearrange norms and convey structures of meaning that people need in order to make sense of their lives. If a religion develops through its leaders an adequate comprehension of the processes of change, it can then play an important role in providing a meaningful sense of direction, while maintaining the cohesion of society.

It is obvious that no religion can maintain its vigor if it avoids coming to grips with change and its attendant problems in the social, economic, political, and technological spheres. There is a growing awareness that poverty and injustice cannot be overcome by charity alone. Increased understanding of the nature and origin of poverty and the structures that perpetuate injustice brings religion face-to-face with the perplexities of power and the complexities of transforming unjust institutions—one of which, in a particular setting, may be an established church or clerical institution.

Social movements designed to reform or transform economic and political structures, no matter how morally pristine their motivations, are historically defined. They bear the imprint of their leaders' personalities, of their specific geographical and social settings. They have their own inner contradictions and their own cycles of inspiration, complacency, and decay. No social movement is permanent. Therefore, a religion cannot and should not be fully identified with a social movement. Nevertheless, religions are called upon to be a part of—indeed to instigate—morally justifiable change. They must recognize and reinforce the moral impulses that drive change and stand against the immoral. But how can they be so deeply involved in social change without setting up particular social or political movements as new—and false—religions?

It is the responsibility of religious leaders to speak out clearly on ethical issues that have a high political content. However, it is wrong for a religious institution to anoint any political party, group, or individual as the sole bearer of the right answers to political questions. It is the proper role of religions to articulate moral positions. Beyond this, however, religions must mediate among the often conflicting demands of public order and social change by relating these to an ethical framework that transcends the particular issues and passions of the day. In so doing, some religions will have to abandon their traditional role as legitimizers of established authority and instead become the moral counselors of a difficult and tempestuous process of change.

The attempt to reunite ethics and policy from a renewed awareness of the religious significance of history is noble and necessary, but it is also fraught with the dangers of dogmatism, intolerance, and absolutism. The exercise of religious conviction in the temporal sphere can—and has—led to the most merciless fanaticism. In order to avoid these dangers, the process of moral reasoning must be clearly articulated, and a profound appreciation of the boundaries between religious judgment and political judgment must be cultivated. Very often, political judgment simply means taking moral judgment one step farther—but the possible directions for that one step are almost infinite. It is essential for the person who is trying to think and act morally to realize that there are many different, valid ways of translating a particular moral judgment into a political act. Zealotry and bigotry begin when only one way is accorded moral legitimacy. Religious leaders have a major responsibility to see that the energy and inspiration of believers does not flow into these dark and narrow channels.

Consider one broad example. Many, if not most, religious people would agree to take a moral stance against poverty. Some of us may believe with utter conviction that the capitalist system generates poverty. To such people, to oppose poverty means to oppose capitalism. To oppose poverty is a moral judgment. To oppose capitalism is a political judgment proceeding from the moral judgment. Another person may proceed from the same moral judgment to the opposite political conclusion. Two such people may oppose each other on political grounds. But they would be wrong to label each other immoral, thereby damaging the possibilities for dialogue and cooperation.

The possibility of cooperation among religions depends on an ability to agree on basic moral principles and on a willingness to respect each believer's way of trying to translate moral judgment into social reality. The ideal is to agree to work against poverty and injustice, for peace, for responsible stewardship of the earth, each through his or her chosen channels, together if possible—but if not, separately.

Beyond any commitment to specific changes, no religion can escape the obligation to try to reduce as much as possible the human cost of change. This implies an abhorrence of violence and an insistence on tolerance, civility, due process, democratic procedures, the rule of law, and human rights.

The problems of society—of social, political, economic, and technological change—are not problems of ultimate truth. The approach to them may and should proceed from moral conviction but they should not be approached dogmatically. What our religious beliefs should equip us with is a heightened capacity for moral reasoning—that is, an ability to put religious perceptions to the test of evolving situations and to derive new modes of action to replace those that have lost their meaning and effectiveness. Here lies the constant challenge for religion with its passionate absolutisms in an age of social transformation. It must provide a structure of meaning that reaches beyond politics and yet relates to present reality; it must link human ethical responsibilities and moral purposes to an active role in the making of history; and it must teach the humility of mind and spirit that is so much needed in a period of rapid and unpredictable change.

A cooperative effort among religions has the power to reawaken a dormant vision of the essential oneness of the human race. The moral common ground among religions is broad enough to permit a cooperative challenge to the enormous problems that threaten to overwhelm humankind and indeed all of God's creation on this planet. The spiritual common ground among religions is probably far greater still, had we but the power and the inspiration to perceive it.

On Different Ways of Knowing:
Science, Technology, and Spiritual Values[2]

The juxtaposition of the terms *science, technology,* and *spiritual values* is deliberately provocative. It appears to accept an implicit contradiction—even an opposition—between science and technology on the one hand and spiritual values on the other. What follows will argue that this implication is dangerous and should be rejected out of hand.

First, what is meant by the term *spiritual values?* Do we mean by this religious values, moral values, ethics? None of these three is precisely synonymous with spiritual values, though they overlap considerably. Religion, for example, is the major source of spiritual values for most people—but even irreligious people may hold spiritual values. Unsatisfactory as the resort to negative definitions may be, the simplest definition of spiritual values is nonmaterial values; values that are held without reference to worldly or bodily objectives.

The highest spiritual value in this writer's view is truth. A vision of the truth is central to all religions that I know of; indeed, it is religions' claim to an understanding of the ultimate nature of truth that gives them their legitimacy.

Seen in this light, is science value-free? Quite the contrary. The ultimate scientific value is also truth, though the aspirations of science are more limited than that of religion. Science seeks the truth about the physical universe. At its best, science has the humility to leave the question of the meaning of the universe to other realms—religions, for example. At its worst, science has the arrogance to deny that there is meaning to the universe or that truth is more than the constructs of verifiable facts.

Hans Morgenthau wrote that "the constituent principle of science is the search for and profession of truth." He went on, however, to inveigh against the corruption in the scientific community of this central value and guiding principle of science. The crisis of meaning that he saw in science stemmed from the perversion of science's commitment to the truth. Science at the service of government—and he might have added of commerce as well—is often used to obscure the distinction between truth and falsehood. It is virtually always used in the pursuit of material as opposed to spiritual values—whether for domination, as in weapons research; physical health, as in medical research; or commercial profit, as in product research. Some governments, however, do support "pure" scientific research for which there is no immediate application.

The modern scientific enterprise is almost wholly dependent on government and industry. The budgets and priorities for scientific research are set by those who control the purse strings.

The great predominance of military research and development is one result. It is roughly estimated that military pursuits engage between one-quarter and one-third of all scientists and technologists in the world. But even when scientific research is not directed toward improving the instruments of destruction, it is often guided by principles of maximizing economic profit rather than maximizing human dignity and the quality of life. The creative impulse may belong to the individual scientist, who may indeed hold truth as the highest value. But the infrastructure and the financial support that make the scientist's work possible are social constructs, reflecting the values of the decisionmaking collective.

Technology is the opposite of spiritual values but is not necessarily in opposition to them. This apparent paradox can be explained as follows. The purpose of technology is to achieve material results. Technology is irrevocably nonspiritual. However, the material objective that is sought through the application of technology may be wholly consistent with spiritual values. Indeed, it may proceed directly from them. Love for our fellow creatures is a spiritual value, and we seek to invent new devices, new methods, and new applications of knowledge that will relieve their suffering from hunger, disease, or violation. Technological objectives may also be in stark opposition to spiritual values, as we have so often seen in the technology of war and exploitation.

The argument presented here is an argument against technological determinism and also an argument against a kind of dualism that sees the material values of technology as necessarily opposed to spiritual values. This may seem so obvious that it does not need stating. Yet we see in many groups of people a rejection of technology in reaction to the very real damage that our technological tools have allowed us to do to one another and to our environment, in violation of spiritual values. During the violent convulsions in Cambodia not too long ago, even wearing glasses was sufficient reason to be regarded as an associate of the modern technology of war that had laid waste to the country. All technology was rejected; cities were virtually abandoned, and agriculture returned to primitivism in a chosen policy under which millions suffered and died. This rejection of technology served values that were as opposed to the spiritual values of the Cambodian people as was the horrific application of technology in the preceding war. So let us be very careful before we reject or embrace technology as an abstraction. The consequences of technology are the consequences of human choices and actions; the machines do not—at least not yet—program and run themselves.

One of the mainstays of religion is some form of a doctrine of consequences. Most religions teach that, whether in this life, the next life, or the afterlife, human beings are responsible for their actions and must bear the consequences. Most religions also offer the possibilities of grace, enlightenment, redemption, or forgiveness—though even these are consequences of actions such as confession, penitence, faith, devotion, petition, or good deeds. To place the blame for all the ills of society on technology is in a peculiar sense to absolve human beings of responsibility for the consequences of actions that are always set in motion by human beings.

The American Protestant theologian Roger Lincoln Shinn wrote, "The big issues cannot be left to technologists who are ethically illiterate or to moralists who are technically ignorant." Yet it is likely that ethics and technical knowledge often reside in the same person but are rarely given scope for simultaneous exercise. The values of the scientist or technician may influence his or her work, but the operative values of society determine the scope for different kinds of scientific work, the degree of support they are given, the enthusiasm for their application, and the restrictions placed on their distribution. In other words, the values that science and technology are made to serve are very much a matter of social choice.

Although it is dangerous to generalize, a few tentative observations about the spiritual values of West and East suggest how they might affect the broad direction of the scientific enterprise and its technological expression. In a celebrated essay written in 1966, historian Lynn White, Jr., argued that the ecological destructiveness of modern science and technology could be traced to the relationship between man and nature posited in European Christianity. He wrote, "Especially in its Western form, Christianity is the most anthropocentric religion the world has seen. . . . By destroying pagan animism, Christianity made it possible to exploit nature in a mood of indifference to the feelings of natural objects." From a world in which animals, plants, and places were believed to be inhabited by divine spirits, Western Christianity molded one in which spirituality was appropriated and vested in God, who made man in his image and gave him dominion over the earth.

In Islam, the concept of the human person as God's vicere-
gent on earth denotes that people have an obligation to care for
nature even as they use it. This concept also gradually evolved in
Western Christianity. Stewardship is a somewhat anthropocentric
notion, though it is a step up from dominion. The religions of
Asia—particularly Buddhism, Hinduism, Shinto, and some of the
Sufi traditions within Islam—have a worldview in which the natural world is much more of a continuum, with humans a part of
nature rather than privileged beings standing outside of nature.
There is here at least the rootstock for a sense of obligation to
the rest of creation that could do much to moderate the more
brutally destructive interface of modern technology with nature.
The very idea of reincarnation expresses a sense of solidarity
with other creatures, just as the idea of an endless cycle of
rebirth expands the temporal horizon of the individual. Having
said this, however, it must also be admitted that these particular
spiritual values have not prevailed over short-term, materialistic
values to protect the integrity of the Asian environment.

Commitment to freedom of inquiry depends on an ethical—
almost a religious—judgment that knowledge is good and ignorance is bad if not evil. Islam enjoins people to seek knowledge
wherever they can find it. The history of Islam, however, has also
shown the constantly shifting tension between this injunction
and piety. There is also ambivalence about knowledge in Christianity. Adam fell from grace by eating the fruit of the tree of
knowledge. Knowledge and innocence are opposed in the myth
of the Garden of Eden, where the acquisition of knowledge cast
humanity out into the world of toil and sorrow. In Buddhism, by
contrast, ignorance and illusion are the root of all suffering.
Here is a worldview consistent with the highest values of science
and technology: to push back ignorance and use knowledge to
relieve suffering.

The unquenchable human thirst for knowledge in the face of
the mysteries of the universe was identified by Aristotle as the
basic motive force of science. In the mystical traditions of Asian
religions (which have remained much stronger than the mystical
traditions of the West) we find another response—a striving to
transcend the limits of empirical observation and achieve a
direct encounter with truth. In this there is a recognition, or perhaps simply a greater acceptance, of the limits of what we can
know—an acceptance of mysteries that are beyond human
understanding. For some Asian civilizations, there is danger in

treating this path toward truth as an alternative to or substitute for scientific inquiry, for the two are, in reality, parallel and complementary paths.

The recognition and acceptance of limits to human understanding and power are qualities that have emerged with increasing clarity in recent decades as a key to human survival. The physicist Edward Teller, in speaking of the development of the atomic bomb, said, "We would be unfaithful to the tradition of Western civilization if we were to shy away from exploring the limits of human achievement." We may be grateful that this view is not part of the tradition of Asian civilization. In both West and East, there is an alternative view gaining ground that operates on the basis of a certain humility in the face of creation. It accords spiritual values at least equality with material values. It recognizes that there are limits to our understanding rather than denying the importance—or even the existence—of that which we cannot grasp. It acknowledges that even if there are no limits to what we can do, there are limits to what we should do. One of the advocates of this alternative worldview is Jakob von Uexkull, a German philanthropist and member of the European Parliament. He described one of the needs of our time as the need "to help the West find a wisdom to match its science and the Third World a science to match its ancient wisdom." Surely that is a call for cooperation between the two, in the interest of all humankind.

Religious Perceptions of Desirable Societies: Islamic Perspectives and Responses[3]

In recent years, there have been a number of efforts at interreligious collaboration on questions of peace and development. But they have been largely directed toward finding common ground for cooperation in the increasingly fragmented situation of today's world. Although these efforts are certainly to be commended, the limitations of this approach have already become visible. A different approach is predicated on the recognition that there is a resurgence and intensification of religious faith in virtually all societies in one form or another. The articulation of possible visions of desirable societies, consonant with the rich diversity of cultural value systems rooted in the world's major religions, may help us understand the different perspectives on the future that impel the major religions to become political actors. The variety of these perceptions, and their compatibility or incompatibility, may explain some of the challenges that lie ahead in the area of peaceful and creative coexistence and mutual tolerance.

This resurgence of faith is perhaps nowhere so manifest as in today's Islamic world. In the many faces of the cultures of Islam across a vast expanse of the globe, there are powerful impulses for self-renewal. Extremely varied social, economic, political, ecological, and historical conditions are embodied in the rubric of Islamic civilization. It is as important to recognize the differences as the common ground—both interreligiously and intrareligiously—in organizing the search for cooperative endeavor. If religion is to play a role in helping humanity's entry into the twenty-first century before it destroys itself, then ways must be found to convert renewed religious intensities into actions relevant to our pluralistic age.

The upsurge in religious feeling is due in large part to the pace and scale of profound social and cultural change that permeates our daily existence. Change of this magnitude is painful. It has left many people bewildered. Old moral certitudes have fallen by the wayside. The change is due to a number of elements that are converging at this moment in history. Advances in science and technology are altering the shape and texture of societies and their institutions. There are vast migrations of hundreds of millions of people—from countryside to city, from nation to nation, from continent to continent—who are cut adrift from their traditional cultural moorings. Values and ways of life are changing swiftly. The weak and the powerless no longer accept poverty and injustice passively—and their outraged voices threaten and disturb those who would maintain the status quo. When injustice becomes unbearable, violence is unleashed.

All this uncertainty and newness has led to a yearning for some greater certitude to guide us in learning to deal with change. There seems to be a growing realization that answers at the materialistic level alone, where present-day political leaders and decisionmakers of various ideologies look for solutions, are essentially leading up a dead-end street. The yearning has led to a breakthrough in the sense of the sacred, defined in many different ways. It is important to recognize that the relevant questions to be asked might not be the same for every religion—or indeed within one religion. The history of Islamic civilization is a tale of a multiplicity of responses to the challenges of the time; it may well be that there is no one single answer to the challenge of the modern world from Islam.

History shows us that all established religions have had great difficulties in accommodating social change. This disjunction between religion and history is an intimate part of the human experience. Life on earth is eternally different from the religious ideal. But human life assumes its significance within that tension; human beings, in trying to walk the straight path, assume both freedom and responsibility.

Some religious "renewal" turns out to be a blind hearkening back to a reactionary fundamentalism. Other efforts are too narrow and rigid. Even those who escape these pitfalls are not sure that they are on the right path in search of a new awareness of the moral dimensions of problems and proposed solutions.

In a setting such as this, a number of new ethical challenges are posed:

- How are we going to manage to live in some measure of harmony and civility on a planet that will number six billion people by the close of this century and ten billion before the middle of the next century? What will this do to our societies—already so sorely afflicted with unemployment, hunger, and poverty? We are faced with concerns on a scale that escapes the religious precepts and ethical norms by which humankind has lived over the centuries. Against the scale and structural character of much of today's poverty, charity is simply not enough.
- How do we face the staggering challenge of creating one billion new jobs to satisfy the job market of the year 2000? What contribution could the major religions, Islam included, make in helping to rethink the relationship between faith and work? Can religion help us fashion a new equation for work, culture, leisure, and learning?
- What are our environmental responsibilities to future generations weighed against our short-term needs? There are basic ethical choices demanded here—what are the rights of our children or of our neighbors up- or downstream?

- Where do we strike the proper ethical balance between the rights of the individual and his or her obligations to the larger community?
- What is the balance between the need for growth and development and the demand for equity? Between personal needs and the need for common survival?
- In an age in which machines are coming to regulate and control so many aspects of our daily lives, how do we foster growth of societies that are not totally depersonalized and that offer space for freedom? Put more broadly, there is the question of governance—governance of our inevitably pluralistic world, governance of the desirable societies envisioned by the revitalized religious thinking.

Cutting across the many faces of Islam is the recognition that it is a religion of personal responsibility. Truth is not just a cognitive matter; it is not passive. Truth is true only when it is acted upon. From this concept flow many important social implications for the role of Islam.

Any attempt to organize the world's religions in a cooperative diagnosis of the world's ills is fraught with disconcerting issues. One important one, of course, is the question of tolerance. But there are other compelling issues, including the need to reconcile religious values and worldly goals, the relationship between religion and modernization, and the danger of reactionary or escapist tendencies.

Like all processes of rejuvenation, the religious resurgence manifests itself in both backward-looking and forward-looking directions. It can deny neither its historical roots nor its continuing commitments and aspirations. Careful and critical questioning may contribute to the forward thrust of the process of spiritual resurgence. The questions most pertinent for each religion can be identified only by looking at the specific contemporary context in which each religion lives. Every major religion has wrestled with its own problems and is continuing to do so. Therefore, the most pressing questions may differ from one religion to another.

The questions that Islamic thinkers feel the need to address may include the following: Why has there been no revival of science and technology after the attainment of independence in any of the Islamic societies? Is it possible to think of a revitalization of Islamic civilization without coming to grips with the age-old encounter between faith and scientific reasoning? Can we avoid considering the decline of scientific reasoning in Islam as resulting from the prevalence of a legalistic approach to life?

This line of questioning leads to a further question: Are the concepts of industrial society and Islamic culture mutually compatible? In the face of the problems faced by humankind, will it be possible for a revitalized Islamic civilization to reconcile the imperatives of its faith and the legalistic injunctions of Islam in ways that might provide important contributions to the solution of these problems?

The unprecedented character, scale, and depth of the social and cultural changes that are taking place, and the rapidity of these changes, will put a premium on the capacity of each religion to discover how to define the meaning of these changes and to interpret their significance in relation to its basic tenets. What crucial factors that affect the capacity for continual reinterpretation will be required if religions are to address these problems in a manner relevant to our times?

Specifically in the case of Islam, should we or should we not reconsider the place of *ijtihad* (interpretation of sacred texts) in the process of moral reasoning, and see it as part of our search for proper responses to new and unprecedented social situations? A second general question is: How are faith, inspiration, religious law, and the spiritual symbolism of Sufism to be related to other facets of human life, collectively as well as individually? In such a value configuration, which elements can be considered Islamic and which not? What constitutes the boundaries between them? What then *are* Islamic values and Islamic norms in such a situation?

A third question is: How should Islam, as a system of faith and belief, interact with other religions and belief systems—as well as with modern ideologies? Should Islam act as an alternative to all of them, or should it seek new areas of understanding that could form a common contribution shared with other religions for the benefit of the human race in general now or in the future? If the latter is the only possible answer in an increasingly interdependent world, then what are the implications for what might be called "institutionalized Islam"—as manifest in the group of *ulamas*, conventional Islamic scientific disciplines, and the

orthodox worldview itself? What might constitute the new orthodoxy of Islam?

Islamic communities everywhere in the world have tried—and
still keep trying—to give at least partial answers to these long-
range questions. Partial and limited answers, such as particular
forms of relationships between Islamic faith and state power, are
already being advanced. They need not be seen, in any way, as
complete or final answers. But they deserve continuous monitor-
ing and examination. They turn on fundamental questions about
the variety of modes of governance and their political, economic,
and social institutions in our visions of desirable societies. Particular patterns of interaction between Islamic legalism and indigenous cultures have taken place. These all merit our careful and
meticulous study. Perhaps most deserving of our attention are
the efforts to formulate an Islamic concept of the human person,
which has been tried in separate locations and diversified man-
ners throughout Islamic history.

It is an enormous task to formulate a response to the enormous challenges now confronting humanity that is consonant
with both Islamic norms and Islamic experience. Reflections of
this nature should not only be legalistic or normative but should
also take into account the variety of historical experiences of the
many Islamic communities in the world, be they majority or
minority groups. It is also incumbent upon us Muslims to reflect
on the kinds of Islamic studies we will have to develop within our
own societies.

We will also want to reflect on the problems of coexistence
and tolerance—not only between Islam and other religions but
also within the varieties of Islamic cultures—at what appear to be
higher levels of religious intensity. This will force us to consider
the various historical experiences of Islam in black Africa, in the
Arab world, as well as in the Turko-Persian-Afghan cultures,
South Asia, and the Southeast Asian Islamic communities. There
are further lessons to be drawn from the experiences of sectarian
communities in Islam and from the Muslim minorities in non-
Islamic countries.

Essential to the success of this undertaking is a recognition
that we are not interested in so-called concrete answers to the
problems we have raised. We are not in search of any technocratic fix or social engineering. Asking for concrete solutions
would be asking the wrong questions; it is important that the

right questions be defined—it is perhaps the main purpose of this inquiry.

It is true, in Islam as elsewhere, that a people is defined by its history as well as its aspirations for the future. The cast that molds the basic values of our cultures prefigures, to a certain extent, the manner in which we perceive and decide our future options. Our flexibility in dealing with the future hinges on the extent to which we are either prisoners of our past or creative inheritors of it. Only the latter are capable of continually reinterpreting their cultures to meet the challenges of the late twentieth century.

A process of reflection within the world of Islamic scholarship may help in the building of appropriate responses to the major challenges the world faces today—responses that are consonant within faiths and across faiths. Above all, we are seeking responses relevant to the survival and growth of the human community in pluralistic and peaceful coexistence.

Religion and the Development Process in Asia[4]

The forward movement of a social system depends on a broad consensus about goals and means. There must be some shared vision relating to the future, capable of arousing new hope. Without such hope, no movement is possible. That vision of the future should not only relate to the character and structure of the society being aimed for but also be capable of providing the principles and guidelines for understanding and working on present problems. Unless realities can be seen with new eyes and hope can be translated into a sense of new profitable opportunities on the individual level, such vision will have little motivating value. The relatively brief history of newly independent nations has made it clear that unless the new goals, objectives, and purposes are related to prevailing notions, attitudes, and values, it is almost impossible to mobilize broad sectors of societies in transition. The politicians' familiar exhortations to progress and develop fail to generate social action unless these new goals are related to motivations that are more deeply embedded in tradition.

The system of social organization in most traditional Asian societies was shaped by religion. The most meaningful language of large parts of Asia's masses is still the language of religion. We cannot begin to understand their social dynamics, nor can we develop ways of utilizing or circumventing them in the development process, unless we understand how religion meshes with social relations and with collective as well as individual human behavior. Religions can be strong motivating and integrative forces. They can also be an obstacle to necessary change. Most religions have played one of these roles, and most have played both at different times. It would be folly to ignore the potential that religions have to facilitate or hamper the processes of development and nation building.

There are other motivating forces that can play a role in the development process. One of them is self-confidence or pride. Success in the attainment of intermediate goals in trade, industry, or politics may have a spillover effect on other sectors of society, stimulating them to greater efforts and generating a climate of renewed hope and heightened activity. Fear of a threat to national survival may spur a society to greater exertions and to the fullest use of its capabilities. Class hatred, fueled by deliberate class struggle and welded into an instrument of power, can act as a trigger for action, but so can a desire for freedom and justice and the yearning for a better life. It is the task of any developmental ideology—secular or religious—to integrate the elements of hope into a consistent structure of thought and perspective. Unless modernization and development are incorporated into new structures of meaning that are capable of relating to the deepest wellsprings for social action embedded in the history and the traditional heritage of a nation, we cannot hope for a new, socially creative dynamic. Models or rational strategies for development are not enough. What is needed is a vision that provides both a sense of direction and a method for struggle toward its attainment.

There is no general strategy for development. Each nation will have to develop its own vision of the future out of the materials of its own history, its own problems, its own national makeup and geographical location. Western models of modernization have dominated much of the thinking on development, but the existence of non-Western models such as the Russian and the Japanese is convincing evidence of the historical freedom that—within limits—each nation has in shaping its own future. It may eventually turn out that adherence to the Western model is not the rule but the exception.

The development process has no built-in guarantee against derailment, nor does it have an automatic mechanism for the maintenance of momentum. We speak in terms of new goals and new purposes and values, but we should not close our eyes to the pains of social transformation. The breakdown of traditional value systems and familiar modes of behavior and standards of conduct, without the emergence of other coherent and authoritative frames of reference, leads to the loss of many of the essential certitudes that people need for guidance, reassurance, and spiritual comfort.

Rapid social change is inevitably accompanied by growing uncertainties and disorientation, deep anxieties and fear. Often, it generates resistance to further change. The capacity of a culture to resist change is perhaps as important to its health as is its capacity to innovate and absorb change. Without resistance there would be neither structure nor continuity. However, the anxieties and fears that come with development tend to stiffen resistance to change—especially when these fears are played on for political reasons. New and dangerous rigidities may develop within the system. Not only institutions and vested interests but also cherished values are threatened. Thus, in cultures where the family is the most important social unit and family loyalty and solidarity are virtues of the highest order, it may be difficult to achieve a superseding loyalty to the nation, which is essential to the solidification and effectiveness of a new nation-state. The persistence of corruption in some nations reflects an incomplete transition to the more impersonal organizational requirements of the modern nation-state.

Adding to the difficulties may be the failures of specific developmental projects as a result of overzealousness and high-handedness on the part of its implementors; mistakes in planning as a result of misconceptions about the need for development itself, its goals, its values, its methods and instrumentalities. Serious problems arise from the increasing irrelevance of traditional conceptions of social reality. As a result, narrow political preoccupations and patterns of conflict persist, though they bear no relationship whatsoever to new and urgent problems that have emerged. Much of the incapacity of the traditional sectors in our transitional societies in this connection stems from the lack of a consistent frame of orientation capable of overcoming the contradictions in the perception of the new dimensions.

In a sense, these inabilities reflect the inner fragmentation and identity crises that individuals and societies experience in the course of social transformation. The establishment of a creative new relationship to social reality and the formation of a new system of commitments pivot around the development of a new sense of identity, on both the collective and the personal levels. What follows is the integrative reordering of one's conceptual and emotional frame of reference regarding man, society, and the divine, regarding history, the present, and the future. The kind of person I want to be, the kind of relations I want to have with my fellows, the kind of society and the kind of world I want to live in are the central issues in the search for this identity and in the process of nation building.

It is, of course, possible to look for answers to these questions from the perspective provided by the humanities and the social sciences. But on the whole, their positivism and operational pragmatism fall short in meeting intensely felt human needs. Some secular ideologies, to be sure, have shown that they can have such integrative and motivational power. However, it would be a serious mistake to overlook the transcendental and essentially religious dimensions in these questions. Few people and very few cultures in Asia are able to live among the happenings of our day-to-day life without some sense of meaning. Mortality, the cycle of birth and death, growth and decay, the seeming senselessness of much of human experience are bearable only with some awareness of eternal truth and reality. Especially in Asia—where religions have not only been roads to the salvation of the individual soul but have also helped shape systems of social organization—this aspect should be taken into account in any analysis of social dynamics.

As claimants to ultimate truth, all religions have had difficulty in their relationship to history and social change. Although both history and social change inevitably bear the stamp of the prevailing religion, both continue to escape the precepts, norms, and injunctions of religion. Of course, the tension between religion on the one hand and autonomous society on the other is a basic and permanent one. Mostly, it is a creative tension. From it many human cultural and artistic achievements flow. Rapid social change, however, aggravates the already difficult relationship between religion and society.

One thing seems to be certain. The attainment of, or failure to attain, the goals of development could be determined by whether or not the religions of Asia are able to absorb and digest the new elements and perspectives that come with social change without losing their own integrity. Insofar as this comes about, they will be able to play the essentially reintegrative and motivating role described here. Further, the manner in which the religions of Asia position themselves in relation to the development process will have a profound impact on the political systems that emerge. In other words, unless the religions of Asia are capable of formulating their own development ideology and learn to use their tremendous influence on the masses toward the attainment of development goals, they may be shunted aside. The secular counterreligions may well be the alternative forces that shape the political processes through which these goals will be achieved.

So far, this discussion has assumed a society that is homogeneous. The relationship between religion and the development process becomes even more complicated in pluralistic societies where nations are composed of different cultures and religions. In those societies in which more than one religion has traditional roots, *modi vivendi* have emerged that make peaceful coexistence possible. In a static society, these unarticulated interreligious balances function relatively well. However, religions and their practitioners do have different capacities to absorb social change and to adjust to modernization. In some cases, extraneous or incidental factors in the development process—for example, the prevalence of particular religious attitudes or the role of particular institutions—may seem to work to the advantage of the members of one religion as opposed to another. The development process, therefore, may at some point upset the delicate interreligious balances that had been worked out and on which religious tolerance had been built. This is bound to resuscitate the fears and suspicions of the various religious groups about one another and to compound the anxieties following in the wake of social change and development. In such a climate, the problems of change then tend to be perceived in terms of religious conflict, provoking major new dangers to the political and social system as a whole. The violence attendant upon the breakdown of systems of interreligious accommodation, which has occurred in a number of countries, has made us realize the necessity of preventing social problems from being identified and fought over as theological or communal problems.

It is of the greatest importance for the viability of the political system in a religiously pluralistic developing nation that no single religion become totally identified with any specific aspect, or with the whole, of the development effort to the exclusion of other religions. Thus, although religious organizations can and should play their part in modernization, these endeavors become counterproductive and dangerous to the political system when fears and anxieties on the part of other religions become a factor. In religiously pluralistic societies there is, of course, room for healthy competition in developmental activities among the religions. Such competition serves to accelerate the rate of change and increases the capacity of the social system as a whole for creative adjustment to the requirements of modern life. But we should be aware of the point at which such competition becomes counterproductive. Each religion in such a pluralistic society has a stake not only in the growth of its own developmental capability and in its own contribution to the development effort but also in the development of a similar capacity in the other religions of the country.

Such involvement of all religions in the country and their organization will therefore be an important step toward the building of a transcommunal consensus for development. All religions within a single society thus have a common interest in developing among themselves the understanding, accommodation, and self-restraint, as well as modes of explicit and implicit cooperation, that will ensure the continued participation of all religions in the developmental efforts at all levels. They also have a common stake in strengthening the capacity of the nation as a whole to deal with conflicts peacefully, with full regard for basic human rights. Although many of our nations are committed to these basic rights, the social preconditions for their effective application are, on the whole, quite fragile. This is bound to remain so unless an effective and militant constituency is forged —out of elements drawn from all religions—on which civility and tolerance can rest.

It is impossible to exaggerate the need for such an effort. Strengthening the "rules of the game" for conflict resolution in our relatively new nation-states is therefore a *conditio sine qua non* for maintaining the political consensus and social cohesiveness on which our national existence depends. At this early stage of nation building, this need transcends some of the more customary concerns and activities of a number of religions and their institutions in our countries.

The foregoing argument points to the desirability, even the necessity, of religions in Asia being involved in the politics of development, at least in some specific ways. Unless they become an unquestioned part of the impulse and momentum for change and development, they cannot play an integrative role in shaping the inner features of the new and expanding national awareness in our countries. A nation's political cohesion and strength for survival do not depend solely on a sense of common material interests but also on a capacity for transcendence. Hence the need that all revolutions have felt to explain and legitimize themselves in terms of universal values. Failure of religion to play this role will open the way for those strong, secular ideologies with eschatological pretensions to perform this essential function in the building of new nations— or will leave the society to stagnation and frustration.

Political involvement of religious institutions in whatever form raises some fundamental questions. How can a religion immerse itself in the political process without losing its soul? This question forces leaders of a religion to reflect on its relationship to power and to history. Although history is significant to some religions in Asia, in no way can this be taken to mean that God simply awaits us at the end of the road toward progress and development. Does the imposed moral significance of a particular historical trend or process relieve people of their personal and moral responsibility for their actions? The many historical episodes in which social and political systems established in the name of God or truth have led to insufferable tyranny and oppression should give second thoughts to anyone who considers subscribing to the politics of salvation.

This search for a clearer understanding of our relationship to history—in which the development process is embedded—takes on a particular urgency in the light of the new eschatological emphasis in some contemporary Western thought, attitudes, and style of action. This emphasis may be important in the revitalization of some religious institutions in the West. In the Asian setting, however, the new utopianism, its political activities, and its constant temptation to violence are bound to have a different significance, evoking responses quite different from those in the developed countries.

Millenarian movements have been familiar features in the history of many parts of Asia. They are rooted in the ahistorical Weltanschauung in which the future is not borne and shaped by the present but merely succeeds it temporally without inner connection. The impulse is visible in the pervasive and persistent expectation among large segments of the Asian population that the "just king" will suddenly appear in order to lead the establishment of a just and prosperous society. The innumerable Asian *jacqueries*—violent outbreaks of peasant rebellions—leading to no appreciable change in the social or political structure are also symptomatic of this outlook. In Asia, therefore, instant utopianism, especially if coupled with violence, may not accelerate structural change but rather resuscitate archaic and regressive patterns of thought and behavior that will seriously set back the struggle for emancipation, modernization, and development.

As one whose life was shaped by revolution and the violence that goes with it, I would be the last person to deny the role that violence can play, under certain conditions, in the shaping of new societies. But historical experience also shows how—after independence—the application of violence in a pluralistic society can result in the total breakdown of traditional mechanisms for intercommunal accommodation, leading to unimaginable waves of bloodshed. That the new utopianism in some of our countries is not peasant based but urban centered, operating among religiously or morally motivated sons of the middle class, should not prevent us from drawing lessons from these phenomena.

History is not simply a morality play where good and evil are easily identified and personified. The complexity of the historical process is such that no final judgments are possible. There is no certainty as to how an action may ultimately affect the course of history. And, so, in acting out a commitment, one cannot but be deeply aware that the meaning of history is opaque, discontinuous, and subject to many interpretations. History has a way of serving unintended purposes. Both revolutionary and melioristic reform movements show the intractability of the big issues of politics and the human condition, the way they keep recurring in different shapes and under different circumstances. This awareness need not reduce commitment, although it does point to humankind's essential insufficiency. But it also serves to emphasize humility, tenacity, perseverance, and patience; the ethos of tolerance and the capacity to fight without hatred will be required before our nations can come into their own.

This essay has discussed the role of religion in terms of the development process. Within this context, it has pointed to the reintegrative role of religion in the process of formulating new systems of values and commitments through the selective rejection, incorporation, and rearrangement of new and old values in relation to new social situations. This essay has said very little about goals. Nevertheless, it is impossible to leave a discussion of religion and its relationship to economic development without saying at least something about the goals of development. The essence of religion escapes us if it is discussed exclusively in terms other than its own.

Because religion is essentially concerned with questions about the meaning and the purpose of life, it cannot unquestioningly abide by the conventional wisdom of economists, sociologists, and political scientists or accept the goals they implicitly assume for the development process. In facing up to the need for economic development, all religions must raise the question of goals as well as of means. Should Asian development aim at duplicating—with minor modifications at best—the American, Russian, or Japanese model of development and the goals implicit in them? Or do the cultural crises in which the industrial and technologically advanced nations find themselves—their spiritual malaise and their high ecological costs—raise the question of whether Asian development should search for different directions? Are there not alternatives based on a different balance between humankind and nature, between society and technology on the one hand and the supernatural on the other? Should not the religions of Asia raise the question of the desirability and possibility of alternative social systems, of an alternative civilization capable of coping with the problems of the twentieth and twenty-first centuries, that could be maintained at a lower human and environmental cost? The religions of Asia cannot escape the responsibility of raising these fundamental issues so that each step, each choice, is made in full awareness of the options that present themselves if we refuse to follow blindly the economic development steps already taken by the industrially advanced nations. In order to be able to play this creative role, it will be necessary for religious leaders to speak to the problems of development not only in terms of the formal precepts or general moral values of their religions but in terms that make sense to their followers in their efforts toward material, intellectual, and spiritual improvement. Because religion points to a transcendental reality and is to some extent a reflection of it, it must be able to speak to the economist and the political scientist as well as to the layperson about development in terms that encompass but also go beyond economics and politics. Although it is not the task of religion to give answers to specific policy issues, by raising the fundamental questions of meaning at each step of the way—and insisting on their being confronted—it may also improve the quality of what we as human beings are making of ourselves in the pursuit of these goals.

8

....

Common Humanity:
An Ethical Framework

Soedjatmoko was an active member of the Independent Commission on International Humanitarian Issues, which met from 1984 through 1986 and was chaired by Prince Sadruddin Aga Khan and Crown Prince Hassan bin Talal of Jordan. Part of its purpose was to extend the consensus on humanitarian issues beyond the traditional framework of Western Judaeo-Christian culture. In 1986, Soedjatmoko and Kathleen Newland presented this paper to the commission. It drew together a number of the threads that had appeared in Soedjatmoko's work over the previous two decades: a sense of the fundamental worth and equality of human beings, a concrete appreciation of global interdependence, a warning against one-dimensional thinking. He did not shy away from the ambiguities and uncertainties of ethical choices but avoided being paralyzed by them. His fundamental values of tolerance, compassion, mutual inclusiveness, and solidarity here find their place in a coherent framework for analysis and action.

Humanitarianism:
An Ethical Framework for Human Solidarity[1]

In a world of shrunken spaces and high density, porous national boundaries and horrifying destructive power, expanding technological capacity and instant communication, we live in imperfect but vivid intimacy with all of our fellow human beings. Our attention to any one segment of humanity may be limited or self-limiting. But our mutual ability to affect one another's lives for better or for worse has never had the scope and immediacy that it has today.

Humanitarianism is a basic orientation toward the interests and welfare of people. This perspective demands that whatever detracts from human well-being must be questioned, regardless of its effects on economic growth, political power, or the stability of a certain order. Abstractions such as growth, stability, and order are not taken as ends in themselves but have value only as means toward greater well-being for people.

Humanitarianism proceeds from the recognition that each one of us is no more and no less than a human being. The quality of human dignity, however defined, belongs to each one of us equally. To emphasize our common humanity is not to deny or downplay the importance of transcendental concerns but simply to recognize that no one definition of a higher truth is universally and unconditionally accepted. Common humanity is a point we can start with as we learn to live with multiple perceptions of the truth. And it has its own value. As soon as we brand our opponents as devils, we deprive them of their humanity—and deprive ourselves of the humane standards we hold ourselves to in dealing with fellow human beings.

The humanitarian perspective necessarily takes a long-range view of human welfare, for one of its essential dimensions is solidarity with future generations. Our first responsibility to our progeny is to assure that they have a future by avoiding catastrophic war. A further one is to assure that they do not inherit a planet whose productive capacity has been substantially and irreparably decreased. A third is not to deprive our descendants of the chance to learn what we do not know, such as the value of species that seem useless to us. In other words, we have an obligation not to foreclose the options available to our successors. Humanitarianism is cautious. It has a strong bias against the irreversible.

Humanitarianism is not a formula for resolving dilemmas. It is a framework for recognizing them. Once human welfare has been placed firmly at the center of concern, however, there are still a host of questions to be resolved in any specific set of circumstances. The humanitarian perspective includes an ethical orientation that equips us to approach these difficult questions: an ethic of human solidarity. Modern communications have played a tremendous role in strengthening the sense of human solidarity. This was seen most dramatically in 1984–85, when the images and descriptions of the continuing famine in Africa burst upon the consciousness of the public in Europe, Japan, the United States, and elsewhere. Coming face-to-face, in an almost literal sense, with suffering on such a scale challenges people's notions of what it means to be human. It brings about an expansion of our moral universe.

An expansion of the moral universe to match the functional interdependence of people is highly appropriate. The expansion needs to take place in several dimensions: horizontal, to cover more of the globe; vertical, to take in new kinds of moral issues; and temporal, to cover future generations. Individual and institutional capacities to respond to expansion are, however, far from adequate. In some cases, the expansion of the moral universe is overwhelming and produces reaction—chauvinism, survivalism, and extreme parochialism are manifestations of this.

There are deep ambiguities in virtually all the ethical choices that people are called upon to make. These arise because worthy goals can and do conflict with one another, because contemporary life is extremely complex, and because we cannot perfectly foresee or control all the consequences of our actions. It is impossible, in any complex situation, to do only one thing, and the unintended consequences of a choice may overwhelm the intended result. Even with a firm ethical orientation toward human well-being, we cannot eliminate risk, the possibility of tragedy, or the real constraints that prevent people from doing what they believe to be right. The distance and disjunction between intention and result make caution an ethical imperative.

Certain other ethical imperatives follow from the fact that we cannot control or foresee consequences in a complex environment. They include the responsibility to examine and try to understand the full range of consequences of an action—in other words, to avoid one-dimensional thinking. Another is to make every effort to minimize harm and to compensate the sufferers when harm is unavoidably brought about in pursuit of a competing good. A third is to exercise discernment in the face of unintended harm. Justifiable actions may bring harm to some people, and it is important to acknowledge bad consequences for what they are rather than insisting that they are tolerable because they are unavoidable.

The need to act without perfect knowledge or certainty is a major dilemma for those who hold power. Inaction is no alternative—it can be as decisive as action, and just as damaging. No single person or institution has the capacity to marshal all the facts, understand all the alternatives, or predict all the reactions to and interpretations of an action. Therefore no one can be self-sufficient in making complex ethical decisions. This fact underscores the crucial importance of continual discourse on ethical issues. The broadest possible discourse, within and among different cultures, can at the very least uncover differences of conviction and their sources. Exposure to different ways of looking at a problem may increase understanding and, in so doing, enlarge areas of agreement. These are the prerequisites for an expanded consensus on humanitarian issues.

The preoccupation with humanitarian issues arises out of a sense of the tremendous vulnerability of the human person in today's world. Violence has become a fact of life in the daily lives of millions as well as in the wars that continue to plague the developing world. Civilian casualties have shown a steady tendency to rise in proportion to military casualties in recent history. Torture is reportedly institutionalized as an instrument of repression in more than 100 countries. Indiscriminate weapons are being used in actual conflicts and as the basis of strategic doctrine—nuclear weapons being the leading example in the latter category. Starvation continues to be used as a means of suppressing opposition, and control over civilian populations serves as a tactic as well as an objective of armed conflict. State authorities seem to be increasingly willing to use violence not only in their relations with other states but also in extrajudicial proceedings against their own citizens: political opponents, criminals, misfits, or outcasts—extending even to the children who inhabit the street.

Man's inhumanity to man is not an invention of the modern era, but the scope of our capacity to act it out is historically unprecedented. Ancient themes such as greed, betrayal of popular will, lust for power, and ethnic hatred combine with more recently emerged economic and social strains to create new sources of conflict. Rivalry over land and resources has intensified, spurred by the need to satisfy the requirements and aspirations of growing populations. Developments in science and technology raise new ethical challenges by endowing human beings with powers that far outstrip their collective good judgment.

Many kinds of environmental problems show no respect for international borders, such as the air pollution that produces acid rain or the destructive land-use practices that disrupt hydrological cycles.

Increasingly, impelled as refugees, expelled as misfits, or volunteering as migrants, people too ignore international borders. The vast population movements that are taking place give rise to a plethora of humanitarian problems. Those who succeed in moving often become targets of resentment, exploitation, discrimination, or debilitating dependency; those who do not succeed are often stopped by inhumane methods.

Around the world, poverty holds more people than ever in its grip, while income disparities fuel tensions that can erupt into violent between or within countries. Even the search for solutions to these basic problems can lead to conflict, as ideological disputes over economic strategies degenerate into violent confrontation. Meanwhile, the frustration of heightened popular aspirations generates political discontent, and there are almost always internal or external forces willing to exploit that impatience.

National governments, clearly, are not in control of the processes of change. Their ability to direct the course of events is being eroded from two directions at once: from below by subnational groups that have lost faith in the government's commitment to represent their interests, and from above by transnational processes and institutions. The nation-state is on the defensive. In many cases, this has prompted governments to respond to internal challenges with repression and to external forces with the refusal to cooperate in common endeavors. The pursuit of national security has come to place excessive reliance on the use or threat of force. This has led to the militarization of whole societies and the neglect of the economic, social, and political factors that determine in large part a nation's vulnerability.

It is important to recognize the nature of the historical process in which contemporary humanitarian issues are embedded. It is one of tremendous turmoil, fragmentation, and vulnerability—in the developing countries in particular. In some cases, the turmoil is part of the struggle to throw off the remnants of colonial structures and power relationships. But in many more cases, the end of the colonial era has been followed in short order by a new period of contention, as mechanisms for political representation have failed to take hold. In a number of countries, the state apparatus has been captured by one class or ethnic group that has used it for its own advancement. But even without the willful appropriation of the benefits of state power, the development process itself generates inequalities that a representative government must mediate. All too often, however, states have failed in or abandoned their mediating roles and substituted repression for social management. Increasingly, therefore, resistance to inequality and the violation of humanitarian norms manifests itself in opposition to the state.

An important consequence of this process is the prominence of new actors, both within the government structures of new states (or states that have radically changed their political systems) and outside of state structures. Humanitarian norms are based on the consensus of what we loosely call the community of nations; they evolved in the nineteenth and early twentieth centuries—most in the context of wars among European states. The new actors referred to above spring from movements and cultures that did not participate in formulating the international consensus on humanitarian norms and have never been asked to give their views on these norms. It is not surprising that they feel little obligation to maintain them.

Many of the new contenders have no experience of real national politics, which is necessarily consensus politics, much less of international politics, which is even more so. Moreover, many states that accept international standards in external conflicts still refuse to apply humanitarian norms to internal opposition groups. These groups thus lack the incentive of mutual restraint to apply the norms themselves.

One additional explanatory factor in the fragility of the humanitarian consensus may be that the consensus itself has not drawn sufficiently upon non-Western cultural, legal, and religious traditions. The historical reasons for this are comprehensible. Humanitarian law grew out of European experience and was codified initially by Europeans. Naturally, it drew upon European moral and intellectual sources. However, the norms of humanitarian conduct might become more firmly entrenched in non-European cultural areas if they were more explicitly related to non-European sources of inspiration. The holy texts of non-Western religions and the legal traditions, philosophies, and customary practices of other cultures abound in implicit or explicit moral injunctions that imply an ethic of human solidarity.

A broader consensus on humanitarian issues requires a search for the highest common values that are widely shared despite all the negative, conflictual elements of human societies. All cultures and religions accredit human beings with a moral dimension and expect to see it manifested, in however fragmented and diluted a form. Values such as respect for innocent life, responsibility toward future generations, protection of the human habitat, an obligation to aid and protect the weak, and altruism at least within the family circle and the immediate community—if not the nation and the world—are widely if not universally acknowledged in some form. This ethical core is the basis on which a wider consensus can be built.

Disregard for humanitarian values is not found only in situations of overt conflict. It is also manifest in the willingness of the international community to stand by while hundreds of millions of people sink into the depths of absolute deprivation. This amounts to the acceptance of a "doctrine of dispensability" applying to the poorest and most helpless members of society. Although the first line of responsibility for these people rests with their own communities and states, these entities are often helpless to remedy a bad situation. Often they lack the resources or the skills to combat deprivation or are in the grip of larger forces in the national or world economy over which they have no control.

The international community can easily condemn violations of humanitarian standards. But it can hardly claim to be surprised when desperate people lash out violently and disregard basic humanitarian principles in the process. The first reaction of the perpetrators to pleas for restraint is likely to be: Where was the outrage of the international community, whose norms we are now being asked to respect, during the quiet crisis that killed our children through malnutrition and disease, that despoiled out lands through environmental destruction, that imprisoned us in ignorance and oppression? This keen sense of victimization and people's determination to resist it, is the link that joins long-term humanitarian issues of poverty and injustice to the acute outbreaks of violation of norms in wars or violent internal struggles. The contenders in such struggles are not likely to observe the norms set by the international community until they are acknowledged to be part of it themselves.

To illustrate: In 1979, a papal envoy went to Iran to intercede with the revolutionary government in behalf of the American

hostages—hostage taking being one broadly acknowledged violation of the humanitarian principle that noncombatants should
not be made to suffer. Ayatollah Khomeini replied to the envoy:
"Our people were massacred for fifty years, and the best sons and
daughters of our nation were thrown into inhuman prisons
where they died under brutal torture, yet the question of mediation never arose, nor did it ever occur to His Eminence, the
Pope, to show any concern for our oppressed people or even to
mediate with the plea that oppression cease." The eye-for-an-eye
impulse may be flawed as moral reasoning, but the episode
demonstrates that the essential characteristic of a workable
humanitarian ethic is universality. It cannot be applied selectively
without losing all credibility. Only if it is based on human solidarity can it function at all.

Dual standards, or multiple standards tailored to specific circumstances or to the perceptions and ideologies of separate societies, are a luxury that can no longer be afforded. With all
societies so vulnerable to the actions of others, and all faced with
the possibility of extinction, standards must be fashioned that are
acceptable across a wide spectrum of cultures and ideologies.
Embodied in these standards must be the notion of the human
species as a single and indivisible but pluralistic unit.

Growing population densities, improved communications and
transportation technologies, the unification of world markets,
and above all the powerful means of violence now available
mean that the world has become like a small island; there is no
way to escape from or avoid the aspirations and ambitions of our
neighbors. People who live on an island or in conditions of
extreme population density learned long ago that in such circumstances it is foolish to seek complete control over one's
neighbors or total victory over one's adversaries. The ability to
tolerate differences, and to empathize with those who are different, is a mechanism for survival.

General rules and principles of human conduct have evolved
in specific historical settings, and within those settings they have
acquired strong presumptive authority. But in a situation of rapid
social, cultural, and technological change, the old presumptions
may lose their reliability as ethical guidelines. Still, it is possible,
if not easy, to define some of the outer limits of ethical behavior
that would be widely recognized in the modern world. The question is, do these outer limits help us very much in the ambiguous

and complex circumstances in which we must operate today? As the American theologian James Gustafson wrote,

> Slavery and murder are always wrong . . . but that principle does not in itself resolve the question of how to deal with the massive dependence of large numbers of people on the choices made by those who have power to determine national or international economic arrangements and developments. Those arrangements put masses at the mercy of others, but we do not call that slavery; they may lead to malnutrition and death, but we do not call that murder.

These ethical issues are not residual questions; they are absolutely central to the dilemmas of our times.

Stanley Hoffman, a professor of government, made the point that "we should not pose the problem of ethics and international affairs as a problem of morality versus politics. . . . It is through the right kind of politics that some moral restraints can become observed and practical." The right kind of politics begins with a sober consideration of which self-interested reasons will persuade states and other actors to accept the precepts of common humanity. These reasons emerge from the inescapable fact of interdependence, from which no nation can insulate itself.

With the development of nuclear weapons, the destructive power of the instruments of war has reached levels never before imagined, so that even those states not directly involved in a conflict have a strong interest in mediating it. Powerful conventional weapons are easily available even to small groups, so that every country with an aggrieved minority faces a substantial risk. Furthermore, the volatility of a world that is going through a period of fundamental transformation creates a tinderbox effect in which conflict cannot be easily contained and isolated. Each time a violation of international law or a norm of civility is tolerated, it sets a dangerous precedent that makes it more likely that similar violations will be attempted.

The willingness voluntarily to blunt the sharp edges of national sovereignty can be seen in all successful efforts to manage interdependence. It is no less essential to the task of preserving and extending humanitarian values, which are truly indivisible. Each violation in whatever sphere diminishes our common humanity. But trimming the edges of sovereignty does not imply undermining or superseding the nation-state. It does imply the need to agree on some methods of holding states accountable for their actions or for their inaction in the face of another's dereliction of humanitarian obligations.

In 1915, when Europe was overtaken by the horror of World War I, Sigmund Freud observed that restraint originates in dread of the opinion of the community. "When the community has no rebuke to make," he wrote, "there is an end of all suppression of the baser passions, and men perpetrate deeds of cruelty, fraud, treachery and barbarity so incompatible with their civilization that one would have held them to be impossible." When there is no sense of community, when the community remains silent or cannot find its voice, restraint breaks down.

The refinement and extension of international legal instruments provide one important avenue for the explicit acceptance of humanitarian norms and the obligations that flow from them. There are serious gaps in the law as it stands, and there are even more serious failures to secure general ratification of some of the existing instruments. But the greatest failure of all is not in coverage or ratification but in implementation. In the face of gross violations of humanitarian principles, the community of nations too often "has no rebuke to make" unless it is a politically motivated one.

The weakness of international enforcement mechanisms in a world of highly politicized nation-states forces a return to the emphasis on consensus. The importance of wider participation in consensus building and a universal standard of accountability has been noted. There may also be a need for additional and more effective institutions in which states can be called to account. To some extent, the United Nations provides such a forum, but there should be more outlets in which the voices of nongovernmental actors and claimants can be heard, as well as those of people who feel themselves unrepresented by existing political structures. Regional organizations may be effective settings for such exercises in accountability. But there is little doubt that the most powerful channels of expression for the powerless will continue to be through nongovernmental channels: through organizations, movements, and courageous individuals. It is essential that such voices have access to means of communication so that others may have access to their message.

Calls for strong international consensus are often dismissed as unattainable. They raise fears of a tyrannical imposition of a uniform system of values on a highly pluralistic world. Uniformity is neither necessary nor desirable, for an international consensus can and should be a flexible, dynamic, and minimalistic one. It requires identifying a few irreducible values—but these may have a different configuration and a different relation to other values, depending on their cultural setting. What is important is not the configuration but that within each culturally specific setting the irreducible values can be found. Each nation and people has a stake in helping to identify the core of the humanitarian ethic and in tolerating many different expressions of it. As political philosopher Terry Nardin wrote, "Not everyone is committed to a pluralistic world, but everyone must live in one."

The idea of human solidarity implies an almost Copernican change of perspective, from a view centered around the nation-state to one in which the state system revolves around the commonality of human interests, with human well-being as its primary goal. It requires the extension of personal loyalties and commitment beyond the community or the nation to the human race as a whole.

For centuries, the great religions have taught the essential oneness of the human race. That transcendent perception of common humanity seems to have waned, though it may yet be reawakened. It is strongly buttressed by the exigencies of interdependence as well as the logic of moral philosophy. And it is fully consistent with the reality of international pluralism.

Living together on this finite planet, where we all have the ability to damage if not destroy one another, requires an enlargement of our concept and our sense of neighborhood. Neighbors are bound together in mutual dependence, and on that functional score all people today surely qualify as neighbors. But we lack the positive qualities of neighborliness: empathy, an acknowledgment of mutual obligation, and a reasonable level of tolerance. The classic neighborhood can also be the ground for intense suspicion, jealousy, and even hostility. But its members know that they must live together and that the expression of open antagonism leaves them all poorer and less comfortable. There is also a degree of acceptance, within bounds, of the weak and the nonconformist—the town drunk, the village idiot, the black sheep—on the grounds that they display weaknesses that we all possess to some degree. In the final analysis, they too belong.

The greatest obstacle to the achievement of a sense of neighborhood based on an inclusive ethical consensus is the drifting apart of the rich and the poor into two separate worlds. Today, this is a far more complex phenomenon than the geopolitical division of the world into North and South, industrialized and developing countries. Today, the well-to-do in Cairo, New Delhi, Lima, and Lagos have far more in common with the well-to-do in Chicago or Paris than they have with the poor in their own countries. The affluent also communicate more easily with one another across national boundaries than with their poor compatriots. Technologies of communication and transportation, to say nothing of pervasive commercial culture, have aided a new stratification of the world's people into transnational classes that share very little information, experience, or common concern. The psychological distances between the strata are in imminent danger of reaching the point where the only form of discourse between the top and bottom is violence, punctuated by occasional spasms of charity. Preventing the split between the two worlds from widening, and restoring the sense of solidarity among people, is a matter of the greatest practical as well as ethical urgency.

The business of building a consensus around an ethic of human solidarity is a long-term proposition, but this should not be a source of discouragement. There is plenty to do in the meantime, step by step, to remove the causes of human suffering and ease the lot of the victims of humanitarian disasters.

Three kinds of victims claim immediate attention. They are the victims of armed conflicts, the victims of natural or man-made environmental disasters, and—perhaps the most tragic for being locked into a seemingly unending state of misery and suffering—the victims of circumstance. These last are the most vulnerable members of the human family. Included in their ranks are the displaced, the stateless, various indigenous populations, the street children of urban slums, and a host of others who are neglected, exploited, or bypassed by society.

Efforts to improve the plight of these victims need to be set within the larger context of a shared set of human values, ones that can both honor the diversity of the world's peoples and cultures and undergird the notion of our oneness on this troubled planet. The turbulence, confusion, and dangers of our age are such that we must somehow find an overarching ethical framework for action, before it is too late to begin.

Notes

Introduction

1. Mochtar Buchori, "He was a Great Moralist" (in Indonesian), *Amanah*, December 23, 1989.

2. Citation for the Magsaysay Awards (Manila: Ramon Magsaysay Foundation, 1983).

3. Aswab Mahasin, "Soedjatmoko and the Human Dimension: An Introduction" (in Indonesian), *Dimensi Manusia dalam Pembangunan* (Jakarta: LP3ES, 1983).

4. Galuh Soedjatmoko, "A Child of the Revolution." Unpublished paper, Swarthmore College, 1985.

5. Mahasin, "Soedjatmoko and the Human Dimension."

6. *Ibid.*

7. *Ibid.*

8. *Ibid.*

9. Magsaysay Awards.

10. *Ibid.*

11. Soedjatmoko, "Why 'Confrontation'?" (in Indonesian). Paper written to introduce the first issue of *Konfrontasi* (July/August 1954).

12. Soedjatmoko, "Creativity as an Absolute Element" (in Indonesian). Paper presented at a seminar on Creativity and Development, Bogor, Indonesia, August 1961.

13. Soedjatmoko, "Economic Development as a Cultural Issue" (in Indonesian), *Konfrontasi* 22 (1954).

14. Soedjatmoko, "The Role of the Intellectual in a Developing Nation." Paper presented at the Asia Society, New York, 1970.

15. Soedjatmoko, "Indonesia: Problems and Opportunities." Paper presented at the Dyason Memorial Lectures, 1976.

16. Soedjatmoko, "Exploring the World of Diplomacy" (in Indonesian). Indonesian Ministry of Foreign Affairs, 1989.

17. A selection of Soedjatmoko's English-language works was published: Anne E. Murase, ed., *The Primacy of Freedom in Development* (Lanham, Md.: University Press of America, 1985).

18. Soedjatmoko, "Perceptions of Social Justice in Southeast Asia." Paper presented at a meeting of the Southeast Asia Study Group on Cultural Relations for the Future. Bangkok, September 22–25, 1975.

19. Soedjatmoko, *Development and Freedom* (Tokyo: Simul Press, 1980).

20. *Ibid.*

21. Soedjatmoko, "Nationalism and the Third World: Some Dilemmas." Paper presented at the Yomiuri Colloquium, Tokyo, October 1974, and concurrently used at the Asia Society's Williamsburg Conference, Hong Kong, 1974.

22. Soedjatmoko, "Soul and Society." Address at the Opening Convocation of Cedar Crest College, Allentown, Penn., September 18, 1969.

23. Soedjatmoko, Farewell Statement to UNU Council, Helsinki, 1987.

Chapter 1

1. A lecture under the auspices of the Indonesia Council of the Asia Society, New York, 1970.

2. Edward Shils, "The Intellectuals and the Powers," *Comparative Studies in Society and History* 1:5–22 (1958); "The Intellectuals in Political Development of the New States," *World Politics* 12(3):329–68 (April 1960).

3. *Asia*, a Special Report by the Asia Society on Social Science Research in Southeast Asia, 1968, p. 84.

Chapter 2

1. Soedjatmoko, "Religion in the Politics of Economic Development, Parts I and II," *The Stanford Journal of International Studies* 6 (Spring 1971).

2. The first Hans J. Morgenthau Memorial Lecture on Morality and Foreign Policy, Council on Religion and International Affairs (now the Carnegie Council on Ethics and International Affairs), New York, 1981.

Chapter 3

1. The Tenth Vikram Sarabhai Memorial Lectures, sponsored by the Vikram Sarabhai Memorial Trust, Ahmedabad, India, January 19, 1985.

2. Barbara Tuchman, *The March of Folly* (New York: Knopf, 1985), p. 32.

3. The Tenth Vikram Sarabhai Memorial Lectures, Ahmedabad, India, January 20, 1985.

4. E. S. Dunn, Jr., in *People-Centred Development,* David Korten and Rudi Klauss, eds. (West Hartford, Conn.: Kumarian Press, 1985).

5. Jeremy Rifkin, *Algeny* (New York: Viking Press, 1983), p. 223.

6. C. R. Wharton, Jr., "Education 1985: Renaissance and Reform." Address to Education Commission of the States, St. Paul, Minn., August 2, 1985.

7. D. Mazzonis, U. Colombo, and G. Lanzavecchia, "Cooperative Organization and Constant Modernization of the Textile Industry at Prato, Italy," unpublished paper, n.d.

Chapter 4

1. Address to the Fourth National Science Congress of the Indonesian Council of Sciences, Jakarta, September 9, 1986.

2. William Bennet, quoted in Helene Moglen, "Erosion in the Humanities," *Change* 16(7) (October 1984).

3. Elting E. Morison, "The New Liberal Arts: Creating Novel Combinations Out of Diverse Learning," *Change* 18(3) (March-April 1986).

4. A similar list appears in *The Humanities in American Life: The Report of the Commission on the Humanities* (Berkeley and Los Angeles: University of California Press, 1980).

5. Address to the Sixth Biennial Conference of the Association of Asian Social Science Research Councils, Denpasar, Indonesia, September 2, 1985.

6. Address to the Eighth General Conference of the International Association of Universities, held at the University of California, Los Angeles, August 12, 1985.

7. George Keller, "Trees Without Fruit: The Problem with Research about Higher Education," *Change* 17 (1) (January-February 1985).

Chapter 5

1. Paper presented to the Nobel Symposium on the Study of War and Peace, Noresund, Norway, June 1985; published in *Studies in War*

and Peace, Oyvind Osterud, ed. (Oslo: Norwegian University Press, 1986).

2. The difficulty of specifying what sort of conflict constitutes a war makes this a very imprecise figure. Estimates range widely from about 100 upward, including the count of 259 "wars or warfare incidents" made by the historian of the U.S. Joint Chiefs of Staff and the 307 "conflicts" counted by Dr. Nazli Choucri in *Population and Conflict: New Dimensions of Population Dynamics* (Cambridge, Mass.: MIT Press, 1983).

3. John Paxton, ed., *The Statesman's Year-Book, 1977–1978* (London: Macmillan Press Ltd., 1977).

4. Quoted in Lloyd Timberlake, *Africa in Crisis: The Causes, the Cures of Environmental Bankruptcy* (London: International Institute for Environment and Development, 1985).

5. Johan Galtung, *There Are Alternatives! Four Roads to Peace and Security* (Nottingham: Spokesman Press, 1984).

6. *Ibid.*

7. See, for example, Michael Howard, "The Causes of War," in *Studies of War and Peace*, Oyvind Osterud, ed. (Oslo: Norwegian University Press, 1986).

8. Jackson Diehl, "Argentina Takes Steps against a Rightist Paramilitary Group," *International Herald Tribune*, June 3, 1985.

9. Gerry S. Thomas, *Mercenary Troops in Modern Africa* (Boulder, Colo.: Westview Press, 1984).

10. Anthony Short, review of *Armed Communist Movements in Southeast Asia: Issues in Southeast Asian Security*, edited by Lim Joo-Jook and S. Vani, *Survival* 27(2) (March-April 1985).

11. Maria Elena Hurtado, "Colombia: So Who Writes to the Coloreis?" *South* 56 (August 1985); "CPT No Longer Poses a Threat to Thailand," *Thailand Foreign Affairs Newsletter*, No. 15/84 (November 1984).

12. "Central America: Revolution and Counter-Revolution," in *Strategic Survey 1984–85* (London: International Institute for Strategic Studies, 1985).

13. *Ibid.*

14. Sergio Gonzaléz Gélvez, "The Arms Race as a Factor of Instability in Latin America." Unpublished manuscript, United Nations University, Tokyo, 1986.

15. Address to the Swedish Institute of Foreign Affairs in memory of Olof Palme, Stockholm, May 5, 1986.

Chapter 6

1. The Oscar Iden Lecture, Georgetown University, Washington, D.C., October 9, 1987; published as an Occasional Paper of the Institute for the Study of Diplomacy, Edmund A. Walsh School of Foreign Service, Georgetown University, under the title "Policymaking for Long-term Global Issues: The Oscar Iden Lecture."

2. This paper was presented to the International Leadership Forum sponsored by the Center for Strategic and International Studies of Washington, D.C., in Brussels on April 4, 1986; it was published in *The Washington Quarterly* 9(4):67–72 (1986).

3. This paper was presented at the *Asahi Shimbun* International Symposium, "A Message to the 21st Century," Tokyo, October 24, 1984.

Chapter 7

1. Opening speech at the International Seminar on "The Future of Mankind and Cooperation among Religions," Tokyo, April 13, 1987.

2. Introductory speech to the Symposium on Science, Technology, and Spiritual Values held at UNU headquarters, Tokyo, May 25, 1987.

3. Opening address at the Planning Meeting for the UNU Project on "Islamic Perceptions of Desirable Societies," Bangkok, March 12, 1984.

4. Soedjatmoko, "Religion in the Politics of Economic Development," Parts III–V, *The Stanford Journal of International Studies*, 6 (Spring 1971).

Chapter 8

1. Paper presented to the Independent Commission on International Humanitarian Issues in consideration of the Final Report of the Commission, Stockholm, May 1986.

Select Bibliography

Bellah, Robert N., ed. "Introduction." In *Religion and Progress in Modern Asia*. New York: Free Press, 1965.

Daubert, Amy, ed. "An Interview with Soedjatmoko" (transcript). Living History Program, Duke University, 1989.

Feith, Herbert, and Lance Castles, eds. *Indonesian Political Thinking: 1945–1965*. Ithaca, N.Y.: Cornell University Press, 1970.

LP3ES (Institute for Social and Economic Research, Education and Information). *Mengenang Soedjatmoko: Kumpulan Berita dan Obituari*. Jakarta: LP3ES, 1990.

Legge, John D. *Intellectuals and Nationalism in Indonesia: A Study of the Following Recruited by Sutan Sjahrir in Occupation Jakarta*. Monograph Series. Ithaca, N.Y.: Cornell Modern Indonesia Project, 1988.

Ramon Magsaysay Foundation. *The Ramon Magsaysay Awards: 1976–1978*. Manila, 1983.

Soedjatmoko. "Point Four and Southeast Asia." In *Indonesie: Tweemaandelijks Tijdschrift Gewijd aan het Indonesisch Cultuurgebied: 1950–1951* 4(6) (May 1951).

———. "Why 'Confrontation'?" (in Indonesian). *Konfrontasi* 1: 3–12 (July-August 1954).

———. "Economic Development as a Cultural Problem." Translation Series. Ithaca, N.Y.: Cornell Modern Indonesia Project, 1958.

———. "Clearing the Path to the Future" (in Indonesian). *Konfrontasi* 22:23–47 (January-February 1958).

_____. "Cultural Motivations to Progress: The 'Exterior' and the 'Interior' Views." In *Religion and Progress in Modern Asia,* edited by Robert N. Bellah. New York: Free Press, 1965.

_____. "The Indonesian Historian and His Time." In *Introduction to Indonesian Historiography,* edited by Soedjatmoko, Mohammad Ali, G. J. Resink, and G. McT. Kahin. Ithaca, N.Y.: Cornell University Press, 1965.

_____. "Indonesia: Problems and Opportunities." *Australian Outlook* 21(3) (December 1967).

_____. "Soul and Society: An Asian Commentary on Western Counterculture." Address at Opening Convocation of Cedar Crest College, Allentown, Pa., September 18, 1969.

_____. "Nationalism and the Third World: Some Dilemmas." Paper presented at the Yomiuri Colloquium, Tokyo, and concurrently used at the Asia Society's Williamsburg Conference, Hong Kong, 1974.

_____. "Perceptions of Social Justice in Southeast Asia." Paper presented at a meeting of the Southeast Asia Study Group on Cultural Relations for the Future, Bangkok, September 22–25, 1975.

_____. "Political Systems and Development: Reflection on an Asian Research." *Prisma* 19:25–38 (1980).

_____. *Development and Freedom.* Tokyo: Simul Press, 1980.

_____. *Dimensi Manusia dalam Pembangunan: Pilihan Karangan.* Jakarta: LP3ES, 1983.

_____. *Etika Pembebasan: Pilihan Karangan tentang Agama, Kebudayaan, Sejarang dan Ilmu Pengetahuan.* Jakarta: LP3ES, 1984.

_____. "Has Freedom a Future in Asia? A Study Outline." Unpublished paper. Jakarta, 1987.

_____. "Exploring the World of Diplomacy" (in Indonesian). Jakarta: Indonesian Department of Foreign Affairs, 1989.

_____. Interview with Yuwono Dwi Priyantono. Oral History Project, Indonesian National Archives, Jakarta, 1989.

Soedjatmoko, Galuh. "A Child of the Revolution." Unpublished paper, Swarthmore College, 1985.

Index